QUESTIONING
PLATONISM

SUNY series in Contemporary Continental Philosophy

Dennis J. Schmidt, editor

QUESTIONING PLATONISM

*Continental Interpretations
of Plato*

DREW A. HYLAND

STATE UNIVERSITY OF NEW YORK PRESS

Published by
State University of New York Press
Albany

For information, address
State University of New York Press
90 State Street, Suite 700, Albany, NY 12207

Production by Diane Ganeles
Marketing by Fran Keneston

Library of Congress Cataloging-in-Publication Data

Hyland, Drew A.
    Questioning Platonism : continental interpretations of Plato / Drew A.
Hyland.
        p. cm. — (SUNY series in contemporary continental philosophy)
    Includes bibliographical references and index.
    ISBN 0-7914-6195-5
    1. Plato.   2. Philosophy, Modern—Europe—20th century.   I. Title.
II. Series.

B395.H95 2004
184—dc22   2003064720

10 9 8 7 6 5 4 3 2 1

For my grandchildren:
Jake, Aidan, Alexandra, Phoebe, and Drew

Contents

Preface

This book brings together two philosophic interests that have long sustained me: the Platonic dialogues, and so-called continental philosophy. Several of the chapters began as papers that I have delivered here and there over the last several years, and I want to acknowledge and thank my many listeners at those occasions for their astute and helpful comments. Since virtually every one of those papers was presented first at Trinity College, I want explicitly to thank my colleagues at Trinity who have always given me their best attention and advice. They are challenging friends indeed. Those friends surely include my students who have participated in courses on one aspect or another of this book. Their challenging questions and comments have aided me immeasurably. Second, several of the early versions of these chapters were presented at meetings of the International Philosophical Seminar at Castelrotto, Italy, in a wonderful setting that always encourages the utmost thoughtfulness. I want to thank all the participants in those meetings for their warm reception and helpful comments, but to single out the founders and co-directors of IPS, Hugh Silverman and Wilhelm Wurtzer, who may have discovered the Platonic Form of Philosophical Conferences. The two anonymous referees who read my manuscript made astute and thought-provoking comments, for which I thank them both. Finally, as always, I acknowledge and thank my wife, Anne, for her support, her love, and her art, which always enriches our lives.

Introduction

Imagine that you are Plato. Quite impossible, I know, but I have in mind a much more focused image. Imagine that you are Plato deciding, presumably after long reflection and against the practice and probably the strong advice of your mentor, Socrates, to *write* in the light of philosophy. I say "in the light of philosophy," not "write your philosophy," because, if the Seventh Letter can be believed, you decided early on that you would not "write your philosophy" because philosophy "cannot be put into words like other studies" (Letter VII, 341c). In any case, you come to the long and no doubt complicated decision to go ahead with it and risk the old man's displeasure. Now the question becomes, how to write?

The first thing we should note is that modern, and especially contemporary, philosophers almost never have to confront that question seriously. By the time we are sufficiently educated in our discipline that we decide to write philosophically, it quite literally usually *goes without saying* how we shall write. If it's philosophy we're going to write, it will be in the form of treatises, whether of article or book length, in which we develop our arguments for whatever philosophic view we want to espouse, or at least as often, want to refute. It is important to recognize that the dominance of this format is closely tied to what philosophy has become. Since philosophy is now widely regarded as a matter of asserting ones convictions about this or that issue and presenting ones arguments for them, or presenting the views of others and the arguments as to why those views are wrong, it is clear that in almost all cases the best way to accomplish those goals is in a treatise format. (As will soon become obvious, this book will take that very form, hopefully and at least in part *sous rature*.) For reasons such as these the treatise form has become, again quite literally, the canonical format in which philosophic writing is done today. Present company not excluded.

Not so with the young Plato. Having decided to write, he must have thought long and hard about the writing of the philosophers previous to him and perhaps been daunted by the amazingly rich palette before him. Would he write "concerning nature" treatises, as some of the earliest philosophers had done? The treatise format for presenting philosophy was clearly already an option. Or philosophical poems, like Parmenides and Empedocles (this must have been a special temptation for the young, poetically inclined thinker)? Or perhaps write aphoristically, in the style of Heraclitus? The point is, the young—and later, the old—Plato had a decision to make in a way that few of us writing philosophically today do. He had to consciously and conscientiously decide which among a variety of writing formats would best accomplish what he wanted to accomplish in writing in the light of his philosophy. Which means, in turn, that his fateful choice of a writing format simply must have been a more reflective, careful decision than most of us ever have to make.

And so, as we know, he chose to write dialogues. But these reflections force us to ask, what might he have thought he would accomplish best by writing in the dialogue form? Suppose that Plato, against the teaching of the Seventh Letter but like the majority of the philosophers after him, had as his primary objective something like this: to express his own philosophic views as clearly and persuasively as possible. Would he, could he, have chosen the dialogue form, have thought that writing in a dialogical form (and moreover, one in which no character named "Plato" ever speaks and so no clear "mouthpiece" for his own views was presented), would best present his own views? That is hardly possible. Surely, if that were his intention, the treatise format, already before him in the case of the *concerning nature* treatises, would have been the best choice, as it has been, by and large, ever since. Even in the case of the utterly fragmentary remains we have of those pre-Socratic *concerning nature* treatises, we at least know that, for instance, Thales wanted to espouse the view that the *arche* of all things is water. Can we therefore conclude anything else than that whatever were Plato's intentions in choosing to write dialogues, he could not have been motivated primarily by the guiding one of most philosophical treatises? If indeed, he had chosen the dialogue format in the belief that it was the best way to present clearly and persuasively his own philosophic views, that is, to accomplish what treatises best accomplish, he surely made an obtuse choice. And Plato, I think we can all agree, was not an obtuse man. Which is to say, are we not forced to conclude that Plato did *not* have as his primary goal the clearest and most persuasive presentation of his philosophical position? If so, do we read the Platonic dialogues fairly and fruitfully by assuming that Plato must have been attempting what most treatise writers obviously are attempting, the clear presentation of his own philosophic views? Yet most, we might say almost all, of the Platonic scholarship of the last two centuries has proceeded on just that assumption. How else explain why that scholarship is full of accounts of "Plato's metaphysics," "Plato's epistemology,' Plato's moral theory," and so on?

Plato, for whatever reasons, never tells us anywhere in his published writing, in first person prose, just why he wrote dialogues rather than treatises, although as I suggested above, the Seventh Letter (as well as the Second, though it is even more controversial as to authorship than the Seventh) surely offers us some clues. But we can look at what is actually presented in the dialogues, what happens in them, and from there perhaps we can infer something of Plato's project in writing dialogues. So what *is* happening in the Platonic dialogues, if not primarily the clear presentation of Plato's views?

Perhaps the most striking feature of the dialogue form, differentiating it from the standard philosophical treatise, is the presence in the dialogues of different characters, different locations, different times, in sum, the presentation within dialogues of the dramatic situation in which whatever philosophic discussions might ensue will take place. In some dialogues, of course, the characters, location, and time are presented in elaborate detail and play an overtly significant role in what is said. The *Phaedo*, for example, occurring in jail on the day of Socrates' death, is an instance of this elaborate presentation of context. Other dialogues, such as the *Meno*, are less explicit about, say, the dramatic location or the dramatic time. Indeed, the presence or relative absence of this dramatic elaboration is, or should be, an important part of the interpretation of any given dialogue. But it is important to emphasize that *every* Platonic dialogue presents the philosophic discussion that ensues as occurring within a given dramatic context, whether that context is presented richly or sparsely. There is a clear if quiet lesson to be drawn from this fact. It suggests, especially by contrast to the treatise form, that Plato thought that philosophy could not be abstract, in the sense of being presented with no reference to the existential situation out of which it arose. A given philosophic position must always be understood as arising out of a given set of conditions: these sorts of people, with these abilities and limitations, in these sorts of situations, facing these problems, at these times in their lives, holding this or that conviction. This is not to infer from the dialogues the relativistic position that no philosophic view can transcend the situation out of which it arises. But it is to say that the position cannot be adequately understood without at least considering the situation out of which it arises. As I have put this point elsewhere, a philosophic view may indeed be able to transcend the situation out of which it arises, but it will always be a *finite transcendence*. Judging from the Platonic dialogues, it would seem that Plato held that there is no such thing as a position that is "the view from nowhere," no absolute or totalizing position that bears no reference to any human situation (notwithstanding the fact that certain characters, *within* the dramatic context of the dialogue and in contradiction to that situation, suggest the contrary. The dialogues, while existentially presenting the view that a philosophic position is always related to its context, nevertheless recognize that one existential possibility is to claim a radical transcendence of any context). There is, that is to say, no such thing as abstract philosophy, at least not abstract Platonic philosophy.

Since a character named "Plato" never speaks in the dialogues (and this itself was a clear choice on Plato's part), we cannot assume without convincing argument that any single character—certainly including Socrates, as I shall eventually argue—simply speaks for Plato, articulates Plato's view of this or that. But again, if something like "Plato's philosophy" is not what is primarily presented in the dialogues, what is? What are presented with incomparable power are philosophic situations, dramatic portrayals of the remarkable variety of human situations in which philosophy might arise, and how it might arise with those people, in those situations. In jails, at trials, in gymnasia, at parties, in the city, in the country, in the daytime, at night, with youths, with old folks, with lovers, with haters, one could say that an implicit teaching of the dialogues is that there is almost no human situation that is not shot through with philosophic issues, although the particular issues, and the manner of their elicitation, will always vary with the context. In that sense, every Platonic dialogue is an *imitation* of philosophy, an imitation of a given philosophic situation, of how philosophy might arise out of that situation. One crucial difference between treatises and the Platonic dialogues, then, is that the dialogues are in every case imitations of philosophy. Plato, that is, writes for a public audience always and only *mimetically*. As everyone knows, certain characters within certain dialogues criticize imitation as characteristic of art, which is represented as inferior to philosophy. There is irony here.

But the dialogues are not only imitations of philosophy. They are also *invitations* to philosophy. That is, every dialogue, as a dramatic portrayal of philosophy, invites the reader into that philosophic situation, invites the reader to think about how he might respond in and to that philosophic situation, whether, for example, he would answer in the same way or ask the same questions as the interlocutors. This is nowhere more powerfully presented than in the so-called aporia dialogues, those dialogues where a given topic is discussed—say, friendship in the *Lysis*, courage in the *Laches*, piety in the *Euthyphro*, or knowledge in the *Theaetetus*—but no satisfactory conclusion is reached. Socrates often concludes those dialogues by suggesting that they will have to return to the issue another time and keep on trying. How could that not be an invitation to the reader to pursue the issue further herself, with friends? But this invitational dimension to the dialogues is true of every Platonic dialogue, not just the aporia dialogues.

Are the various philosophical positions presented in the dialogues *Plato's views*? It is almost impossible that they are all his views. Many if not most get refuted, and even in the case of those that are tentatively accepted by the respondents (tentatively in the sense of within that context, with those people, and so on), we are given no indication that they would all be espoused personally by Plato, or which ones of them would be. What, then, are the views presented?

Many of them might be characterized as "the opinions of the day." Consider the various definitions of justice presented in Book I of the *Republic*. They would seem to be there because they are commonly held opinions at the time of what justice is, representative views, we might say. It is noteworthy, in fact, how often the Platonic Socrates does begin with the opinions of the day, begins not by presenting his own view on a given topic but by asking what the people with whom he is talking believe about a given subject. In an especially striking example, Socrates, in the *Sophist*, begins by asking the stranger from Elea not even what *he* believes about the difference between the sophist, statesman, and philosopher, but "how the people who live over there tend to regard these things, and how they've named them" (*Sophist*, 217a).[1] So one thing that very often happens is that the dialogues present to the reader the opinions of the day to be considered and examined.

Second, a very particular set of opinions of the day, of the day in which the Platonic Socrates lived but not just of that day, is that of that notorious set of figures in ancient Greece known as the sophists. It is remarkable how many dialogues, among them the *Protagoras, Gorgias, Republic*, and *Theaetetus*, focally present positions held by well-known sophists for the reader to consider. To be sure, those positions are usually criticized, but the reader is surely invited to examine for himself the efficacy of the refutation as well as the position itself.

Another set of views that Plato would seem to have thought it particularly important to consider are those of the Pythagoreans. Plato usually signals the presence of those Pythagorean views by having them espoused by a Pythagorean (as in the *Timaeus*) or by having the primary audience be composed of Pythagoreans (as in the *Phaedo*). The case is similar with the oft-presented Parmenidean position, sometimes presented by Parmenides himself, as in the *Parmenides*, sometimes by someone deeply influenced by Parmenideanism (as in the *Sophist and Statesman*).

In each of these presentations, the positions are put in front of the reader for evaluation, along with, often, a set of objections put to the position by a particular interlocutor (often Socrates) that must *also* be evaluated by the reader. In this sense, we can employ the extremely helpful term suggested by Mitchell Miller, and say that the Platonic dialogues, each and every one of them, are *"Platonic provocations,"* literally positions "called forth" for the reader's critical evaluation.[2] This seems to be an altogether more efficacious way of thinking about the various positions presented in the dialogues than to think of them in the more orthodox manner as Platonic doctrines. Nothing in the dialogues advocates that we take these positions as ones actually espoused by Plato, and everything about the dialogues suggests that they are presented for our thoughtful consideration and evaluation.

If something like all this makes sense, then a remarkable portrayal of the activity of philosophy begins to emerge from the Platonic dialogues. If we were, against all the above, to take the dialogues as primarily a vehicle for Plato to assert his own philosophical views, then, as with most of the subsequent history of philosophy, we could conclude that for Plato, too, the fundamental mode of philosophizing, its fundamental speech act, as it were, would be *assertion*, the assertion of one's own philosophic views, the assertion of proofs for those views, the assertion of arguments against other views, and so forth. But if we take the various positions presented in the dialogues, whether commonly held views, sophistic positions, Pythagorean or Parmenidean positions, as primarily *provocations* to the reader, then we would be led to conclude that Plato himself, by the testimony of what happens in the dialogues, never abandons the conviction of Socrates his teacher that philosophy is not fundamentally an assertive but an interrogative activity, that the fundamental speech act of philosophy is not the assertion but the *question*. In this case, the Platonic philosophy that one might find in the dialogues would be less a series of Platonic positions on this or that (as in "Plato's metaphysics," Plato's moral theory," Plato's epistemology," etc.) than a presentation of *what the fundamental questions are*. That is, what Plato is trying to teach us in the dialogues—and he is most certainly trying to teach us something—is what some of the fundamental questions are, what we most need to ask about, and how we ought to ask those questions. Once more, Plato's philosophy would then not be a set of doctrines about this or that, but the development—and encouragement in the reader—of a stance of questioning by which one might live one's life.

Let me cite an example of just one dialogue to try at least to suggest how our reading of the dialogues would have to change if we take them as Platonic provocations rather than as vehicles for the assertion of Platonic doctrines. Let us consider briefly the *Phaedo*, which I choose because it is widely regarded by doctrinalists as a primary locus of the assertion of core Platonic doctrines: the "theory of forms," the "proofs for immortality," the "theory of recollection," and the supposedly strong influence on him of Pythagoreanism.

The dialogue begins on the day of Socrates' death, and he is in his jail cell. Among the many peculiarities of this altogether peculiar man is that on this day, the day of his death, he wants to do what he does every other day; he wants to engage in dialogue, in philosophy. But he cannot, for an obvious reason; everyone is crying, and one can hardly conduct a dialogue while the potential interlocutors are crying (a phenomenological insight to which most of us can attest). In order for Socrates to do what he wants, therefore, he must get them to stop crying. His wife, Xanthippe, is one of those crying: Socrates, rather callously it seems, sends her away (much and very much more needs to be said about this incident. One might begin by noting how utterly out of character it is; Socrates' regular habit is to *introduce* women into previously all-male gatherings. In the *Symposium* he introduces Diotima, in the *Menexenus*, Aspasia, in the *Theaetetus*, his mother, Phaenarete, from whom he learns his midwife's calling, in the *Republic*, the insistence that the Philosopher-rulers will include women as well as men. But here, the weeping Xanthippe is dismissed). How to stop the others from crying?

They are crying because they are about to lose Socrates, whom they love and respect. How can Socrates get them to stop crying about his death? By convincing them that he will not really die. How can he do that? By appealing to what they believe anyway. What is that?

Almost everyone present in the jailhouse gathering, certainly including the primary participants, Phaedo himself after whom the dialogue is named, Simmias, and Cebes, are Pythagoreans. Even Echecrates, to whom Phaedo relates the story, is a Pythagorean (he is from Phlius, the leading center of Pythagoreanism in the Peloponnese). As Pythagoreans, they hold, or should hold, to certain doctrines: to a dualism of soul and body, to a belief in immortality tied to a doctrine of reincarnation, to a predilection for the abstraction from the body captured paradigmatically in mathematics, and to a tendency toward a mathematization of the universe. How does Socrates, then, get them to stop crying? By appealing to the very doctrines that their deepest convictions ought to lead them to believe in any case. Socrates, that is, gets agreement from them on a set of doctrines they are already predisposed to believe. The most striking exception to this Pythagorean prevalence in the dialogue is Apollodorus, who is not a Pythagorean, and he, apparently if understandably unmoved by the appeal to Pythagorean beliefs, keeps on crying throughout the dialogue. Socrates, by contrast, regularly laughs along the way.

Are these Pythagorean views—dualism, immortality, reincarnation, abstraction from the body, otherworldliness, mathematization of the universe—Platonic doctrines? Or are they not rather Platonic provocations, positions well-known and popular at the time, which Plato is setting before the reader to critically examine? It is worth noting yet again that in this dialogue more than any other, Socrates regularly laughs: that in discussing the so-called proofs for the immortality of the soul he refers to them not as "proofs" (*tekmeria*) but only as "convincing reassurances,"[3] and things to be "hoped for."[4] Are these *Plato's* views? Then why are we told at the very beginning of the dialogue that Plato is *absent*?[5]

It is in the context of this situation, with these people, with these predilections, with these predicaments, that Socrates, appropriately enough, introduces in a way altogether conducive to mathematicians the notion of formal essences, and carefully chooses as examples forms that will be particularly congenial to them and their concerns: The Equal Itself, Largeness Itself, Smallness Itself, precisely those forms that can be measured by mathematics. That is, Plato has Socrates present to them not his abstract, comprehensive "theory of forms," but precisely those aspects of the notion of formal structure that he knows will be congenial to mathematically oriented Pythagoreans.

I suggest that a reading of the *Phaedo* that paid heed to the fact that it is a dialogue, not a treatise, would begin, but only begin, from considerations such as these. Obviously, however, this has only rarely been done. For the most part, the *Phaedo*, like the other dialogues, is read as if, like a treatise, it was primarily a vehicle, if a curiously artistic one, for the presentation of Plato's doctrines. Hence interpreters find in the dialogue versions of "Plato's theory of forms," "Plato's epistemology," "Plato's theory of recollection," "Plato's proofs for immortality," etc. Other dialogues, read as if *they* were covert treatises, reveal to these interpreters, in addition to the doctrines just mentioned, things like "Plato's metaphysics," "Plato's moral theory," "Plato's early epistemology," "Plato's late ontology," among others. These are precisely the set of doctrines that have come to be known, by supporters and critics alike, as "Platonism."

It is crucial to note that not once, in any dialogue, are any of these doctrines labeled as such. They are in each case *impositions* of later—mostly 19th and 20th century—scholarship on the dialogues. What the attribution of these abstract theories or doctrines to Plato ignore is the very thing that most strikingly distinguishes the dialogue form from treatises: the location of every philosophic discussion, every philosophic view, in *the concrete situation out of which it arises*. I hasten to reiterate that I am not suggesting that the teaching of the dialogue is that any view is limited to the existential situation out of which it arises—who articulates it and to whom, under what conditions, etc. That would entail a form of relativism that is regularly refuted in the dialogues. But the dialogues, by their very form, do seem to suggest that the situation out of which a given position arises must be considered in any adequate understanding of it. Again as I have developed the point elsewhere, a given view may, under certain circumstances and in an appropriately nuanced way, be able to transcend the situation out of which it arises, but it will in every case be a *finite transcendence*.[6] But finite transcendence is not the stuff of the sort of totalizing abstract theories that go under the name of Platonism.

One might put the point in a slightly different way. If the implicit teaching of the dialogues is a notion of finite transcendence, in which philosophical thinking must always begin out of a concrete existential situation and see, from there, what more general things can be said, then one might say that the Platonic view is that philosophy must begin from the ground up; that is, from the particular to the more general (but not universal). Yet that set of views that constitute Platonism—and quite especially the so-called theory of forms—are all paradigmatically top down theories, abstract, totalizing theories that we are presumably supposed to impose on any possible human situation.[7]

On the interpretation I espouse, which takes into account such features of the dialogues as differences in time, existential situation, and especially characters, it is hardly surprising, indeed it is altogether natural given the different contexts, that different things would be said in different dialogues, even about similar issues. Even more, it is understandable, taking these dramatic differences into account, that occasionally even contradictory things would be said regarding the same issues, even by the same person (say, Socrates) when he is talking to different people in different situations. That is part of the existential drama of lived experience as it is portrayed in the dialogues.

However, for those readers of Plato who do *not* consider such dramatic aspects to be germane to the philosophy at play in the dialogues, such differences become a problem. If Plato is presenting his "doctrines" in the mouths of one or several of the speakers, and those speakers with some regularity contradict themselves from one dialogue to another on those very doctrines, what is a reader to say (again, the case of Socrates is especially problematic here insofar as Socrates is so often taken as "Plato's mouthpiece," the primary articulator of "Plato's views" at the time)? The most common response to these disparities on the part of Plato interpreters (especially in the analytic tradition but also in the continental school) has become known as the "developmental" view.

According to the developmental view, the disparities in doctrine presented from one dialogue to another, and again ignoring the exigencies of the dramatic context, are best explained as signs of Plato's development in his position from one dialogue to another. If someone—again often but not only Socrates—says different things in different dialogues about forms, or about knowledge, or about virtue, that shows that *Plato*—whose doctrines these presumptively are—has changed his position on these issues. This assumption has generated a veritable scholarly industry concerning the dating of the Platonic dialogues, since it is also presumed that what are speculated to be "later" dialogues will be more sophisticated than earlier ones. A decisive problem facing the partisans of this view is that Plato never gives us any explicit indication as to when *he* wrote this or that dialogue, or the order in which they were written. He does gives us many, many indications within the dialogues of the dramatic time in which the dialogue is to take place (how old Socrates is, indications of historical events, etc), but these are curiously ignored by the partisans of development because they suggest a very different chronology to the dialogues from the one they seek. They are therefore reduced, in the end, to a series of more or less (and often less) educated guesses as to the actual period of Plato's life in which he wrote this or that dialogue, and it is on these guesses, as well as a host of other assumptions, that the developmental hypothesis hinges.

Despite its continued popularity, the developmental hypothesis has been soundly refuted by a number of authors.[8] I need not repeat those arguments here, for the particular deficiency on which I want to focus is the one I have emphasized, that such a hypothesis ignores a much more plausible interpretation of the differences in views presented, one that Plato has *written in* to his texts: the existential differences in dramatic situation of which I have spoken. Those differences ought to, but alas, have not, encouraged interpreters to *avoid* interpreting the dialogues as vehicles for the presentation of Plato's doctrines of this or that and so seeing as a problem the fact that the doctrines presented by this or that person vary from dialogue to dialogue. Instead, we get readings of Plato's doctrines, doctrines whose so-called development from dialogue to dialogue present, in truth, an insurmountable interpretive problem.

If I am right, then, the set of theories and doctrines that constitute Platonism are not articulated in the dialogues themselves but are imposed from without by later scholars. It is striking how widespread this imposition has been. Interpreters of Plato today tend to divide into standpoints that are often regarded by each other as opposed and mutually incompatible: "analytic" interpretations and "continental" or sometimes "postmodern" interpretations. The former take their interpretive bearings from the predominantly English-speaking standpoint widely known as "analytic philosophy." Their failure to pay careful heed to the dramatic aspects of the dialogue form in which Plato wrote, and so their attribution to Plato of the various theories and doctrines known as Platonism, is a function, in my view, of their consistent adherence to a fundamental premise of analytic philosophy that they see no reason not to apply to the dialogues. That is the conviction that philosophy is inseparable from the presenting of arguments for this or that view, indeed, in its strong versions, that philosophy *just is argument*. Armed with that conviction, when such scholars turn to the Platonic dialogues, where are they going to look for the philosophy? Certainly not in the dramatic portrayals of existential situations, of characters, of personal attractions, of playful teasing, of the telling of myths. No, from their standpoint, such literary accoutrements can be safely ignored, perhaps explained away in a preface as a kind of hangover from Plato's youthful aspirations to poetry. The philosophy in the dialogues, given their construal of philosophy, can be found in and only in the rather narrowly construed arguments therein, to which they can safely turn without much attention to the various literary flares in which Plato might have indulged. In the case of the analytic tradition, then, the ignoring of the dialogue form, and so the imposition on the dialogues of the various doctrines that constitute Platonism, is at least a consistent consequence of their very construal of the nature of philosophy, even if there is no reason to believe that it was a construal held by Plato himself.

For interpreters of Plato in the continental tradition, the situation is at once more complex and more curious. On the one hand, not one of them, so far as I can see, would accept the presupposition of analytic philosophy that effectively reduces philosophy to a series of arguments for this or that position. On the contrary, one of the great contributions of continental philosophy is to have disturbed the boundaries between philosophy and other disciplines, especially the arts and literature, and so to have brought to philosophic thinking the sensitivity to literary style, to drama, to myth, to the poetic character of thinking, that has been largely missing from the analytic tradition but which is exhibited *par excellence* in the Platonic dialogues. Thus Martin Heidegger, for example, finds in poetic thinkers from Sophocles to Holderlin, Rilke, and Trakl, the stimulus to profound philosophical meditations. Not surprisingly, his own writing, especially his late writing, becomes increasingly infused with poetic gestures, poetic tropes, poetic spirit. The same is true, perhaps even more so, of thinkers such as Jacques Derrida, Luce Irigaray, or Adriana Cavarero.

One would expect that these thinkers, when they turn to the reading of Plato, would be much more attuned to the dramatic, literary dimensions of the dialogue form, and so would not simply assume that Plato was trying primarily to assert his own philosophical views, as if he were writing treatises. Yet strangely, quite to the contrary, most of these continental writers, including the ones I just mentioned, make almost exactly the same assumptions as their analytic counterparts, although the judgments they make on that basis may be quite different. For the most part paying scant attention to the literary and dramatic dimensions of the dialogue form (I will turn to the exceptions in the body of the book), they find in the dialogues what their analytic counterparts find: Plato's metaphysics, Plato's theory of forms, etc. What is distinctive about continental interpretations, however, is that they tend to see in these doctrines, and especially in their construal of Plato's metaphysics, the very foundations of that metaphysical tradition that they strongly criticize and wish somehow to get beyond, whether that metaphysical tradition be construed as "the forgetting of Being" (Heidegger), "logocentricism," (Derrida), or "phallologocentricism" (Irigaray et al.). So, having construed Plato as presenting his own doctrines in the dialogues, they tend to view those doctrines as the foundation of the very metaphysical tradition they wish to criticize and to the extent possible, transcend.

Because the attribution of doctrines to the dialogues on the part of analytic interpreters of Plato follows coherently from their very conception of philosophy as argument, they have been perhaps understandably reluctant to seriously consider alternative ways of reading the dialogues and so of interpreting Plato. For clearly, to read Plato in a fundamentally different way would be to call into question not just their reading of the dialogues but their very conception of philosophy as fundamentally about "arguments." If the *philosophy* (as opposed to the gratuitous literary flourishes) in the dialogues resides not just in the explicit arguments but in the myths, the interactions between personalities, the jokes and erotic playfulness, then philosophy must be rather different from the way in which it is typically construed, and to rethink the very nature of philosophy on the part of a tradition would be a daunting undertaking.

But, I want to argue, the case is different for the continental philosophers I shall address. They *are* committed to a much broader, less limiting, conception of philosophy. They *do* find in literature, art, poetry, drama, rich sources of philosophic reflection. Therefore they *should*, by their very conception of philosophy, be much more receptive to the manner of interpreting the dialogues that I wish to espouse.

I write this book, then, to challenge continental philosophers to an interpretation of the Platonic dialogues that I believe is fully consistent with their guiding convictions about the nature of philosophy, but at the same time is utterly different from the rather standard interpretations that they usually attribute to Plato and criticize in him. Indeed, as I hope to show in this book, what emerges from a more appropriate reading of the dialogues is a Plato altogether more congenial to the kinds of philosophic stances and concerns that motivate so many continental philosophers. If the book is successful, therefore, it should lead continental philosophers both to open themselves to a reading of the dialogues more congenial to their own convictions, and at the same time lead them to call into question their characterization of Plato—and their criticism of him—as the founder of a metaphysical tradition they want to leave behind.

To accomplish this, I have selected some of the major thinkers in the continental European tradition who have addressed the Platonic dialogues in some depth. The bulk of the book will address some of those who tend to be critical of Plato in the sense that they find in his work the doctrinal source of the metaphysical tradition they wish to call into question. I shall begin, therefore, with Martin Heidegger's reading of Plato, then consider the Platonic interpretations of Jacques Derrida, Luce Irigaray, and Adriana Cavarero in that order. For reasons that I hope will become clear, I reserve consideration of Hans-Georg Gadamer's interpretation of Plato for the end. Each of these continental thinkers has addressed Plato focally, in lecture courses, articles, or books. They are by no means the only continental philosophers who have had occasion to address Plato in their works. One thinks especially of Foucault and Deleuze, both of whom have referred to Plato on more than one occasion. But in no case that I know of have they had as their focal intent in an article or book a consideration of Plato, and for that reason I have not included them in this book. Moreover and in any case, my intent is in no sense to give an exhaustive account of the continental interpretations of Plato. Rather, I want to address a sufficient number of the seminal continental thinkers who themselves address Plato focally, in order to establish that there is a certain trend of interpretation among them that I want to call into question.

It should be clear, then, that the focus of my critique of these writers will be on their way of reading the dialogues, the (inappropriate) interpretive principles they bring to Plato's texts. Given the genius of the authors I address, it should hardly be surprising that, along the way and in spite of what I regard as flawed hermeneutical standpoints, they nevertheless give us often insightful and challenging readings. I do not mean at all to deny those insights, but I also shall not focus on them. Even less do I mean to infer from their readings of Plato larger flaws in their philosophic standpoints as a whole, standpoints with which I am often very sympathetic. To the contrary, as I have stated, part of my argument is that their larger positions and commitments should lead them to a different reading of Plato than they often present. Moreover, in no case do I intend these readings as complete interpretations of Heidegger's, Derrida's, Irigaray's, Cavarero's, or Gadamer's accounts of Plato. My point in each case (with the interesting exception of Gadamer) will be that those occasional insights are indeed *in spite of* their interpretive principles, and that if they would pursue interpretations more true to the dialogues themselves and to their own understanding of philosophical textualities, they would find in the Platonic dialogues a much more challenging and engaging Plato than they tend to discover.

Two final qualifications: first, this book is not about the history of Plato scholarship, and I have therefore tried to keep my references to scholarly literature to a minimum, whether that literature be on Plato or on the interpreters of Plato I address. For the most part, I have tried to limit such references to articles or books that explicitly address the interpretive principles these writers bring to bear on the Platonic dialogues. For that reason, much of the fascinating scholarship both on Plato and on the continental thinkers I address here will not be cited or considered in what follows. That is in no way to imply that it is not full of insight and provocation in its own right.[9]

Second, one direction of my critical remarks on the continental philosophers I address focuses on their tendency, as I have already indicated, to find that metaphysical view in the dialogues that has come to be labeled "Platonism." I want to be clear that my critique here is limited to their claim, in effect, that *Plato* is a Platonist in the metaphysical sense that they wish to criticize, that the positions of Platonism are actually Plato's positions that are espoused in the dialogues. A second, very different issue that I will not address, is the question of the development of Platonism as a movement, a dominant movement, in the history of philosophy after Plato. I am often quite sympathetic to their critiques of Platonism, as opposed to their claims, explicit or implicit, that Platonism is actually espoused in the dialogues as Plato's intent. A fascinating and worthwhile study could be made of the history of Platonism, of how the dialogues came to be (mis)interpreted by subsequent philosophers as espousing Platonism. That would be a long but different book from the one that follows.

Chapter One

Heidegger's Plato

Nietzsche, who is such an important influence on what becomes the tradition of continental philosophy, evidently regarded Socrates throughout his career as a "problem." In his early *Birth of Tragedy*, he both severely criticizes Socrates as "the opponent of Dionysus,"[1] and therefore the enemy of tragedy, yet at the same time acknowledges in Socrates "the one turning point and vortex of so-called world history," without which there would have been generated in the world "a gruesome ethic of suicide."[2] This ambivalent attitude toward Socrates continues to his very late work. An entire section of *Twilight of the Idols* is devoted to "The Problem of Socrates."[3] Socrates is always "a problem" for Nietzsche because he is at once enormously attractive and repulsive.

Martin Heidegger, too, is troubled by Plato and the Platonic Socrates throughout his writing career, although his attitude, as we shall see, tends to be more consistently critical. I shall consider several texts and identify three broad stages in Heidegger's own attitude toward Plato. I shall begin with Heidegger's early (winter semester, 1924–25) lecture course on Plato's *Sophist*, where Heidegger, still very strongly under the influence of Husserlian phenomenology, interprets

Plato (and Aristotle) largely from the standpoint of the extent to which they prepare the way for something like philosophy as scientific research in the phenomenological mode. From this vantage point, as we shall see in detail, Plato is to be criticized as falling far short of Aristotle. Since this is the only work of Heidegger's that engages in a thorough interpretation of an entire Platonic dialogue, I shall examine it in the greatest detail. The second text to be considered will be, significantly, Heidegger's only formally published work on Plato, "Plato's Doctrine of Truth," from 1931 to 1932 (although I shall also consider briefly several lecture courses from the same time period). There, Plato will again be criticized, but this time more as the thinker who begins the fateful transformation of *aletheia*, truth as "unhiddenness," into truth as "correctness," and so the beginning of the "forgetting of Being" that becomes the Western metaphysical tradition. As such, Plato's thinking is, so far as possible, to be got beyond, if not indeed overcome. Later, as Heidegger becomes more oriented toward the poetical and even mythic, both in his writing style and the matters he addresses, he becomes somewhat more sympathetic to Plato and to the dialogue form, while remaining in the end still profoundly suspicious of Plato's thought. I shall consider third, then, an example from this later, more poetic period in Heidegger's thinking, his 1943–44 lecture course on *Parmenides*. I shall there suggest that Heidegger's own movement away from philosophy as science and toward a more poetic way of thinking *ought* to make him much, much more sympathetic to Plato than he in fact becomes. Finally, I shall consider two works of Heidegger's in which Plato is never mentioned, but in which it might be argued that the influence of Plato is—or ought to be—most apparent: Heidegger's two later attempts at writing dialogues, the "Dialogue with a Japanese," and "Conversation on a Country Path." There, we shall evaluate Heidegger's engagement not so much with his assessment of Plato's so-called doctrines, but with the Greek's choice of writing format.

THE LECTURE COURSE ON PLATO'S *SOPHIST*

In the winter semester of 1924–25, still at the University of Marburg, Heidegger gave a lecture course on Plato's *Sophist*.[4] It is a remarkable and remarkably important text, both as one of Heidegger's most thorough studies of Greek philosophy (certainly of a Platonic dialogue) and as an important precursor to *Being and Time*. Before turning to Heidegger's interpretation, however, let us, in the spirit of the introduction, consider the dialogue the *Sophist* itself, or rather, let us consider some of the aspects of the dramatic situation presented therein, which we would need to take account of in a thoughtful interpretation of the dialogue. This is in no sense a substitute for a comprehensive interpretation of the dialogue as a whole.[5] Rather, we need to consider as a crucial propaedeutic to an interpretation that dramatic or existential situation in which Plato has placed what is said in the dialogue. In the light of that propaedeutic, we can turn to Heidegger's own reading of the dialogue.

In the introduction, I discussed critically a widespread view that interprets the many differences and contradictions in the dialogues in terms of Plato's supposed development throughout his career. That view involves a series of guesses as to when Plato actually wrote each dialogue, and so what was the order of that composition. Plato, we noted, gives us no indication of his own as to the order of composition of his dialogues. He does, however, give us, in varying degrees of explicitness, the *dramatic* date of each dialogue, the approximate time, and in particular the time of Socrates' life, in which it supposedly took place (that is, at the level of the probably fictional drama). As I mentioned at that time, in some dialogues, such as the *Meno*, say, or the *Laches*, that time is indicated only generally. In other dialogues, however, the dramatic time, and especially the time of Socrates' life, is very explicit and precisely indicated. The *Sophist* is one of those dialogues. Particularly given that in many dialogues Plato seems to feel that only a general indication of the time period is necessary, in those dialogues such as the *Sophist* where a very explicit indication is given, we are presumably invited to consider the significance of that explicit indication with care. The first thing we need to do, then, in reading the *Sophist* is to consider the significance of the dramatic date.

As a consideration of the *Theaetetus* makes clear, the *Sophist* takes place toward the very end of Socrates' life, indeed, the day *after* he has been indicted for impiety and corrupting the youth, and so very shortly before the trial for his life that Plato memorializes in the *Apology*. Indeed, it is part of a series of at least seven dialogues that dramatically take place at the very end of Socrates' life: the *Theaetetus* took place "yesterday," and at the end of that dialogue Theodorus and Theaetetus agree to meet Socrates "tomorrow," presumably to continue the discussion (which in the *Theaetetus* ends in *aporia)* about what knowledge is. But not before Socrates must go to answer the charge of the king archon for which he will be brought to trial. On the way to that destination, Socrates meets Euthyphro and has the dialogue named after that respondent. Thus, again in terms of dramatic time, these two days are ones of extraordinary intensity and urgency: yesterday Socrates engages in two dialogues (the *Theaetetus* and

Euthyphro) and today he will participate—even if less dominantly—in two more (the *Sophist* and *Statesman*). Are we not invited, then, to consider each pair (and perhaps all four) together? In any case, today Socrates keeps his appointment with Theodorus and Theaetetus that occasions the *Sophist* and *Statesman*. Shortly after that, the *Apology*, *Crito*, and *Phaedo* occur, whereupon Socrates' life ends.[6]

By placing so many dialogues within so short a space of time toward the very end of Socrates' life, Plato portrays a powerful sense of urgency as Socrates confronts his end. He is soon to go on trial (and in the *Sophist* he knows this) for which, if convicted, his life may end. To accentuate the sense of impending death, Plato has the telling of the *Theaetetus* take place in the shadow of Theaetetus' own death (it is one of those second-hand dialogues in which the story is told long after the event). Clearly, there is a sense presented of the impending urgency brought about by the nearness of this double death. Heidegger himself has given this sense of urgency in the face of our possibly impending death a name: Being-toward-death. There could hardly be a more dramatic portrayal of this experience than that presented by Plato in the short time before the end of Socrates' life.

As Socrates will soon emphasize in his own defense in the *Apology*, part of the reason for his having been charged with impiety and corruption of the youth, as he sees it, is a crucial confusion on the part of his accusers and the Athenians between philosophy, of which he is a representative, and sophistry. His defense will include in part an explanation of the difference between his work and those of the sophists.[7] Especially since, in the drama of the *Sophist*, Socrates only answered the charge yesterday, the question he eventually asks the Eleatic Stranger at 217a, what do the people in Elea say the differences are among the philosopher, sophist, and statesman, can hardly be innocent, abstract, or theoretical. The distinction among these, or their easy confusion, must be very much on Socrates' mind, and what he learns today may, he might well hope, be useful in his defense. So the guiding question of the *Sophist* about the difference between the philosopher and the sophist is one, at this point in his life, of the utmost existential urgency. This must be kept in mind as one evaluates the Stranger's answers, so formulaic, so methodical, so abstract, indeed, at crucial junctures, formulated in such a way as to make more, not less, problematic the difference between the philosopher and sophist.[8] Of what use can they be in the life of Socrates? Does not this practical uselessness of the results of the Stranger's diareses call into question the efficacy of the method? At very least, we are invited to consider the stark contrast between Socrates' own efforts to get clarification on matters of importance to life with the stranger's much more abstract and intellectual pursuit of what turn out to be elaborate definitions.

As I argued in the introduction, the fact that Platonic dialogues take place among distinct individuals of varied character, ability, and interest is a crucial beginning point for the adequate interpretation of any dialogue. Accordingly, let us consider briefly the cast of characters in the *Sophist*. With one striking exception, the cast of characters "today" is the same as those of "yesterday" in the *Theaetetus*. First is Theodorus, a mature mathematician of some renown, and apparently the teacher of Theaetetus. His conduct today in the *Sophist* must be understood and evaluated in the light of his conduct yesterday in the *Theaetetus*. There, he several times exhibited a distinct reluctance to participate in the give and take of dialogue with Socrates, despite Socrates' repeated efforts to get him into the discussion, quite explicitly preferring to have the much younger Theaetetus undergo the questioning.[9] Indeed, at 146b, early in the discussion when Socrates is trying to lure the older mathematician into dialogue, Theodorus explicitly admits that he is unused to dialectical discussion of the sort in which Socrates engages. It would hardly be an exaggeration to say that Theodorus here explicitly denies that he is a philosopher, at least in the Socratic sense. This is especially striking as we turn to the *Sophist*, for there, at the beginning of the dialogue, Theodorus introduces the stranger with considerable pomp as "a very philosophical man," (216a) and a bit later, under Socrates's playful chastisement, calls him not a god but godlike, "For that is what I call all philosophers" (216c). He certainly did not call Socrates godlike yesterday! Given Theodorus's conduct yesterday, how confident should we be of his self-assured assertion about the Stranger's status? Moreover, again joining his conduct yesterday with his opening statements today, there is at least the strong implication that Theodorus considers the Eleatic Stranger a philosopher *but not Socrates*. In that light, how should we take his judgment? In sum, despite Theodorus's assertion that the Stranger is "very philosophical," or rather, precisely in the manner in which he does so, the actual status of the Stranger, whether he is a genuine philosopher or not, even whether he is perhaps a sophist, becomes a problem in the *Sophist*, not something that can be taken for granted.

Second, there is Theaetetus. He is also a mathematician, indeed, he becomes a very distinguished one, although at this time he is a young adolescent, perhaps sixteen years old or so. We learn in the *Theaetetus* that he is genuinely intelligent, and that in addition to becoming a distinguished mathematician he also later distinguishes himself by his courage in war, dying as a result of battle, even if from "the flux."[10] We know from that dialogue that, in marked contrast to his teacher, Theodorus, Theaetetus has a genuinely philosophical spirit, and he shows himself fully open to having his views tested and even refuted by Socrates. As we shall see presently, this should be contrasted to what happens in the *Sophist*, where the Stranger emphatically does *not* test Theaetetus's views. Instead, the Stranger uses Theaetetus basically to gain assent to the Stranger's own suggestions and directions. The most Theaetetus does in this dialogue is indicate when he doesn't quite understand something and needs further explanation.

Third, of course, is Socrates.[11] Surely today, in the *Sophist*, we must imagine Socrates as thinking about the events of yesterday, the two dialogues—*Theaetetus* and *Euthyphro*—and quite especially his experience in court, where he has now been formally charged with impiety and corrupting the youth. We should recall that piety is the explicit theme of the *Euthyphro*, underlining just how much the charges against Socrates must be on his mind. This may in part explain Socrates' utterly strange behavior today, for he is indeed out of character. Theodorus, as we have seen, ostentatiously introduces the stranger from Elea as a "very philosophical man." If Socrates were his usual self today, how would we expect him to respond to this purported philosophical stranger? Just as he responded yesterday with Theaetetus and with Euthyphro: to enter into dialogue with him! Yet strangely, Socrates almost immediately falls silent (to be sure, after determining what the topic of discussion will be and pressuring the Stranger into conducting his presentation via Socrates' own preferred procedure of question and answer) and lets the Stranger conduct the rest of the dialogue without response from Socrates. What are we to make of this behavior, so out of character for Socrates? Is it a mark of his preoccupation with the events of yesterday? Is he genuinely hoping for practical help from the Stranger in distinguishing philosophy—and so his own calling—from sophistry? This much is surely clear: one striking existential question raised by the drama of the *Sophist* is what to make of the silence of Socrates. We will have to take special note of what Heidegger makes of it.

Finally, there is the Stranger from Elea, who will basically conduct the dialogue to ensue. That he is from Elea immediately invokes Parmenides and, more generally, Parmenideanism. Later in this dialogue, the Stranger will risk "parricide" by criticizing father Parmenides' injunction against speaking of non-being (241d). By contrast, yesterday, after having rather harshly criticized the partisans of flux, including Heraclitus, Socrates pointedly refuses to engage in what he and Theaetetus recognize should follow next in the argument, a critical evaluation of the Parmenidean position (*Theaetetus*, 183e). Nevertheless, the Stranger, despite his eventual critique, remains heavily influenced by Parmenideanism, especially in its development by Zeno. This is exemplified in his emphasis on the method of diaresis, a method, despite its many flaws, characterized at least by the appearance of procedural rigor (not to mention its propensity for abstractness). So between the mathematicians Theodorus and Theaetetus on the one hand, and the Parmenidean Stranger on the other, Socrates is in the presence in this dialogue of what we may call a strong bias toward the mathematical in a broad sense.[12] Yesterday, with Theodorus and Theaetetus, Socrates countered this mathematical bias with regular use of metaphors and images. Today he is silent. Should we take that silence as consent? Hardly! Surely part of the drama of the *Sophist*, part of the problematic of the dialogue for the reader, is to wonder what the silent Socrates must be thinking of the appearance of argumentative rigor that characterizes the method of division soon to be exhibited by the Stranger.

Indeed, one of the first things Plato invites us to do by the juxtaposition of Socrates' examination of Theaetetus yesterday and the Eleatic Stranger's today is to contrast the two procedures. The contrast is striking indeed, and nothing about it suggests what Heidegger and many other scholars have claimed, that the Eleatic Stranger's procedure is meant to be taken as straightforwardly superior to that of Socrates.[13] Let us briefly examine what happens in the two procedures.

In the *Theaetetus*, perhaps more than in any other dialogue, Socrates explicitly comments on his own interrogative procedure in addition to exhibiting it in his discussion with Theaetetus. In his famous self-characterization as a philosophical midwife, Socrates emphasizes that he does not have wisdom of his own that he gives to those with whom he talks. Rather, he draws out and thus helps give birth to the ideas that are within the souls of his interlocutors. Thus it is that in that dialogue Theaetetus himself is genuinely interrogated; his own views on what knowledge is are elicited, they are critically evaluated with the help of Socrates, and Theaetetus is again and again made to see that what he thought was a well-founded view is not. The point to be emphasized here is that Theaetetus personally is examined. His own views are elicited, his own views called into question, he himself is forced to acknowledge his lack of wisdom. Socrates' last speech in the dialogue testifies to the benefits he believes will ensue from this very personal examination:

"And so, Theaetetus, if ever in the future you should attempt to conceive or should succeed in conceiving other thoughts, they will be better ones as a result of this inquiry. And if you remain barren, your companions will find you gentler and less tiresome; you will be modest and not think you know what you don't know. This is all my art can achieve—nothing more" (*Theaetetus*, 210c).

The contrast with the Stranger's procedure in the *Sophist* could hardly be more striking. For the Stranger almost never genuinely questions Theaetetus about the boy's own convictions. Instead, having explicitly asked for docility in the respondent before rather reluctantly agreeing to conduct his discussion via question and answer (*Sophist* 217d, a passage to be discussed in more detail later), the Stranger for the most part simply gets Theaetetus's assent to, or checks to see if he understands, the cuts or divisions that the *Stranger* in almost every case suggests. We are very far, today, from the intensely personal examination of Theaetetus's soul of yesterday. The most Theaetetus does with the Stranger is ask for clarification of difficult cuts. The Stranger's procedure, then, is nothing like the Socratic elenctic of self-examination. It is an altogether more abstract, less personal procedure.

Second, as mentioned earlier, the Stranger gives a strong impression—which, as we shall see, does not hold up to careful examination—of methodological rigor in his procedure: hence the "method of division," or "method of diaresis," as it is regularly called. By contrast, Socrates' procedure of questioning that we witnessed yesterday, of eliciting from Theaetetus his views and then calling them into question, is far, far looser in its formal structure. Indeed, in any strict sense, it could hardly be called a method at all. Socrates' questioning, there and elsewhere, makes ample use of metaphors, asides, digressions, myths, jokes, in sum, all of the characteristics of a genuine if informal conversation. The Stranger, instead, claims to proceed by carefully dividing each cut in two, leaving aside one and pursuing the other with further cuts until the process is completed. As we shall see, Heidegger will regard this appearance of methodological rigor as a distinct advance. We should not hasten to that conclusion.

Third, a crucial contrast is that whereas Socrates' procedure is one of discovery, the Stranger's procedure, despite the superficial appearance of question and answer, is in fact didactic. That is, in Socrates' questioning we actually discover what Theaetetus believes and subsequently discover whether it is a viable position or not. The Stranger, by contrast, proceeds by drawing divisions that are always and only ones that the Stranger *already knows* and suggests to the compliant Theaetetus. His procedure, then, is not one of discovery, since he presumably discovers nothing that he did not already know, but rather is one in which he discursively presents the divisions that he must have decided upon in advance in each case. After all, the stranger would have been just as happy to present his position, which he already knows, discursively rather than via question and answer. Socrates' earlier pressuring of the Stranger to employ Socrates' preferred procedure of question and answer, we now see, has a distinct bite. Despite the superficial similarity, in the hands of Socrates and the Stranger, then, the two procedures are in fact utterly different.

Given these differences and this confrontation of procedures, should we simply say that Plato is espousing one procedure over the other? Or does it not make more sense, in these two dialogues that dramatically occur one day apart, to contrast thoughtfully the two procedures, to notice the strengths and weaknesses of each? To be sure, many, perhaps most modern scholars take the Stranger's method of division in the *Sophist* as "the later Plato's view." As we shall presently see, Heidegger does precisely this as well. But I suggest that we do not do so. I suggest instead that we are invited by Plato to consider each of the ways of philosophy exhibited yesterday and today and measure their relative strengths and weaknesses. Can we imagine the intelligent young Theaetetus, who undergoes these two very different procedures one day apart, doing anything else? Perhaps we should choose one or another. But perhaps, as well, Plato's view lies in the interstices between them, in the critical evaluation of each toward which he is leading us.

Theodorus, as we have seen, introduces the Stranger from Elea as a "very philosophical man" (*Sophist*, 216a). We have already said that this judgment is not necessarily to be accepted without skepticism. Indeed, it should be taken as a question. Just who is this man who, rather bizarrely, remains a stranger throughout the two following dialogues. Why do we never, even after extended conversation, learn his name? What is it about the stranger, or the position he represents, such that it does not occur to Theodorus to introduce him by name, and, perhaps even more strange, does not occur to either Socrates or the others present to inquire of his name, Socrates, who seems always interested in names and indeed even in the parentage of those whom he first meets? What is it about the stranger or his position that such anonymity is appropriate? We might note in advance that the Stranger, almost in imitation of the method he espouses, remains strikingly impersonal, didactic. Perhaps we do not need to know much about the person of the Stranger precisely because his method is so impersonal, so abstract as to be indifferent to time, place, and personal situation. Is this, we must ask from a Socratic standpoint, say the standpoint of yesterday, a virtue?

Socrates, too, immediately expresses skepticism about Theodorus's judgment of the Stranger. He puts it politely: perhaps the Stranger is a god, a god of refutation (216b). Not a god but godlike, replies Theodorus (whose own name, "gift of god," Plato is no doubt having Socrates play upon), an epithet he says he would apply to all philosophers (216c). One wonders immediately and again: would he consider *Socrates* godlike? There is certainly no evidence from his conduct of yesterday that he would. Does he, then, even consider Socrates a philosopher? If not, what confidence will we have in his judgment that the Stranger is one? One wonders secondly: would Socrates agree that all philosophers are godlike? Has he not throughout his career pointedly *distinguished* the aporia and lack of wisdom that is the human condition with the divine, who are wise? Will he not do so again most pointedly of all in a few days, in the *Apology*? "God-like," we might speculate in anticipation of Heidegger's lectures, would be a more appropriate epithet applied to *Aristotle's* portrayal of philosophers than either Socrates' or Plato's. Heidegger, as we shall see, accepts Theodorus' portrayal, and proceeds to read Plato through Aristotle. It is as if the problematic status of that procedure is prefigured in this very passage.

Socrates now introduces the topic of the next two day's discussion (assuming that the putative dialogue the *Philosopher* takes place tomorrow in dramatic time). He has a problem, one for which in part he is about to be put on trial. It is not clear to most people what the difference is between three kinds of people: sophist, statesman, philosopher. Could the Stranger explain what the people "over there" (in Elea) think about this? (217a). It is instructive, and in keeping with the earlier mentioned anonymity of the Stranger, that Socrates pointedly does *not* ask what the Stranger himself thinks, but what the folks in Elea think. This from the man who just yesterday—and characteristically—had emphasized to Theaetetus the intensely personal character of philosophic inquiry. For some reason the Stranger as a person is so irrelevant that he can remain unnamed, and his own views are of insufficient interest to invite the kind of personal questioning that went on yesterday. Once again, does this have something to do with the abstract methodology that is about to be introduced? At very least, Socrates' lack of interest in the Stranger's personal views anticipates the abstract, impersonal methodology the latter is about to espouse. It also starkly contrasts to Socrates' own procedure and to his own conception of philosophy.

That the question of the relation between, especially, the sophist and philosopher is on Socrates' mind is particularly striking in the light of the events of yesterday. In the *Theaetetus*, Socrates developed an extensive critique of that sophist of all sophists, Protagoras. One would think that, at least in the minds of Theaetetus and the others present at both discussions, the difference between sophist and philosopher would now be relatively clear. But the charges that Socrates had to answer before the king archon must have reawakened in Socrates' mind the problematic relation of sophistry and philosophy, and the ease with which they can be confused. Perhaps he reintroduces the issue today because he realizes that he is going to need all the help he can get. We have to ask again, is he likely to be helped in his forthcoming defense by the definitions of the sophist in the dialogue today? Will the Stranger's method be helpful to him at all?

The last thing Socrates does before falling silent and before the Stranger begins his demonstration of the method of division is to pressure the Stranger into using at least a superficial version of his own procedure of questioning. He does so (while apparently politely asking the Stranger which procedure he prefers) by reminding the latter that the great Parmenides had used question and answer on Socrates when he was a young boy. The Stranger, with obvious reluctance and only with the qualification that the respondent be docile and untroublesome (217d) agrees to proceed by question and answer. We have already seen how little his use of that procedure resembles that of Socrates.

So the diareses begin. Before concluding this brief inspection of the dramatic situation in which the *Sophist* takes place and in the context of which it must surely be interpreted, I want to make a few very general remarks about the various divisions or definitions of the sophist and the discussion that takes place in the rest of the dialogue. First, to reiterate, the Stranger's method, by making the various cuts and leaving one side alone while continuing the cuts in one direction, is surely intended, by the stranger at least, to give the impression of methodological rigor. This is the source of the oft-espoused view that the Stranger's method somehow represents an advance on the much looser procedure of Socrates, and so represents the later, more mature Plato's own view. This will in fact be Heidegger's position. But Plato early on in the procedure gives the reader every indication of his awareness that the rigor is superficial, that in fact it is not a genuinely rigorous procedure at all. Two brief examples will suffice. In the exercise meant to demonstrate the gist of the method, the definition of the angler, the Stranger, at 220a, gets Theaetetus to agree to the division of "animal hunting" into two kinds: footed animal hunting and wetlands animal hunting. This hardly exhausts the alternatives or constitutes a comprehensive cut, unless one supposes that the Greeks had never heard of snakes. Even more explicitly, at 222b, in the midst of the very first division that yields a formulation of the sophist, the Stranger, having arrived at the cut "animal hunting on foot," asks Theaetetus's assent to the next cut, tame vs. wild animal hunting. Theaetetus expresses bewilderment at the notion of tame animal hunting, and the Stranger replies,

> If man is a tame animal. But put it any way you like, whether you set down no animal as tame, or some other animal as tame but man as wild, or again, whether you say that man is tame but you consider there to be no hunt for men—whichever of these ways of saying it you consider congenial, mark off that one for us. (222b)

There could hardly be a more explicit indication on Plato's part that we are supposed to recognize that these divisions are not at all natural or necessary, but arbitrary in the highest. To an important extent, it simply does not matter what divisions are made; an adept practitioner of the method will be able to proceed successfully. Yet as we shall see, Heidegger, like many scholars, will accept as Plato's own intention the apparent goal of methodological rigor, and will criticize Plato (in favor of Aristotle) for obviously failing to succeed at being genuinely rigorous. I suggest instead that Plato *wants us to see* the lack of rigor as a problem with the Stranger's procedure. We shall consider this in greater detail when we turn to Heidegger's own lectures.

It is also noteworthy that, under the Stranger's conception of philosophical procedure, there is no "Socratic elenchus" of each of the diareses and resulting "definitions." When the first one is finished at 223b, it is not examined, questioned, or criticized. Instead, it is simply *accepted* as they move on to the second definition. In turn, when the second one is finished at 224d, it is simply added on to the first without comment, and so on with the others. Nor is there any indication that, say, the second one is somehow superior to or an advance upon the first. This underlines how the Stranger's procedure, by contrast to Socrates' and in spite of the superficial use of question and answer, is in fact a didactic, not an interrogative method. By his method, we accumulate what could apparently be an indefinitely large series of definitions of what we are seeking. In this dialogue we stop, depending on how one counts, at six (or seven?). Why stop there? There is no real indication that closure is reached. Presumably one could go on indefinitely with varying characterizations of sophistry. Or, one could ask, if there is a closure point or a definitive characterization, how would we know that we have reached it, rather than simply having discovered yet another formulation? How would one know that one had exhausted the search for the sophist by this method? Without an internal critique or elenchus of the succeeding definitions, there seems to be no way to know, or even to suspect, that one has achieved closure. Is this method superior to Socratic elenchus? Could it possibly be so?

In sum, the Stranger's method is clearly a didactic one, not an interrogative or discovery procedure. As such, it depends for what success it might have decisively on the previously accomplished insight of the practitioner. One might put this point less graciously: it depends on the prejudices and agenda of the practitioner. The very arbitrariness of the method opens it to the possibility of manipulation.

Several other features of the Stranger's procedure need to be identified before we turn to Heidegger's treatment of the dialogue. First, at a decisive passage at 227b, the Stranger has occasion to emphasize to Theaetetus what we today would call the "value-neutral" character of the method. Perhaps we would even want to say that the method is "beyond good and evil." The Stranger's own way of putting it is quite dramatic. Commenting on the ridiculousness of some of the names they have used in the divisions, the Stranger cautions:

> Altogether ridiculous, Theaetetus. But as a matter of fact, the method of argument happens to care neither more nor less for sponging than for drinking medicine, for whether the one type of cleansing benefits us a little or the other a lot. The reason is that, in trying to understand—for the sake of getting insight—what is akin and not akin in all the arts, it honors them all equally and does not, in making its comparisons, consider some any more ridiculous than others; nor has it ever regarded the one who clarifies hunting through the general's art as any more awesome than one who does so through louse-catching, but only, for the most part, as more vain. And now. . . . (*Sophist*, 227b)

This value-free attitude stands obviously in the starkest contrast to the interests and procedures of Socrates, for whom the idea of the Good is the idea of all ideas (*Republic*), for whom the issue of what is good, what is best, is always at stake, and who, in the *Phaedo*, carries to the point of self-parody this teleological concern of his, telling how he has always believed that if the earth is flat or round, part of our understanding should be the knowledge of how and why it is *best* that it is flat or round, and so on (*Phaedo* 97c–98d).

Are we to take the Stranger's value-free method as a philosophic advance over the naïve teleology of Socrates? Then why does Plato surround the very passage in which the Stranger introduces this issue (227b) with the drawing of distinctions that *could not be drawn* within a value-free framework? At 226d, just before the passage quoted above, in discussing "the separating art," the Stranger draws the distinction between "the removing of worse from better, and also that of like from like." How are we to distinguish the worse from the better within a value-free framework? Then, immediately following the quoted passage, at 227d, the Stranger asks Theaetetus, "Do we say that in the soul villainy is something other than virtue?" Again, how would such a distinction be coherent on the basis of the Stranger's value-free stance?

Heidegger, as we shall see in detail presently, affirms this value-free stance articulated by the Stranger as an important advance in *Plato's own philosophic position*. In the spirit of the foregoing remarks, we ask, is the Stranger's view to be taken as Plato's own, or are we being asked both to compare it with the way of Socrates and to notice that it itself cannot make the distinctions it needs to make on its own terms and thus risks incoherence?

The same issue arises again, implicitly but no less crucially, toward the end of the dialogue when the Stranger introduces the notion of the five "greatest kinds" (249 aff.). They are, as is familiar, Being, Motion, Rest, Sameness, and Difference. But with Socrates sitting silently by, and keeping in mind the discussion of yesterday, is not one invited to ask, if these are the five greatest kinds, what about the Good? Is it not the greatest kind of all? Or justice? Courage? Sophrosyne? Once again, are we to take the Stranger's view, with Heidegger, as Plato's, or are we being presented with a profound philosophic provocation: can we, or can we not, coherently discuss the structure of being without reference to the Good?

The discussion of the greatest kinds presents us with our last general consideration before we turn to a more detailed inspection of Heidegger's interpretation. At the apparent end of the diareses, the Stranger points out to Theaetetus that they are still left with an enormous problem: the sophist can avoid being caught because of the apparent inability of the "friends of the forms," certainly including the Parmenideans, to deal with non-being. How can the sophist have a sham wisdom, how can he say what *is* false, if non-being can in no sense be? The concluding portion of the dialogue is taken up with the question of non-being, oriented toward explaining how the sophist can deceive, how he can speak what is not true. It is crucial, in the spirit of the discussion of the dialogue form so far, to keep in mind that nothing about this important passage suggests that it is presented as "Plato's theory of Being and Non-being." It is a focused, targeted account dictated by the problem of coherently saying that sophistry is sham wisdom. Although we may well want to generalize what is said beyond the limitations of that context, we must be very careful in doing so. Certainly it is *not* careful, to leap to an interpretation of the dialogue as "Plato's doctrine of Being." Armed with these observations about Plato's use of the dialogue form and about the dramatic situation in which the *Sophist* takes place, we are prepared to turn to Heidegger's detailed interpretation of the dialogue. Let us do so.

One must begin a sympathetic understanding of Heidegger's interpretation of Plato—and of Greek Philosophy—by appreciating first how deeply imbued he was at that time with the spirit of Husserlian phenomenology. One sees this almost immediately that one turns to the text, in Heidegger's emphasis on philosophy as "science" and his conception of philosophic thinking at the time as "research." From the very beginning, he makes it clear that he understands his own phenomenological procedure as science, and that the scientific spirit of phenomenology finds its roots in the Greeks. Speaking of his intentions in this lecture course on the *Sophist*, Heidegger says, "Our lectures do not intend to train you to be phenomenologists; on the contrary, the authentic task of a lecture course in philosophy at a university is to lead you to an inner understanding of scientific questioning within your own respective fields. Only in this way is the question of science and life brought to a decision, namely, by first learning the movement of scientific work and, thereby, the true inner sense of scientific existence."[14] Moreover, Heidegger's insistence, which he is about to announce, on reading Plato through Aristotle, is justified in part because Aristotle is *more scientific* than Plato. Heidegger assures us that "What Aristotle said is what Plato placed at his disposal, only it is said more radically and developed more scientifically" (PS, 9). By approaching Plato through Aristotle we shall thus "secure the ground on which Plato moved in his research into the Being of beings as world and into the Being of beings as human Dasein, the Being of philosophically scientific existence. We will be brought into position to participate in the possible ways of Plato's research into Being" (PS, 16). (We shall address the appropriateness of reading Plato through Aristotle in detail presently.) Later, preparing to turn to the *Sophist* itself, he adds, "Our considerations thus far have had the sense of a preparation for understanding a *scientific* dialogue of Plato. I expressly emphasize 'a *scientific* dialogue' in order to indicate that not all Platonic dialogues attain this height of scientific research, although all of them in a certain way aim at knowledge. There is no scientific understanding, i.e., his-toriographical return to Plato, without passage through Aristotle" (PS, 131; Heidegger's emphases). And even later, in words of praise, he adds, "In other words, genuine existence resides in the idea of scien-tific philosophy, as Socrates first brought it to life and as Plato and Aristotle developed it concretely" (PS, 160).[15] At this point, I want to emphasize in these passages Heidegger's language. It is full of the appeal to "science," "scientific philosophy," "scientific research," and "research into Being." Clearly, Heidegger is at this point deeply under the influence of the Husserlian notion of phenomenology as "rigorous science," and he is interpreting the greatness of Greek philosophy precisely in terms of its proximity to his own conception of philoso-phy as science. This is crucial to understanding the interpretive deci-sions that Heidegger makes in this lecture course: his occasional praise of Plato is nearly always in terms of his movement toward scientific philosophy; his preference for Aristotle is that Aristotle is more scien-tific than Plato, etc. However much I shall presently contest these judgments, I think they must be understood as grounded in Heidegger's own construal of phenomenological philosophy at the time.

This is particularly important in understanding the otherwise bizarre guiding insistence on Heidegger's part that Plato must be read through the eyes of Aristotle. We must do so, first, he says, because Aristotle is "clearer" than Plato. Early on, Heidegger asserts,

> If we wish to penetrate into the actual philosophical work of Plato we must be guaranteed that right from the start we are taking the correct path of access. But that would mean coming across something that precisely does not simply lie there before us. Therefore, we need a guiding line. Previ-ously it was usual to interpret the Platonic philosophy by proceeding from Socrates and the Presocratics to Plato. We wish to strike out in the opposite direction, from Aristotle back to Plato. This way is not unprecedented. It follows the old principle of hermeneutics, namely, that interpretation should proceed from the clear into the obscure. We will presuppose that Aristotle understood Plato." (PS, 7–8; more on the last claim presently).

Later, in developing the same general point, he again speaks of the movement from Aristotle to Plato as "from the clear back into the obscure, i.e., from the distinct, or the relatively developed, back to the confused" (PS, 132). To say the least, many an astute student fails to find Aristotle clearer than Plato. What is the criterion, we must thus ask, by which Heidegger finds it so obvious that Aristotle is "clearer" and more "distinct" than Plato. The very juxtaposition of the terms offers us the clue. Heidegger is clearly thinking in a Cartesian, scientific mode: Aristotle is clearer than Plato precisely in so far as his writing is more scientific, more suggestive of scientific writing, than is Plato's. And by this criterion, Heidegger is surely right. Undoubtedly, Aristotle is more scientific in this sense than Plato. In light of our previous considerations about the dialogue form and Plato's project of writing, we must ask, does this judgment of the greater clarity of Aristotle to Plato and the decision to read Plato by this standard of clarity itself clarify or obscure what is going on in the Platonic dialogues, and in the *Sophist* in particular?

In turn, this helps make some sense both of Heidegger's interest in the *Sophist*, his choice of that dialogue for the course, and of the interpretation he renders. For the Eleatic Stranger in the *Sophist* has a method, diaresis, a method that, however problematic in the details, surely has the look of scientific methodological rigor. It is an easy move for Heidegger from this recognition to the judgment that in this dialogue *Plato* is moving toward scientific thinking. Moreover, it even makes sense, given his earlier association of phenomenology with research into the "Being of beings," that he would interpret the core of this dialogue, with Bonitz (PS, 160–161) as the discussion toward its very end of Being and the other greatest kinds.

But let us move more carefully here. What about the claim, first, that one reason to read Plato through Aristotle is that we can presuppose that Aristotle understood Plato? Can we make that presupposition? Heidegger simply makes the assertion with, apparently, no sense that it needs support. "We will presuppose that Aristotle understood Plato." (PS, 8). In one sense, the presupposition *does* seem obvious. Aristotle, one of the titanic geniuses of the history of thought, who studied with Plato in the latter's Academy for almost twenty years, how could he *not* have understood Plato? Or if he did not, who possibly could? It would seem almost insulting to entertain the thesis that perhaps he did not.

At the risk of such an insult, I want to suggest that two features of Aristotle's thought may have indeed made it impossible for him to understand Plato: that he was such a fundamentally different thinker than Plato, and that in any case, when he considered his predecessors, from the pre-Socratics through Plato, he tended to evaluate them almost exclusively in terms of the extent to which he saw that they paved the way for his own thinking. Let us consider each of these in turn.

One of the dangers of seeing Aristotle as culminating Greek philosophic thinking, and especially believing that he was a clearer version of what Plato was trying to say, is that seeing Plato as leading up to Aristotle involves a tendency to see only the similarities in their thinking; that is, the ways in which Plato does indeed lead up to Aristotle, and in so doing to overlook the great differences between them. We have already quoted the passages where Heidegger says that, "What Aristotle said is what Plato placed at his disposal, only it is said more radically and developed more scientifically" (PS, 8). Shortly thereafter, Heidegger is even more expansive on this assumption: "In order to be able to watch Plato at work and to repeat this work correctly, the proper standpoint is needed. We will look for information from Aristotle about which beings he himself, *and hence Plato and the Greeks,* had in view and what were for them the ways of access to beings" (PS, 9; my emphasis). Moreover, "What Aristotle conceives in a more precise way was already seen by Plato. . . . We see thereby that we will find in Plato the same orientation as Aristotle's. We have to presuppose in them one and the same position with regard to the basic questions of Dasein" (PS, 16). Now, it is no doubt true that in many instances there are common themes, common questions raised by both Plato and Aristotle. But by focusing only on these similarities, by seeing as the differences only those ways in which Plato is less clear than Aristotle on the same or similar topics, one can easily overlook the deep and fundamental differences between them. And in many ways, Aristotle is a deeply and fundamentally different thinker than his teacher.

To begin to see this, one need only consider the way each organized his writing, indeed, even the titles of his works. For Aristotle *has* a "metaphysics," "physics," "psychology," "ethics," "politics," and so on. That is, he explicitly organized his work into these different books, with their relatively carefully defined subject matters, methodologies, and first principles. Moreover, in addition to the explicit titles of his books, Aristotle draws a broad distinction between the theoretical, practical, and productive sciences, once again on the basis of distinctions in subject matters, methodologies, and first principles. This enables him both to organize or classify the subject matters in a relatively clear way, and to study each subject matter in isolation from the others, thus again, presumably, attaining greater clarity in each. To be sure, these divisions are not at all rigid, and there is much appropriate overlap among them. I am not at all claiming that Aristotle is a strict maintainer of rigid categorical distinctions between disciplines. But he does pave the way for that process by first making those distinctions, which become our disciplines, and writing his works in at least the partial light of those distinctions. In more specific ways, for example, he carefully distinguishes in Book VI of the *Nicomachean Ethics* between the five basic modes of knowledge (*nous, sophia, episteme, phronesis,* and *techne*), the set of distinctions from which Heidegger begins his study of Plato's *Sophist*. Lastly on this issue, after an apparent early dabbling in the writing of dialogues, he wrote all his work in a treatise format. Heidegger is so unimpressed by this difference from Plato that at least once in the *Sophist* course he refers to the *Sophist* as a "specifically ontological treatise" (PS, 160).

Now none of this is true of Plato. He writes dialogues, not treatises, the titles of which are not clearly delineated subject matters but usually the names of characters (sometimes, intriguingly, minor characters) in the dialogue. When they do take titles that indicate subjects, they are not names of disciplines but of specific topics: *Sophist, Statesman, Republic,* etc. Moreover, *no* Platonic dialogue can be designated as treating a single, specific subject matter, including the three named just above. To be sure, what after Aristotle will be called metaphysical issues, ethical issues, psychological issues, epistemological issues, etc., are raised in this or that dialogue. But typically, they are raised in something like the manner that they arise in human life: as intertwined in complex and sometimes confusing ways.

What we could call the "existential complexity" in which philosophical issues are raised in the dialogues is of course the source of the presumed (by Heidegger at least) Platonic obscurity. Where *is* Plato's metaphysics (if there is one at all)? His ethics, epistemology, politics, etc.? They are notoriously all over the place, buried here in one dialogue, there in another, and making it thus unendingly difficult to get a hold on what Plato's position on this or that topic really is.

The crucial question to be raised here, in regard to Heidegger, is this: is this Platonic tendency to place issues in the complex and intertwined existential situations in which they actually arise, and the Aristotelean decision to divide them up into separate disciplines with relative clarity, to be interpreted as an advance on Aristotle's part, as his seeing something clearly that Plato only saw obscurely? Or is it perhaps not that Plato had not yet thought of the idea of clearly dividing the sciences, but rather that he *rejected* the idea in favor of a presentation of issues as they arise in a concrete human life and situation? We need not here resolve this question in order to acknowledge that it is a question, one which indicates how utterly different these thinkers were. But the very raising of the question, and so of the issue of the fundamental differences between Aristotle and Plato, is obliterated if we simply assume that Aristotle was doing the same thing as Plato only clearer.

I have developed this line of thinking and questioning in order to allow to be raised as a serious—and not an insulting—question whether Aristotle might not have been such a fundamentally different thinker than Plato that he really couldn't understand him in a deep sense. This hypothesis is made more plausible, I now want to suggest, by the second consideration mentioned above, Aristotle's attitude toward his predecessors, including Plato.

Aristotle reads all his predecessors, from the pre-Socratics through Plato, with a very narrow focus: they seem to interest him primarily in terms of the extent to which they do or do not hold to some aspect of Aristotle's own thinking. Thus the early pre-Socratics are insightful in so far as they see the "material" cause of things. They are criticized in so far as they fail to see the other of the "four causes." Plato clearly sees the significance of formal cause, which is his great insight, but fails to adequately account for material cause. One might indeed speculate that Heidegger at this stage of his career gets his guiding thesis that Plato and the earlier philosophers must be read through Aristotle from Aristotle himself! But a brief look at Aristotle's reading of his predecessors reveals that by interpreting and evaluating them within such a narrow focus, Aristotle obviously passes over, or fails to see, much of the richness of these thinkers. There is nothing in Aristotle's evaluations of his predecessors, for example, that can match the richness and depth of the examination of Protagoras or the Heracliteans in the *Theaetetus*, or of Parmenides in the *Sophist*. It is instructive in this regard that although at this time, in 1924–25, Heidegger is insisting that Plato must be understood through Aristotle, less than a decade later he has begun his series of incomparably rich studies of a number of pre-Socratic philosophers that could not conceivably be understood as Aristotelean. Quite to the contrary. Those studies of the pre-Socratics think those figures in remarkably creative and unorthodox ways that are as far as possible from Aristotle's rather professorial assessments of his predecessors in terms of their proximity to his own thought. As we shall see, it is odd that although Heidegger rather quickly and completely rejects the notion that the pre-Socratics should be read through Aristotle, he never can quite bring himself to reject that idea as applied to Plato, even in his later work.

If these considerations are plausible, they make altogether problematic the guiding interpretive decision that determines the entire course of Heidegger's lecture course, that Plato must be understood through Aristotle and again and again assessed as a less clear version of the Stagirite. But if so, it must be immediately acknowledged that this tendency is not in the least a peculiarity of Heidegger's. Everyone who speaks of Plato's "metaphysics," "ethics," "psychology," and the like—and that means virtually all of us—is doing precisely what Heidegger insists we must do, reading Plato through Aristotelian categories, except that we are too often not even aware of what we are doing. Heidegger makes his guiding assumptions explicit and thereby opens them to be criticized, as I have done here. But to call into question Heidegger's Aristotelian reading of Plato is to call into question every standpoint that speaks of Plato's metaphysics, ethics, epistemology, etc. And that means almost all of us. There is much to be learned from Heidegger's explicit articulation of his presuppositions and assumptions, and much to be praised.

In any case, after his introductory remarks, Heidegger turns, for well over a hundred pages, to Aristotle, through whose thought he will interpret the *Sophist*. The Aristotelian text through which Heidegger will consider Plato is itself striking and instructive: Book VI of the *Nicomachean Ethics,* and particularly Aristotle's delineation of the five modes of knowing, *nous, sophia, episteme, phronesis, and techne.* Let us turn to that study.

The turn to *Ethics* Book VI is not arbitrary. After his introductory remarks, Heidegger begins the course with a development of his now famous construal of the Greek experience of truth (*aletheia*) as "unhiddenness," which implies that the world is initially experienced by the Greeks as fundamentally *hidden.* Knowledge is thus the effort to gain access to the truth of things, which means, to bring things to unhiddenness, *aletheuein* (PS, 10–12). As the Greeks experienced it, the ways of knowing, of bringing things to unhiddenness, are multiple. But what they tended to share is that they are again and again accomplished fundamentally through *language, logos, legein.* It is Aristotle who culminates this Greek experience of truth as bound up with *logos,* with language. "Aristotle was the first to emphasize: truth is a judgment; the determinations true or false apply primarily to judgments" (PS, 10). The place where Aristotle gathers together the multiplicity of the various possibilities of knowledge, *aletheuein,* through *legein,* is in the well-known chapters of *Ethics,* Book VI, and it is to that section that Heidegger now devotes a very careful analysis, gathering support, of course, through references to Aristotle's other works. The understanding of the discussions of truth and falsity, knowledge and sham-knowledge, the pretense to wisdom on the part of the sophist, in Plato's *Sophist* will be prepared by the study of the modes of knowing in Aristotle. This is a good example, for Heidegger, of moving from the clear to the obscure.

There follows a long, full, and often brilliant discussion of Aristotle's account of the five modes of knowing in *Ethics* VI. But it is not an unproblematic one. It begins with what becomes typically unorthodox Heideggerian translations of the key terms in question, *techne, episteme, phronesis, sophia, nous*. Heidegger translates these, respectively, as "know-how (in taking care, manipulating, producing), science, circumspection (insight), understanding, and perceptual discernment."[16] There are a number of problems in these typically unusual Heideggerian translations, but I want to focus on the translation of *nous* as "perceptual discernment," both in terms of the translation itself and what Heidegger will have to say about this particular mode of knowing.

Nous, of course, is typically translated in English as either "thought," "insight" or "intuition." W.D. Ross, for example, translates it in his translation of the *Ethics* as "intuitive reason."[17] It should be noted that both "insight" and "intuition" have "seeing" at their roots, and so also allude metaphorically to sense perception. But no one would take either insight or intuition as referring to, or even being grounded in, literal sense perception. As early as the pre-Socratics, "seeing" was used regularly as a metaphor for knowing.[18] It is thus already odd that Heidegger uses "insight" (*Einsicht*) in his translation of *phronesis*, which is usually translated in English as something like "practical wisdom" (as does Ross in the same passage). Heidegger then emphasizes the oddity by stressing that "*nous* is a discernment that discerns by way of perception,"[19]—an emphasis that underlines the literal sense of perception that he apparently wants to approach here. It is true enough that in his own discussions of *nous*, Aristotle does link *nous* to a certain kind of perception (*aisthesis*), but he there carefully *distinguishes* the sense of *aisthesis* linked to *nous* from any of the *sense* perceptions (*Nicomachean Ethics*, 1142a25ff, 1143b1–5). It seems that the very explicitness with which Aristotle distinguishes the sense of *aisthesis* linked to *nous* from literal sense perception signifies clearly that he, like us, is using the sense of seeing in *nous* metaphorically. Heidegger, it seems to me, is less clear here. Is he, with Aristotle, using the link between *aisthesis* and *nous* metaphorically, or is he in a more profound and controversial sense linking *nous* in a more literal sense to sense perception? This much must be said; the closer one brings the connection to a *literal* sense perception, the more problematic it is and the more carefully nuanced must be ones defense, and in this case at least, Aristotle is much clearer on where he stands than is Heidegger.

More interestingly, a short time later, Heidegger is clarifying the five modes of knowing into "the two basic modes of *logon echon*:

epistemonikon and logistikon" (PS, 19), and places *episteme and sophia* under *epistemonikon, techne and phronesis* under *logistikon* (PS, 20). He comments immediately, "It seems at first that *nous* is not included here. Yet it must be noted that *noein* is present in all four modes of *aletheuein;* they are determinate modes in which *noein* can be carried out; they are *dianoein"* (PS, 20). Now three things are crucial in this passage. First, Heidegger is right to exclude *nous* by itself from *"logon echon,"* since, strictly, *nous* is not by itself and as itself a linguistic experience. Second, Heidegger would also be right if he had said that *noein* is present in all four modes of *logon echon.* This, namely that there are, strictly, only *four* modes of knowing, which are strictly *logical,* would follow from the fact that *nous* is not a linguistic experience. However, third, since he says that *noein* is present in all four modes of *aletheuein,* he therein implies that there are *only* four, and so that *nous* is not, by itself, a mode of *aletheuein.* This implication gets made explicit later, where Heidegger twice says that "In anticipation, it must be said that *nous* as such is not a possibility of the Being of man" (PS, 41) and again that *"nous,* pure perception, is as such not possible for man, the *zoon logon echon"* (PS, 136). Heidegger offers no real evidence for this bold claim, other than what is possibly implied in the last sentence, that since the definition of human being is the "animal having language," no mode of access to truth is available to us that is *not* linguistic. But this is not true either for Plato or for Aristotle.

This is clear enough in Aristotle from the very section of the *Ethics* Heidegger is analyzing. At 1141a5, concluding his argument that "first principles" are known via *nous,* Aristotle concludes, "If, then, the states of mind by which we have truth and are never deceived about things invariable or even variable are scientific knowledge (*episteme*), practical wisdom (*phronesis*), philosophical wisdom (*sophia)* and intuitive reason (*nous*), and it cannot be any of the three (i.e., practical wisdom, scientific knowledge, or philosophic wisdom), the remaining alternative is that it is intuitive reason (*nous*) that grasps the first principles." Shortly thereafter, he adds at 1141a15, "It follows that the wise man must know not only what follows from the first principles, but must also possess truth about the first principles. Therefore wisdom must be intuitive reason (*nous)* combined with scientific knowledge—scientific knowledge of the highest objects which has received as it were its proper completion." (Both quotes from the Ross translation.) Now, against Heidegger, what could these two statements possibly mean if *"nous* were not a possibility for the Being of Dasein"? Clearly they only make the sense they do on the supposition, which is the supposition of the whole section of the *Ethics,* that *nous,* as one of the *five* (not four) modes of *aletheuein*, is indeed a "possibility for Dasein."

The reason why Heidegger may be making this odd claim about *nous* may become more clear in a later section when he has turned to Plato. In a section entitled "The meanings of the expression '*logos*' in Plato," Heidegger outlines what he takes to be seven important senses of *logos* in Plato. The fifth meaning is "an identification of *logos* with *nous*, *noein*. From what preceded, we know that *logos* is the phenomenon which is taken to be the basic determination of the constitution of the Being of man: man is the living being that speaks" (PS, 139). That is, by identifying logos and nous, Heidegger indicates that nous cannot occur to human beings other than *as language*. This is indeed the gist of his earlier claim that *noein* is present in "all four modes of *aletheuein*" (PS, 20). There are now only four, since *nous* by itself is "not a possibility" for humans. But this flies in the face of Aristotle, as I have shown, and the teaching of the Platonic dialogues, as I now want to argue.

I have addressed the question of the relation of *nous* to language in Plato in two earlier books and in detailed arguments.[20] Here, let me try to restate the case as briefly as possible. The reader can look to my earlier works if a longer argument is needed. *Nous*, or more often in the Platonic dialogues, *noesis*, "insight" or "intuition," functions crucially in any *logos* that seeks or claims *aletheuein*, to uncover the hidden, to reveal truth. It does so in two ways. It functions at the beginning of any such discourse, and it functions as the completion, or *telos*, of that discourse. It functions at the beginning to give us the matter for thought that we shall pursue. In order for us to pursue the question of *sophrosyne*, say, or to try to understand knowledge, it must occur to us that sophrosyne or knowledge is at stake, that it matters to us that we clarify these or any other issues. This is not as simple an issue as it might at first appear. What we recognize in a given situation as being at stake, as mattering, not only can vary from situation to situation and person to person; the decision we make as to what does matter or not can deeply, even decisively, affect the quality of our lives. When our originating *noesis* as to what is at stake in a given situation is wrong, it can be disastrous. That originating noetic vision, *noesis*, it is important to recognize, is not itself a speech; here Heidegger is exactly right. But our speech occurs in the light of that originating insight. But second, our speech is directed toward what we may call a *culminating* noetic vision, an insight into the truth of the matter at hand, which is *also* not linguistic. (Sometimes, but not always in the dialogues, this culminating noetic vision is taken to be an insight into the "form" or "idea" of the issue at hand.) The speech of philosophy, speech that seeks *aletheuein,* is thus bounded, must be bounded if it is to be coherent, by two *nonlinguistic* noetic visions, an originating and a culminating one. Our speech seeks to move us from the originating insight into the matter for thought to a culminating insight into the truth of that matter. One might say, as Plato's Diotima says of eros, that our speech seeks to "bind the two together into a whole" (*Symposium,* 202e).

But second for Plato, both noetic insights, the originating and the culminating one, are finite, that is, precarious, unstable, as a function of the finitude of the human situation out of which and in terms of which they arise. Our originating insight might be off the mark; our discursive speech in the light of that insight may mislead rather than benefit us; our completing insight may simply be wrong, it may leave the matter for thought in hiddenness (*lethe*). That is why *aporia* is the paradigmatic stance of philosophy for Plato, and not just in the early dialogues! This is so because the recognition—itself an insight—of the question-worthiness of our best insights is always more striking than the persuasiveness of those same insights. *Aporia* is the Platonic philosophic stance not because he has "not yet achieved philosophy as a science," but because of his recognition of the radical finitude of the human situation. This offers, in fact, one sense of Heidegger's "*Nous* is impossible for human Dasein" that may indeed be appropriate for Plato: *Nous* is impossible *as a totalizing, complete achievement.* But in this sense of impossibility, all the modes of *aletheuein* would be "impossible."

Precarious though they may be, we do have those noetic insights, both the originating and the culminating ones, and we live by them, for better or for worse. It therefore makes no sense for Heidegger to say or even imply that in the dialogues "*nous* is not a possibility for the Being of Dasein." This is no small problem. As we have seen, Heidegger wants to claim that for Plato as for Aristotle, even if less clearly, truth is propositional, the locus of any *aletheia* granted to humans is within logos. It is certainly true that speech is a crucial element for Plato in the human project to *aletheuein.* But the presence, the necessary presence, of *nous* at the beginning and the completion of any human experience of *aletheia,* makes any comprehensive claim that truth is propositional an impossibility in the Platonic dialogues. Aristotle may have put us on the path to the metaphysical view that "truth is prepositional." But that is not the view portrayed in the Platonic dialogues, neither clearly nor obscurely.

Let us return to the guiding reason why Heidegger turns to the analysis in *Ethics* VI of the five basic modes of knowing. It is because, as he puts it, it is there that Aristotle "for the first time and before all else (he) saw and interpreted the multiplicity of the phenomena, the multiplicity of the various possibilities of *aletheuein*" (PS, 13). Aristotle does indeed there recognize that there are a "multiplicity of possibilities" of *aletheuein*, indeed an irreducible multiplicity; this is an important Greek insight, that should always be contrasted with the modern effort to reduce genuine knowledge to a single, unified procedure and methodology. It is also true enough, and important, that Aristotle here gathers these various possibilities together, clearly delineates them one after the other. This is a good example, again, of the way in which Aristotle was supposedly "clearer" than Plato. Presumably, the contrast we are to see is that in the dialogues all five of these possibilities are at work, but never clearly delineated as such.

The Platonic dialogues do indeed exhibit the recognition of the multiple modes of knowing; indeed, those modes seem to be even more multiple than Aristotle's list of five. Moreover, the dialogues seem to exhibit the conviction even more strongly than Aristotle both that there are multiple modes of knowing, and that they are irreducible to each other. That is, different modes of knowing are appropriate for different situations, different human experiences. This means that one crucial issue when thinking about knowledge is to determine what mode of knowing is appropriate to a given situation. For this reason, the modes of knowing cannot be rank-ordered as if somehow homogeneous, as Aristotle appears to want to do in *Ethics* VI and Heidegger appears to want to emphasize.[21] One mode of knowing is not superior to others, simply more appropriate in given circumstances. What the dialogues try to do, then, is not to bring all the modes of knowing together in a determinate collection, but to exhibit something of the multiplicity of human situations and the corresponding multiplicity of possible ways of knowing. Is this less clear than Aristotle, or simply a fundamentally different enterprise?

Certainly, the five ways of knowing gathered together by Aristotle, *episteme, techne, phronesis, sophia, and nous,* are all present here or there in the Platonic dialogues. But there are also a host of other distinctions, making the ways of knowing if anything even more multiple than in Aristotle. In addition to these five, for example, there is the crucial distinction between those phenomena that, it is suggested, are known, in so far as they are known, through an insight into the form of that phenomenon—perhaps "justice," piety," or "the equal itself"—as opposed to those phenomena about which we can gain some knowledge but which do not have forms. Paradigmatic among the latter is eros. It is no accident that in the *Symposium,* the form that Diotima ascends to in the famous ascent passage at 210a is not eros but "beauty itself." We do not ascend to the "form Eros" because, since eros has been determined to be "in the middle" between the divine and the human, and so *not* a divine entity as a form must be (*Symposium, 202b–203a), there can be no form of* eros. Nor is there any suggestion in the other Platonic dialogue that treats eros at length, the *Phaedrus,* that there is anything like a form of eros.[22] Yet we *do* have some knowledge of eros. Clearly, therefore, the mode of knowing by which we have what knowledge we gain of eros is not the same as the mode of knowledge we gain by having an insight into the form of some phenomenon or other.

There is also the crucial case of the altogether strange mode of knowing that constitutes Socratic self-knowledge, the "knowing what I know and what I don't know," whose exhibition is the questioning stance of *aporia.* Almost always, Plato has Socrates use a form of *gignoskein* to express this peculiar mode of knowledge (as does the Delphic oracle: *gnothi s'auton).* This mode is no doubt connected to the sense of knowing at work in the famous Socratic paradox, "virtue is knowledge." What kind of knowledge is that? *Phronesis?* Almost certainly not *episteme.* But is not *gignoskein* at work here as well? Or what about the altogether precarious knowledge we have—to the extent that it can be called knowledge at all—of the "idea of the Good," which we are told in the *Republic* is "beyond Being" (*Republic,* 509). In the same category of precarious knowledge, perhaps even more so, is the famous *khora* of the *Timaeus,* that we know, if at all, by a "bastard reasoning" (*Timaeus,* 52b).[23]

Plato chooses not to gather all modes of knowing together in an exhaustive list, and I certainly do not want to make such a claim to have exhausted the list of modes of knowing in Plato here. The point is, his project is apparently not the quasi-theoretical one of gathering them all in a definitive list once and for all. His is the very different project of exhibiting something of the variety of human situations and the variety of modes of knowing appropriate to them, so that the reader, considering all these, can respond to his or her own situations with greater sensitivity. But this enterprise is surely no science, either theoretical or practical, and so it may be for very good reasons—and not lack of clarity—that Plato chooses not to claim to gather them in an exhaustive list.

In any case, having carefully and at length discussed Aristotle's account of his five modes of knowing, Heidegger is finally prepared to move to Plato's *Sophist,* and we can do so with him. Immediately that we do so, we must note an enormously problematic dimension of

Heidegger's intention, indeed, one which, if the interpretive principles I espouse have merit, undercuts his entire interpretation of Plato. It is a problem every reader of Plato must face, but it is especially acute for those of us who come at the end of a long tradition of Platonic interpretation. It is this: for philosophic writers who write in the first person singular, and that means for the vast majority of philosophers in the history of philosophy, an almost natural assumption is that their writing espouses "their" philosophy, that, as I have put it in the introduction, they seek to argue as clearly and persuasively as possible for the philosophic view that they hold. Once this becomes the natural way of reading a given philosopher, it is an easy step to interpret the writings of *any* philosopher, even those who do *not* write in a first-person treatise form, as presenting that particular philosopher's doctrine. But as I have argued, at least in the case of Plato, it is by no means obvious that the primary intent of his writing was to present as clearly and persuasively as possible *Plato's own doctrines* of this or that. To say this is not, of course, to go to the other extreme and suggest, say in the manner of the Tubingen school, that there is *nothing* of Plato's view in the dialogues. It is just to say that Plato's primary aim in writing seemed to be something other than espousing his doctrines. If we then seek in the dialogues only Plato's doctrines of this or that, we remain oblivious to the larger and richer event that is taking place in the Platonic dialogue: as I have put it earlier, an imitation of, and an invitation to, philosophy.

Now all such considerations are obliterated by a crucial interpretive decision that Heidegger makes regarding the dialogues. It is a decision by no means peculiar to him, but it is no less problematic for that. It is the decision, as Heidegger occasionally puts it most graphically, that "Socrates=Plato." As Gregory Vlastos will subsequently formulate this interpretive principle for an entire generation of English-speaking Platonic scholarship, "In any given dialogue, Plato allows the persona of Socrates only what he (Plato), at the time, considers true."[24] It might seem odd that Heidegger would articulate this interpretive principle while studying a dialogue in which Socrates is for the most part silent, but that does not stop him, especially because he needs to appeal to other dialogues in which Socrates does play a dominant role. In any case, Heidegger explicitly articulates the principle at least four times, though it is clearly at work whenever he interprets anything said by the Platonic Socrates[25] (it is noteworthy that it does not seem to occur to him to interpret the Socratic *silence* in the *Sophist* as "Platonic silence"). One occasion when he makes the identification explicit particularly exemplifies the problem. In the section of the course in which Heidegger turns to a brief interpretation of the end of the *Phaedrus,* where Socrates indicates his problems with writing and so why he himself never writes, Heidegger begins his discussion by saying, "Socrates, i.e. Plato, clarifies the ontological function of the free-floating *logos* in Dasein by means of a so-called *akoe* (cf. 274c1), something he has heard, a legend" (PS, 235). After which follows a discussion of the famous story of Theuth. But here, of all places, it should have been obvious that Socrates could not possibly "=Plato," since the reasons he gives in criticism of writing were sufficient, apparently, to lead Socrates never to write, whereas they were obviously not sufficient to persuade Plato, who wrote the dialogue in which Socrates recommends that one not write. By identifying them, Heidegger misses this profound irony and the enormously rich problematic of what is going on in the dialogues that it raises.

By assuming that Plato's project in writing was essentially the same as those philosophers who write treatises, to present his own doctrines, and by further assuming that "Socrates=Plato," Heidegger, and those scholars such as Vlastos who follow his example, generate for themselves what has become a virtual Plato industry, the "Plato's development" problem. For it is obvious that Socrates says very different things from one dialogue to another, some of them quite incompatible. If these are all doctrines that Plato himself is taken to hold, then obviously Plato constantly "changed his mind" or "developed" from one dialogue to another. It is important to recognize that this development problem only becomes a decisive issue of interpretation once one makes the above two assumptions. If Socrates does not simply speak for Plato, and if Plato is not primarily espousing his doctrines, then the development issue pales into insignificance, or at very least, becomes an altogether different problem. As we shall see, Heidegger, making the above assumptions, enters into the "Plato's development" business when he turns to the question of Plato's attitude toward rhetoric later in the course.

But Heidegger exacerbates the problems (and he is again hardly alone here) by also assuming, with no apparent sense of conflict, that the Eleatic Stranger *also* equals Plato. This is perhaps the most ubiquitous interpretive assumption of the entire lecture course.[26] The problems with this identification are manifold and acute.

First, if Socrates=Plato, and in addition the Stranger=Plato, then what does this imply as an interpretive principle of the dialogues? That anyone who speaks in any dialogue "=Plato"? That seems ludicrous on the face of it. Then should it be that whoever is the dominant speaker in any dialogue "=Plato"? But Heidegger himself has already undercut that hardly less problematic assumption by insisting that early in the *Sophist*, Socrates, who quickly becomes a silent listener for the bulk of the dialogue, speaks for Plato as well. In sum, once one starts identifying the words of any particular character in a dialogue as Plato's view, one gets lost in an interpretive abyss. In the case of the *Sophist*, by assuming that the Stranger speaks for Plato, Heidegger is able to say (or is forced to say) that all the—rather obvious—problems and failings of the Stranger's procedure are *Plato's* problems and failings, and so makes it impossible to see that Plato is inviting us dramatically to contrast the procedures—and the problems—of the Stranger with those of Socrates "yesterday." Therein, I suggest, lies the real "matter for thought" of the two dialogues.

A good example of the interpretive debacle in which these principles leave Heidegger is in his highly critical evaluation of Platonic dialectic. This becomes an important issue in the *Sophist* once one assumes, with Heidegger, that the Stranger's highly technical procedure of diaresis is *Plato's* latest view of how philosophical thinking should be pursued, that is to say, of dialectic. Since this obviously differs significantly from the procedure of *Socrates* in other dialogues, the problem of Plato's development with regard to dialectic becomes an issue. This is deepened by the obvious question of the relation of dialectic to rhetoric, about which, as Heidegger will go on to show, Plato also has his characters say very different things. Hence the problem on this issue of "Plato's development" regarding dialectic and rhetoric.

The first thing of importance to note here is how highly, even harshly, critical of dialectic Heidegger is.[27] The prevalence of dialectic that Heidegger finds in the Platonic dialogues is for him a defect of Plato's thinking. A passage in the section entitled "First Characterization of Dialectic in Plato" sums up Heidegger's attitude well:

> Dialectic is not something like a higher level of what is known as thinking, in opposition to so-called intuition, but quite to the contrary, the only meaning and the only intention of dialectic is to prepare and to develop a genuine intuition, passing through what is merely said. The fact that Plato did not advance far enough so as ultimately to see beings themselves and in a certain sense to overcome dialectic is a deficiency included in his own dialectical procedure, and it determines certain moments of his dialectic, e.g., the much discussed *koinonia ton genon*, the association, the keeping company together, of the kinds. These charac-

teristics are not merits and are not determinations of a superior philosophical method but are indications of a fundamental confusion and unclarity, which, as I have already said, is founded in the difficulty of the matters themselves, the difficulty of such first foundational research. (PS, 137)

Leaving aside the assumption at work here that the Stranger's procedure is Plato's dialectic, and notwithstanding the polite qualification in the last sentence, it is clear from this paragraph, as from his discussion more generally, that Heidegger finds in what he confidently calls "Platonic dialectic" a deep flaw in the Greek's thinking.

This is a flaw that Aristotle overcomes, another example of the superiority and greater clarity of Aristotle to Plato. Shortly after the above passage, Heidegger adds,

Aristotle did deprive dialectic of its dignity, but not because he did not understand it. On the contrary, it was because he understood it more radically, because he saw Plato himself as being underway towards *theorein* in his dialectic, because he succeeded in making real what Plato was striving for. Aristotle saw the imminent limits of dialectic because he philosophized more radically. (PS, 138)

There is considerable complexity in the way Heidegger treats what he regards as Plato's position on dialectic. A number of things need to be noted initially. First, although in the *Sophist* "rhetoric" is treated as characteristic of the sophist who is being defined, and "dialectic" refers for Heidegger to the "method of division" of the Stranger,[28] in his examination of dialectic, Heidegger conflates the two presumably different possibilities into a single discussion. So the examination of Platonic dialectic and of Plato's attitude toward rhetoric proceeds along a single path, from the *Gorgias* to an extended discussion of the *Phaedrus*, then on to the *Sophist*. Second, since Heidegger follows the hermeneutical principle that "Socrates (or the Stranger, or. . . .)=Plato," what Socrates says to the group of rather arrogant and aggressive sophists in the *Gorgias*, and what Socrates says to his young friend Phaedrus in the *Phaedrus*, and what the *Stranger* says to Theaetetus and the others in the *Sophist*, can, without any attention to dramatic context, all be taken as Plato's view. But, third, since these views are fundamentally different, some explanation is needed, and the explanatory principle is "Plato's development." So the "early" Plato, of the *Gorgias*, has one attitude, the "middle" Plato, of the *Phaedrus*, has another, and the "later" Plato, of the *Sophist*, yet another and presumably more mature view.[29] Passing over for the moment all these unexamined assumptions, let us briefly inspect Heidegger's account of "Plato's view" of dialectic (and rhetoric).

Heidegger begins with a brief examination of one passage in the *Gorgias*, which he takes as sufficient to establish the "early Plato's" negative attitude toward rhetoric.[30] In a remarkable exhibition of his unexamined interpretive assumptions, Heidegger not only takes what Socrates says as Plato's view, but takes a question that Socrates asks Gorgias in his elenchus of that sophist as a sufficient indication of *Plato's doctrine* regarding rhetoric at the time. After quoting the passage in Greek, Heidegger translates and then comments:

> 'Now it seems to me, Gorgias, that you have revealed to me precisely what sort of *techne* you attribute to rhetoric, and if I have understood you correctly you are saying "peithous demiourgos estin he rhetorike," the main concern of the entire occupation is to achieve this end. Or are you saying that rhetoric may be capable of something else than the inculcation of a definite opinion in the audience?' *This is Plato's conception of rhetoric in the Gorgias, hence a negative one.* (PS, 215; my emphasis)

So this is taken to establish that the early Plato's attitude toward rhetoric is entirely negative. There follows a much longer and far more engaging examination of the latter part of the *Phaedrus*, the central point of which is to establish that by the time of this dialogue, Plato's attitude toward rhetoric has moderated, and at the same time the conception of dialectic is developing.

It is in the *Phaedrus*, Heidegger argues, that rhetoric, or at least a certain species of rhetoric, becomes in a sense justifiable. That justifiable rhetoric, however, attains its higher status precisely because of its relation to dialectic. Heidegger presents the connection in two steps:

"1) Plato shows that even rhetoric, rhetorical technique, insofar as it aims at *logos*, at *peithous demiourgos*, hence insofar as it deals with what is probable or with opinions, is actually possible only if it has an insight into *aletheia* itself, i.e. into truthful speech (273d3ff.)."

"2) This seeing of the truth is carried out in dialectic" (PS, 221).

The rhetoric that is justifiable, then, is that rhetoric that is based on an insight into truth, which insight is achieved by dialectic. This dialectic, spoken of in the *Phaedrus*, will be identical, apparently to the Stranger's procedure in the *Sophist*. "We will see dialectic actually carried out in the *Sophist*, with regard to a determinate phenomenon, one connected precisely to the accomplishment of deception" (PS, 228).

Oddly, however, this grounding of legitimate rhetoric in dialectic is only a partial advance on Plato's part. For it occurs as part of what Heidegger regards as Plato's excessive emphasis on dialectic as "the only fundamental science," (PS, 234) a defect, which Aristotle will overcome. This is nicely summed up by Heidegger:

> In the *Phaedrus*, Plato does not retain the negative attitude toward rhetoric expressed in the *Gorgias*. We must keep in mind that Plato does not intend to develop a rhetoric, as Aristotle later did. And indeed, it is not simply that Plato does not in fact care to do so, but he even considers it unnecessary, since dialectic occupies a different position within his concept of science than it will later for Aristotle. Plato sees his dialectic as the only fundamental science, such that in his opinion all other tasks, even those of rhetoric, are discharged in it. The reason Plato does not take up the task of developing a rhetoric, as Aristotle will later, lies in his exaggeration of dialectic or, more precisely, in this peculiarity, that although he in a certain sense understands the secondary significance of *logos*, yet he does not proceed to make *logos* itself thematic in its secondary position and to penetrate positively into its proper structure. (PS, 234)

This leads Heidegger into the well-known Socratic critique of writing at the end of the *Phaedrus*, which, rather oddly, Heidegger interprets as a blanket critique of *logos* altogether. While Plato certainly does indicate both the limits and the possibilities of *logos*, as I have developed previously, it is at least odd to suppose that the limitations of *logos* are to be identified with the Socratic critique of writing, which is accomplished precisely in opposition to the superiority of spoken *logos*.[31]

It must again be emphasized that Heidegger is again employing a number of unexamined assumptions. As usual, he assumes that whatever Socrates says in the *Phaedrus* is what Plato believed. Moreover, in part because of this, it is unnecessary to examine the content of Socrates' speeches within the dramatic context of who he is speaking to, what his intentions are, etc. Indeed, it is not even necessary to examine the entire dialogue. Although the *Sophist* lecture course is surely Heidegger's most sustained interpretation of a Platonic dialogue, it is evident from his examination of the *Phaedrus* within that course that he does not consider it *necessary* to examine a dialogue as a whole in order to make judgments regarding Plato's view in that dialogue. In the case of the *Phaedrus* interpretation, no attention is paid to the entire first half of the dialogue where eros is discussed.[32] Heidegger simply turns to parts of the second half of the dialogue on rhetoric and writing, almost as if these were separate chapters in a book that could stand independently of each other. It does not occur to him, for example, that in order to gain access to something like Plato's teaching on rhetoric in this dialogue, what Socrates says about rhetoric would have to be compared, for similarity and for contrast, to the rhetoric that Socrates actually employs toward Phaedrus, both in the discussion of eros and even in the very conversation on rhetoric itself. Nor does it occur to him that the initially odd juxtaposition of a long discussion of eros and a discussion of rhetoric and writing is a provocation on Plato's part, that we cannot understand the one without considering its relation to the other. Again, since whatever Socrates says at any point is what Plato believes, Plato's view is rather easily determined, without the need for a complicated interpretation of the entire dialogue.

In any case, employing these interpretive principles, Heidegger establishes to his satisfaction that at the time of the *Phaedrus* "Plato" believed that "true rhetoric" was grounded in dialectic, that this is essentially the same dialectic that the Stranger follows in the *Sophist*, and that in the critique of writing toward the end of the *Phaedrus* we can already see Plato's skepticism about *logos*. He is prepared to turn to the *Sophist* to discover Plato's view of dialectic in that dialogue by seeing what the Stranger does.

As we have already seen, Heidegger takes it as obvious that the Stranger's method of division by which he defines first the angler and then—at least six times—the sophist is what Plato now believes dialectic to be. This is odd on the face of it, since it is striking that the Stranger pointedly avoids ever using the term *dialectike,* or any of its cognates, in regard to his method of division. Perhaps Heidegger is moved to his identification by the reference Socrates makes in the *Phaedrus* to being "a lover of divisions and collections." (*Phaedrus,* 266b), though it is neither suggested nor exhibited in that dialogue that this remark implies a putatively rigorous formal procedure or method.[33] More importantly, the word *dialectike* and its cognates *is* taken up by the Stranger, but only toward the end of the *Sophist*, after the formal divisions have been completed, and in reference, first, to "all those who have discoursed (*dialexthentas*) concerning Being," (251d). Shortly thereafter, he attributes "the dialectical science" (*tes dialectikes epistemes*) to those who "divide according to kinds (*gene*) and do not regard the same form (*eidos*) as other nor the other as the same" (253d). Finally, he attributes dialectic (*to dialectikon*) to those who "philosophize purely and justly" (253e). Since it is these activities that the Stranger actually calls dialectic, and especially since they occur so closely together, one would think that a reader as careful as Heidegger would wonder about the connection of the three formulations, and notice that it was by no means obvious that the three together refer paradigmatically—or even at all—to the earlier diareses of the Stranger in coming up with his definitions of the angler and sophist. Nor does it occur to him to wonder whether *Plato* would necessarily accept as his own view the highly formalistic, eleatic procedure followed by the Stranger in his *diareses*. So convinced is Heidegger that Plato is "on the way" toward the construal of philosophy as science that he finds in Aristotle and that he holds himself at this period, that he simply identifies the Stranger's procedure as the one Plato holds. The very obvious flaws and even contradictions in that procedure that I pointed out earlier thus become flaws that Plato himself fell prey to, not provocations that Plato is placing before the reader for our thoughtful consideration.

Nevertheless, having "established" all this, Heidegger turns, for most of the rest of the lecture course, to a very detailed analysis of the detailed distinctions of the Stranger. Since this is not an entire book on Heidegger's *Sophist* lectures, I shall not examine them each in detail. It is important to emphasize that my critical evaluation of Heidegger's reading of Plato is largely directed toward his way of reading the dialogues more than the technical analyses of this or that passage in the *Sophist*. My problems with Heidegger have largely to do with his hermeneutical principles. Many of the technical analyses of specific passages are quite excellent, and one can learn much from them. As a particularly fine example of this, I would cite the closing discussion Heidegger presents in the last 20 pages or so of the course, of the concluding sections of the *Sophist*.

At this point, Heidegger is taking up one of the last sections of the *Sophist*, the section where the Stranger suggests that the sophist, in a last-ditch effort to avoid being caught by the ability now to identify non-being in terms of the five greatest kinds, and especially the kind, "difference," might try to hide in language. Therefore they must discover how non-being not only can somehow *be*, but also how we can speak of it coherently. This engenders the famous section in which Plato supposedly "discovers" the difference between nouns (*onoma*) and verbs (*rhema*). Heidegger, in a most imaginative and provocative discussion, suggests that what is really at work in this section is not merely the grammatical distinction between nouns and verbs, but the far more momentous presentation of the relation between what he calls the "onomatic" and "delotic" structures of *logos*. Here is the way Heidegger articulates the basic issue: The analysis of *logos* will show

> The exhibition of the 'onomatic' and 'delotic' basic structure of *legein*. I have to use these terms because our language contains nothing comparable. 'Onomatic' means 'naming,' *legein* as linguistic expression. 'Delotic,' from *deloun,* denotes *legein* as revealing, letting be seen. A unitary consideration will thus show discourse as: a) self-expression and b) a discussion that addresses the matter at issue and that has the sense of disclosure, *deloun.* It will be clear afterwards how precisely these two phenomena of discourse, expression (or utterance) and the function of disclosure, are taken together here. (PS, 403)

What is especially powerful about this final section of the lecture course is that in it, Heidegger finds in the final section of the *Sophist* not just a rather primitive discussion of the basic structure of grammar, but also the beginnings of a phenomenological account of the disclosive capacity of *logos*. It is a brilliant and insightful analysis.

The question is, how do we interpret it vis-à-vis Plato's intentions? Heidegger makes it easy for us. The Stranger said it, so Plato believes it. I hope that by now I have established that such a hermeneutical principle is altogether too simplistic, failing to take with due seriousness the profound significance of Plato's use of the dialogue form for philosophic thinking and interpretation. I suggest instead that this final passage in the *Sophist,* and for that matter all the technical analyses of the details of the *Sophist* that make up the bulk of Heidegger's lecture course, should be understood as part of a critical evaluation on Plato's part of a certain kind of philosophizing already becoming popular in Plato's time and one that would become a dominant paradigm of philosophy for centuries: the highly technical, formalistic, quasi-mathematical procedure exhibited by the Stranger as a representative of a tendency among Parmenideans and Pythagoreans as well. Obviously, Plato's *Sophist,* as well as a number of other dialogues, suggests that such a standpoint has very much to offer. It is a rich and challenging paradigm for philosophic thinking, and it would be mindless not to take it very seriously. But it is not The Way of Platonic philosophy, late or early. Rather, almost in the manner of a

Kantian critique, Plato writes in such a way as to make visible both the powerful possibilities as well as the limits of such a technical procedure. To use Heideggerian terminology that he was already developing at the time, Plato allows us to see how such a technical procedure both *reveals* and *conceals*.

Heidegger misses all this. Assuming that "the Stranger=Plato," he quickly concludes that the very visible limits of the Stranger's view are limits of Plato's view, and so easily criticizes the dialogues as the "obscure" of which the books of Aristotle are the more "clear" version. But as I have argued, this inability of Heidegger to take with adequate seriousness the significance of the dialogue form, and the concomitant critical stance toward Plato in favor of Aristotle, could easily be attributed in good measure to Heidegger's own strong predilection at the time toward a Husserlian version of philosophy as phenomenological science, and what that view entails. If so, as Heidegger gradually moves away from the paradigm of philosophy as science, as he moves toward a much more poetic conception of philosophical thinking, one would reasonably expect that his attitude toward Plato (and perhaps Aristotle) would change radically if not reverse. Such, as we shall now see, is, alas, not the case.

PLATO'S DOCTRINE OF TRUTH

This text was composed, according to Heidegger's notes, in 1940 and first published in 1942.[34] Heidegger indicates in a note that the origin of this text is the 1931–32 lecture course on "The Essence of Truth," which contains a long interpretation, first, of the cave analogy in the *Republic*, then of a portion of the *Theaetetus*, principally the discussion of Theaetetus's second (though Heidegger calls it the "first") answer to the question of what is *episteme*, "knowledge is perception."[35] The relationship between the published text, "Plato's Doctrine of Truth," and the lecture course is curious and deserves some initial comment. First, the lecture course contains the most careful, nuanced development of which I am aware of Heidegger's now well-known understanding of *aletheia* as "unhiddenness." Within its pages are careful, often rich reflections on certain implications both of the cave analogy and of the section of the *Theaetetus* that he treats. For example, in a remarkably sensitive comment on the cave as an *allegory*, Heidegger says this: "There is thus an inner necessity to the fact that when Plato wants to say something fundamental and essential in philosophy, he always speaks in an allegory and places us before a sensory image. Not that he is unsure about what he is speaking of; on the contrary, he is *quite sure* that it cannot be described or proved" (ET, 13; Heidegger's emphasis). Despite the continued assumption that it is "Plato" speaking here, this kind of sensitivity to Plato's writing is just what one might expect and hope for from a thinker as sensitive to literature as Heidegger. Moreover, I think it is fair to say that, consistent with the more nuanced discussion, a somewhat greater sympathy to Plato's project is exhibited within its pages than shows up in the published text. Indeed, perhaps the most striking and puzzling contrast between the two is that in this, the one text on Plato that Heidegger ever formally published, he withdrew from the more sympathetic, nuanced treatment of the lecture course in favor of what is perhaps his single most critical text on Plato. That the one text he formally published on Plato is also arguably the most critical surely gives us pause. Why did Heidegger, when he wrote as it were for the world and not primarily for his students, go on the attack against Plato most strongly?

Nevertheless, despite this greater sympathy in the lecture course and the sometimes brilliant individual insights contained therein, Heidegger is still using the same flawed interpretive assumptions as he did in the earlier *Sophist* lecture course. As the quote above indicates, it is still the case that whatever anyone says, and especially what Socrates says in any context whatsoever, is "Plato's" view. Second and perhaps most damaging, both in the case of the cave interpretation and of the section of the *Theaetetus*, Heidegger not only ignores the larger dialogical context but explicitly claims that considering that context is unnecessary. Two citations, the first at the beginning of the cave interpretation, the second at the beginning of the *Theaetetus* reading, will make this disappointingly clear. In his preliminary considerations regarding the cave, he says,

> In the following interpretation, we deliberately leave unconsidered the precise placement of this allegory within the dialogue. To begin with we leave aside all discussion concerning the dialogue as a whole. What is crucial about the allegory is that it can stand entirely on its own, so we can consider it by itself without in any way minimizing its content or meaning. (ET, 12)

Then, at the beginning of the *Theaetetus* discussion, we are told:

> The necessary method of interpretation leads to the centre of our *question*. We do not therefore go schematically through the dialogue from beginning to end; we completely aban-

don the attitude of the mere reader. In somewhat imperti-
nent fashion we cut into, as *co-questioning* auditors, the already progressing conversation, without knowing the
beginning or end, yet at a point where we immediately feel
something of the whole. (ET, 109; Heidegger's emphases)

We can, alas, only assume that Heidegger would consider the
interpretive standpoint for which I have been arguing, one that insists
that the context, characters, situation, etc., must be considered in any
adequate interpretation, to be that of a "mere reader." Nevertheless,
despite the many particular insights along the way, Heidegger's understanding of Plato's project continues to be deeply infected by his
flawed interpretive assumptions. No better indication of this could be
had than to see what happens when Heidegger crystallizes the results
of the lecture course into what, presumably, he considered the essen-
tials of his interpretation, his one published text on Plato, "Plato's
Doctrine of Truth." We can turn directly to that text.

Let us begin with a consideration of the remarkable set of assumptions embodied in the title: *Platons Lehre von der Wahrheit*: "Plato's
Doctrine of Truth." We need to examine the significance of each of the
nouns in the title. The foundation of the essay, as we shall see, is an
examination of the famous cave analogy at the beginning of Book VII
of Plato's *Republic*. Begin with the notion that Heidegger will elicit
Plato's *doctrine* (*Lehre*) of truth therein. This means, obviously, that he
joins with so many orthodox interpreters of Plato in assuming that
Plato does indeed present in the dialogues a set of "doctrines," which
are his. We have already addressed the enormous set of problems
involved in this assumption. It implies that Plato was doing in his
dialogues what most more orthodox philosophic writers are doing in
the treatises they write: presenting his doctrines as clearly and persuasively as possible. But as we have seen, this makes the use of the
dialogue form altogether problematic, not to say an astonishing bad
choice on the part of Plato. But for Heidegger, the attribution of a
doctrine to Plato is if anything even more portentous. For around this
same period of his life, Heidegger is embarking on his well-known
and important studies of the pre-Socratic philosophers, in which one
of his important points is that these great thinkers precisely did *not*
have doctrines, and that was part of their greatness. Thus in his sum-
mer semester, 1944 lecture course entitled "Logic," (later published as
Logos: Heraclitus Fragment B 50) Heidegger says of Heraclitus, in reference to the purported "pantheism" ascribed to him, "Heraclitus does
not teach this or any doctrine (*Lehre*). As a thinker, he only gives us to

think."[36] If Heraclitus, writing in his stunning aphoristic style but nevertheless speaking in the first person, did not teach doctrines, why should Heidegger—or anyone else—think that Plato, who never wrote in his own name but wrote those dialogues that established dialogue as the paradigmatic discourse of philosophy, presented doctrines? I would suggest that Heidegger's insightful remark about Heraclitus is true of no one in the history of philosophy so much as of Plato: he did not teach doctrines, but gives us to think. But Heidegger, almost two decades after the *Sophist* lecture course, still holds that Plato does teach doctrines. Hence he can speak of Plato's doctrine of truth.

And it is *Plato's* doctrine of truth. Let us trace carefully the assumptions here. Suppose we were to grant (which I never would) that there are indeed doctrines presented in the cave analogy. Heidegger, with a modicum of caution, might then have entitled his essay "Socrates' doctrine of truth in the cave analogy." For it is the cave analogy, and no other part of the *Republic* or any other dialogue, that Heidegger here addresses. So if there is a doctrine there, since Socrates is the one doing most of the presenting in the analogy, one might say that the doctrine is "Socrates'" (in the cave analogy). Whether it was a more pervasive doctrine of Socrates' in the *Republic* would be a further question. If Heidegger had wanted to be bolder and imply a more controversial claim, he might have entitled the essay more broadly, "Socrates' doctrine of truth in the *Republic*." That would entail showing that the doctrine of truth supposedly presented in the cave analogy was also at work in the rest of the *Republic*; Heidegger never does this. He might have made the still broader claim that this conception of truth was at work not only in the cave analogy, not only in the *Republic*, but throughout the dialogues in which Socrates appears, thus entitling his work "Socrates' doctrine of truth." That, obviously, would involve a broad examination of a number of Socratic dialogues to show that such was indeed the case. But on top of all those assumptions, Heidegger then makes the most monumental one of all, that what is being presented in the cave analogy is not Socrates' but *Plato's* doctrine of truth. Imagine the work that would have to be done to show that this claim was plausible! Alas, Heidegger avoids that work by assuming, as he did in the *Sophist* course, that wherever Socrates speaks, he speaks for Plato.

Ironically, Heidegger begins the *Plato's Doctrine of Truth* essay by acknowledging this very problem. In the second paragraph of the essay he says, "In order to experience and to know for the future what a thinker left unsaid, what that might be, we have to consider what he said. To properly satisfy this demand would entail examining all of

Plato's 'dialogues' in their interrelationship. Since this is impossible, we must let a different path guide us to the unsaid in Plato's thinking" (155). Unfortunately, Heidegger does not follow through on the implications of this very insightful caution. For the rest of the essay, he ignores it, and proceeds with utter confidence that through his discussion of the cave analogy he is eliciting the "unsaid" of "Plato's doctrine of truth."

I have already indicated the defects of this procedure in our discussion of the *Sophist* lecture course. It ignores entirely the significance of the dialogue form, ignores the crucial facts of the context in which the analogy is presented, ignores the limitations and virtues of the people to whom Socrates is speaking, and most of all, ignores the immense problems we have addressed of attributing to Plato whatever Socrates says in any dialogue.

The third noun in the title is "truth." Heidegger proposes to elicit Plato's doctrine of *truth* in the cave analogy. But as is obvious and as Heidegger immediately admits, truth is not in any sense the theme of the cave analogy. That brings us to the important issue, announced in the lines quoted above, with which Heidegger begins the essay: the notion of an "unsaid" doctrine. The explicit theme of the cave analogy, announced by Socrates, is *paideia*, "education." It begins, "Next, then, I said, make an image of our nature in its education and want of education . . ." (*Republic*, 514a). Though Heidegger later in the essay addresses the connection between truth and education, he immediately indicates that what interests him here is not the explicit but the "unsaid," doctrine in the cave, which, he announces, is *aletheia*, truth.

The first thing we must recognize is that to say that he will elicit the unsaid doctrine of Plato changes nothing regarding the problem of attributing doctrines to the dialogues and of attributing them to Plato. An unsaid doctrine remains a doctrine. The dialogues are still being treated as vehicles for the expression of doctrines of Plato. Nevertheless, let us turn to Heidegger's text and follow the outlines of his argument for the elicitation of this doctrine.

Heidegger announces on the first page his guiding thesis: the "unsaid doctrine" that he will elicit in the cave analogy is "a change in what determines the essence of truth" (155). That change, we discover, is from the more originary notion of truth as *aletheia*, "unhiddenness," to truth as "correctness of vision," a change which, as Heidegger tells us toward the end of the essay, puts us on the fateful path toward modern subjectivism. Let us trace the crucial steps of this change, as Heidegger develops it.

Heidegger's first point is to show, very convincingly, that *aletheia* in its originary sense of unhiddenness is still very much at work in the cave analogy. He notes that the deeply visual character of the analogy, the notion of moving from shadows to seeing the fire to moving outside the cave to see the things that are "more unhidden," makes sense only within a framework of truth as unhiddenness. As he puts it, "Only the essence of truth understood in the original Greek sense of *aletheia*—the unhiddenness that is related to the hidden (to something dissembled and disguised)—has an essential relation to this image of an underground cave. Wherever truth has another essence, wherever it is not unhiddenness or at least is not co-determined by unhiddenness, there an 'allegory of the cave' has no basis as an illustration" (172). So truth as unhiddenness is still present in the cave analogy.

But no longer purely. Heidegger now announces that truth as unhiddenness is already infected, as it were, by another, different and more problematic conception of truth that is also at work here. "And yet, even though *aletheia* is properly experienced in the 'allegory of the cave' and is mentioned in it at important points, nonetheless in place of unhiddenness another essence of truth pushes to the fore. However, this also implies that unhiddenness still maintains a certain priority" (172). This fateful other essence of truth is truth as "correctness of vision."

Heidegger begins his development of this momentous change by returning to the role within the cave analogy of the fire and, crucially, the sun outside the cave, as the source of the light by which we see the things themselves. The sun is, of course, the analogue to the idea of the Good, to which Heidegger turns presently. Here, he emphasizes the role of that sunlight, to make the other things—in the analogy, the other ideas by which we know the things that appear—visible, to make them shine. "Everything depends on the shining forth of whatever appears and on making its visibility possible" (172). It is important that this "making visibility possible" function is true only of the sun, that is, only of the idea of the Good. The idea of the Good, by the analogy, makes the other ideas *visible*, in the sense of making them accessible to our intellectual vision, our nous. Yet strangely, Heidegger collapses the crucial distinction between the sun (idea of the Good) and the other ideas by attributing this "shining" capacity to the *ideas as such*. He says, "The 'idea' is the visible form that offers a view of what is present. The *idea* is pure shining in the sense of the phrase 'the sun shines.' The 'idea' does not first let something else (behind it) 'shine in its appearance;' it itself is what shines, it is concerned only with the shining of itself. The *idea* is that which can shine. The essence of the idea consists in its ability to shine and be seen" (173). It is important to see the crucial ambiguity here. Only the sun (idea of the Good) shines in the active sense. The other ideas shine only in the sense that the moon (or the other things that are) shines. *It shines in the light of the sun.* The shining (visibility) of the other ideas is a passive shining in the light of the active shining of the idea of the Good. This collapsing of the distinction between the idea of the Good and the other ideas, and so the overlooking of their crucially different roles and ontological status, is at the core, as we shall see in a moment, of Heidegger's interpretation of the change in the essence of truth to correctness of vision.

Next, Heidegger continues, this emphasis on visibility and shining, thanks to the emphasis on the shining of the ideas (actually, however, on the shining only of the idea of the Good), begins a movement toward an emphasis, or overemphasis, on *seeing,* and so on the role of the "seer." " 'Unhiddenness' now means: the unhidden always as what is accessible thanks to the idea's ability to shine. But insofar as the access is necessarily carried out through 'seeing,' unhiddenness is yoked into a 'relation' with seeing, it becomes 'relative' to seeing" (173).

Heidegger's next step again depends on the confusion of the idea of the Good and the other ideas. Reversing the order here, he says, "The 'allegory' mentions the sun as the image for the idea of the good. What does the essence of this idea consist in? As *idea* the good is something that shines, thus something that provides vision, thus in turn something visible and hence knowable," (174). There are two crucial confusions here: first, it is not "as idea" that the good shines; that is its *unique* quality, differentiating it from the other ideas and separating its ontological status from them. Moreover, second, a crucial dimension of this different status is that while the other ideas are knowable in the light of the good, the good is itself not knowable in anything like the same way. This is part of the genius of the sun analogy that Heidegger overlooks. We see other things thanks to the light of the sun. We do not see the sun in the same way. If we look at the sun the way we look at other things, we will be blinded. The sun, the source of visibility, is not visible in the same way as the things seen in its light. We see the sun only obliquely, indirectly, not with the sharpness with which we see other things. Heidegger here overlooks the altogether problematic ontological and epistemological status of the idea of the Good.

This discussion of the idea of the Good also leads Heidegger to another move that is similar to one that he made in the *Sophist* lectures, the almost perplexing insistence that terms that manifestly refer to questions of virtue have nothing to do with virtue. Here, he insists that the idea of the Good, in effect, has nothing to do with goodness. Heidegger is surely right that, as we have seen, the idea of the Good has as one of its functions the capacity to make visible the other ideas. But Heidegger now treats this as its *only* function, and so denies to it any sense of "the good." The term "idea of the Good" is "quite misleading," (165) and "all too misleading for modern thinking" (175). By treating visibility as its only function, Heidegger ignores the more normative dimension of the idea of the Good. Even within the allegory, we are told that the sun itself gives visibility to the things that are *and being* to them (*Republic*, 509b). By denying the normative relevance, Heidegger fails to ask a crucial question regarding the notion of the idea of the Good. Why does Plato have his Socrates call it the idea of the Good rather than, say, the idea of "Intelligibility" or the idea of "Knowledge," or even the idea of "Truth"? By denying any possible normative significance to this idea, Heidegger enables himself to ignore this crucial question.[37]

The upshot of this collapsing of the distinction between the idea of the Good and the other ideas, for Heidegger, is that since the ideas are visible, that is, can be brought to unhiddenness, only thanks to the idea of the Good, "*Aletheia* comes under the yoke of the *idea*. When Plato says of the idea that she is the mistress that allows unhiddenness (*Socrates* says this, and only of the idea of the *Good*), he points to something unsaid, namely, that henceforth the essence of truth does not, as the essence of unhiddenness, unfold from its proper and essential fullness but rather shifts to the essence of the *idea*. The essence of truth gives up its fundamental trait of unhiddenness" (176; my parenthesis). It is by no means evident, as we shall see, that the function of the idea of the good to make visible the other ideas gives up the trait of unhiddenness. On the contrary, it is precisely what makes it possible.

Nevertheless, Heidegger's next step is to draw out what he takes to be the crucial consequence of this change in the essence of truth. In his view, it makes *correct vision* on the part of the knower take on an exaggerated and fateful significance. "The movement of passage from one place to the other consists in the process whereby the gaze becomes more correct. Everything depends on the *orthotes*, the correctness of the gaze. . . . Truth becomes *orthotes*, the correctness of apprehending and asserting. With this transformation of the essence of truth there takes place at the same time a change of the locus of truth. As unhiddenness, truth is still a fundamental trait of beings themselves. But as correctness of the 'gaze,' it becomes a characteristic of human comportment toward beings" (177). We are on the way toward subjectivism.[38] In the rest of the work Heidegger outlines this historical movement. It means that Plato has become the founder of "metaphysics" (180).

Without question, Plato does have his Socrates use the term "correctness" (*orthotes*) several times in the cave analogy, and Heidegger cites them. The issue is, does Socrates' occasional reference to the importance of "correct looking" constitute the "change in the essence of truth" that Heidegger claims? I think it does not. It seems rather than the importance of correct looking is implicit from the beginning in any possible notion of truth as unhiddenness. How, for example, can truth be wrested from hiddenness to unhiddenness unless it is brought to unhiddenness to someone who looks correctly? Consider, for example, the pre-Socratic Heraclitus, who would seem to embody paradigmatically the notion of truth as unhiddenness in his famous aphorisms, "nature loves to hide," or "A hidden harmony is better than an apparent one." What would it mean for nature to "hide" unless it hides *from someone* (presumably us) who, in order to find it, to bring it to unhiddenness, will have to look correctly? Or consider the proem to Parmenides' poem, where the young man (presumably Parmenides) is brought by the goddess on a journey, through the gates of justice, to a point where he can see "well-rounded truth" (Parmenides, Fragment 1). Does that not entail, almost in a prefiguration of the movement out of the cave in the cave analogy, that he will be brought to a point where he can look correctly? The important point is that to observe that looking correctly is an element in any notion of truth as unhiddenness does not at all constitute a change in the essence of truth but is simply to point out that correct looking is a necessary dimension of the very notion of unhiddenness.

Remarks in two later essays suggest that Heidegger later came to realize this very point, although, unfortunately, that realization did not lead him, as it should have, to rethink his critique of Plato. In the 1958 essay, "Hegel and the Greeks,"[39] he remarks, "It indeed has often been remarked that there cannot be an unconcealment in itself, that unconcealment is after all always unconcealment 'for someone.' It is thereby unavoidably 'subjectivized' " (334). He goes on to show that the charge of subjectivism does not follow from the recognition that unconcealment happens to someone, exactly the point I made a moment ago. We see how close the association of unconcealment and correct looking is to Heidegger's own thought when we consider his claim in *Being and Time* that "Being needs man"[40] and the later favorite metaphor of Heidegger's that man is the "shepherd" of Being. Good shepherds, after all, must watch, and so "look correctly at" their flock.

Even later, in the essay "The End of Philosophy and the Task of Thinking," Heidegger seems to put the point even more strongly, apparently disavowing his earlier position, but again without rethinking his critique of Plato:

> In the scope of this question, we must acknowledge the fact that *aletheia*, unconcealment in the sense of the opening of presence, was originally only experienced as *orthotes*, as the correctness of representations and statements. But then the assertion about the essential transformation of truth, that is, from unconcealment to correctness, is also untenable.[41]

The implication here is odd. It seems to suggest that the Greeks never experienced truth as unconcealment but always and only as correctness of vision. To the contrary, the very notion of unhiddenness is incoherent *without* correct looking. The two are not only compatible but necessarily connected.

Recall that Heidegger begins *Plato's Doctrine of Truth* by asserting that the "doctrine of truth" therein is an "unsaid" doctrine. He neglects to ask just why it is "unsaid," that is, why the notion of truth does not become the apparently explicit theme of the *Republic* or of any other dialogue. If Heidegger had paid more attention to the dialogue form, he might have noticed that in fact, truth as *aletheia*, as unhiddenness, is present again and again in the dialogues, not as the explicit theme of the discussion, something that might be "defined," but as always at work in any movement of thinking. Let us cite just a few examples of how this happens in the dialogues.

An important and sustained dimension of Heidegger's understanding of the Greek experience of truth as *aletheia* is the way in which the very word points to the finitude of every revelation of truth. Truth is always finite in the sense that it is always also "in the untruth." In the very way that it reveals what it reveals, any given experience of truth also conceals. Indeed, truth must always be "wrested" from the concealment toward which it always tends. This understanding of truth is an important antidote to the more modern notion, perhaps finding its clearest statement in Descartes, of truth as an unadulterated, unqualified revelation, a "clear and distinct idea." The later Hegelian notion of absolute knowledge is a near descendent of this view. Only within its influence can we speak colloquially of "the truth, the whole truth, and nothing but the truth." By Heidegger's analysis of the Greek experience of *aletheia*, no such absolute revelation is available to finite Dasein.

Could there by a more dramatic and powerful way of exhibiting this finitude, this revealing/concealing of truth, than by placing every experience of truth within the very situation that at once makes it possible and gives it its limitations? For that is precisely what the drama of the dialogue form does. Socrates is in jail, as in the *Crito* and *Phaedo*, or he is on trial, as in the *Apology*, or he is talking to very young boys, as in the *Lysis* and *Theaetetus*, or to surly sophists, as in the *Gorgias* or in the early part of the *Republic*. He may be addressing an enthusiastic but not overly astute dilletante, as with Phaedrus, or nonphilosophical types whose understanding will be limited, as with Crito, or who simply will not listen, as with Philebus. He may be coerced into speaking, as he is in the beginning of the *Republic*, or have to coerce others to speak with him, as in the *Theaetetus*. These are just some of the most obvious instances of what is demonstrated dramatically within every Platonic dialogue. Every revelation of truth occurs within a given context, including the situation and the participants, a context that at once makes the particular revelation appropriate and possible, but at the same time places limits on its possibilities, qualifies any claims it might make to universality. If only we pay attention to these dramatic elements, we see presented not a theory or doctrine of truth but a concrete exhibition of truth as *aletheia*, as what must be wrested into unhiddenness from an often recalcitrant existential context. Alas, Heidegger never notices this concrete portrayal of truth, so in attunement with his own thinking. This understanding of truth in the dialogues is indeed "unsaid;" it is unsaid because it is *concretely exhibited*. For those who have eyes to see, for those who can "look correctly."

Indeed, the unsaid in the sense of that which is not explicitly articulated as a theory or doctrine is all over the place in the Platonic dialogues. If we modern readers fail to pay heed to these unsaid revelations in our obsessive attention only to the explicit doctrines, that can hardly be blamed on the dialogues. Consider as one more example one that also should be congenial to Heidegger, the significance of silence or of absence.

To be sure, there is no "theory of silence" presented in any dialogue, no "doctrine of the significance of absence." But if we read the dialogues with sensitivity to the dramatic structure and not just to explicitly presented doctrines, we notice these themes in play again and again. We have already looked at one of the most striking examples in our examination of Heidegger's *Sophist* lecture course: the significance of the silence of Socrates in the *Sophist*. The same issue would have to arise in the *Statesman*, as well as in the *Timaeus*. Just as we would in any real existential situation that we actually lived, we have to look for clues within the drama of the situation as to what the significance of Socrates' silence is. Is it silent ascent? Or silent disagreement? Is Socrates' position being superceded by what is said by the Stranger? Or is Socrates' silence not rather an invitation to look at the Stranger's view critically from the Socratic standpoint? We have already addressed these issues earlier. Here the point is to reiterate that the significance of silence is very much at play in these dialogues, even if not thematically, even if unsaid. But here "unsaid" does not mean "unthought."

The same is true of the significance of absence, or withdrawal. The *Timaeus* begins, "One, two, three, where is the fourth . . . ?" How could we not wonder about who is absent here, and what that absence signifies? Or perhaps even more strikingly, we are told in the *Phaedo* that Plato is absent from that dialogue (59b). That clue invites us to realize that with the striking exception of the *Apology*, where Plato writes himself into the dialogue as present but silent, Plato is *always* absent from Platonic dialogues. Or is he, and in what sense? Plato could, of course, have written himself into many or every dialogue. By not doing so, he pointedly raises for the reader who will listen the complex issue of his presence and absence, and so the issue of presence and absence more generally.

Themes such as these are missed by Heidegger as he pays exclusive attention to Plato's supposed doctrines, both said and unsaid. What is especially unfortunate is that given Heidegger's own standpoints, attention to these dramatic happenings should have appealed to him. Had he noticed them, he would have realized that the thinking of the dialogues is much more congenial to his own concerns than he allows in this, the "middle" period of his work. But what about the "later" Heidegger? As he turns more and more to poetry, more and more to a poetic thinking of his own, we might hope that Heidegger would also turn to a rethinking of the poetic character of the Platonic dialogues. Let us see if he does so.

PARMENIDES

In Winter Semester 1942–43, just two years after the composition of *Plato's Doctrine of Truth,* Heidegger offered a lecture course on "Parmenides and Heraclitus" that would seem at first to exhibit this greater sensitivity to Plato's complex writing project.[42] Although ostensibly dealing for the most part with Parmenides, the course often refers to Plato and includes a sensitive interpretation of several phrases from the closing myth of the *Republic*, usually referred to as the "myth of Er."

Several passages in that text suggest at first that Heidegger's doctrinal attitude toward and interpretation of Plato is undergoing significant modification. First, he at least twice indicates a new recognition that there may be a serious problem with interpreting Plato in terms of the history of interpretation of the dialogues that constitutes Platonism. Preparing for his interpretation of the myth of Er, he warns,

> But what could be more self-evident than the conviction that the most appropriate interpretations of the philosophy of Plato are those approaching it with the aid of Platonism? Yet this procedure is one that is comparable to one that would 'explain' the fresh leaf of the tree on the basis of the foliage fallen to the ground. A Greek interpretation of Plato is the most difficult, not because this thinking contains in itself special obscurities and abysses, but because the following ages, and still we today, are inclined to discover immediately our own later thinking in this philosophy. (94)

A few pages later, in his recapitulation of the lecture, he reiterates,

> What could our objection be to this practice of thinking Plato 'Platonically'? Is it not the only appropriate way, or at any rate more 'correct' than interpreting Plato's philosophy with the help of the philosophy of Kant or Hegel? Nevertheless, the attempt to interpret Plato with the help of some sort of Platonism is certain perdition. (97)

Because he refers to "we today," presumably including himself, it is tempting to interpret this passage as a strikingly accurate self-criticism of his previous reading of Plato, for on the basis of the interpretation I have presented so far, I would level precisely this criticism against Heidegger's own previous readings of Plato which we have examined. Does this, then, point the way to a new, more sympathetic, more "Greek" reading of Plato on Heidegger's part?

The second indication that this might be happening is Heidegger's subtle and imaginative interpretation of several phrases from the myth of Er that closes the *Republic*. In particular, he concentrates his attention on the phrases toward the end of the myth (and the end of the *Republic*) that refer to *to tes Lethes pedion*, (621a), usually translated as "the plain of forgetfulness" but which Heidegger renders as "the field of withdrawing concealment in the sense of oblivion" (118), and on the river that flows through that plain, which Socrates calls *ton Ameleta potamon*, "the river Carelessness," which Heidegger renders as "Carefree." The upshot of Heidegger's rich interpretation of these phrases is that they sustain in the strongest way the Greek experience of truth as *aletheia*, unhiddenness, and moreover, that they connect as deeply as possible the experience of *un-* hiddenness to the founding experience of *lethe*, of hiddenness and concealment, out of which any possible revelation arises, and to which it inevitably returns.

Without question, this is a sensitive and rich interpretation of these phrases, one that indeed rings with plausibility. But does it point to a genuine sea-change in Heidegger's attitude toward Plato? Unfortunately, if we place it in the context of what he says elsewhere in the book, and indeed of the myth of Er itself, our answer must be no.

The first thing we should note is that Heidegger continues the practice that we saw in *Plato's Doctrine of Truth* of not feeling any need to place the interpretation in the context of the book as a whole. Indeed, in this case, he does not even render a full interpretation of the entire myth, not to mention that he fails to place the myth in its very strange context, at the end of the *Republic*, at the end of Book X wherein poetry was once again chastised severely and its virtual banishment from the "city in speech" justified again. To be sure, he acknowledges in passing, as he also did in *Plato's Doctrine of Truth*, that a fuller interpretation would be necessary, but he will not give it. His words are instructive:

> The myth of *Lethe* concluding the dialogue on the *polis* is so far reaching and rich that already for that reason it cannot be presented here in full. Besides, any merely reportorial presentation is otiose if it is to take the place of a meticulous interpretation. But we are lacking what is essential to carry out such an interpretation: an experience of the basic character of myth in general and of its relation to Plato's metaphysics. (92)

Again we see a perfunctory acknowledgement of the inadequacy of what he is about to do, which is then ignored. But notice as well that the last words quoted indicate that notwithstanding the sensitive interpretation he is about to render, he still sees it as related to "Plato's metaphysics." He is still thinking within the larger context of a doctrinal Plato, the Plato of Platonism.

Indeed, Plato is still the very founder of metaphysics. Toward the end of his interpretation of the myth of Er, Heidegger says,

The *muthos* understands the necessity of *aletheia* and its essential relatedness to *lethe,* as the ground preceding it, on the basis of the essential provenance and destiny of man. This emphatic reference to man already indicates a transformation of the basic position of thinking among the Greeks. This transformation signifies the inception of metaphysics. (130)

The parallel to the interpretation of Plato in *Plato's Doctrine of Truth* is striking. In the dialogues there is still at work the more primordial experience of *aletheia;* but it is being transformed into modern metaphysics. We are also told earlier that, "That means that the aesthetic attitude toward art begins at the moment the essence of *aletheia* is transformed into *homoisis,* into the conformity and correctness of perceiving, presenting, and representing. This transformation starts in Plato's metaphysics" (115). And even earlier, we are informed that "With Plato and Aristotle, who speak the beginning of metaphysics, the word becomes *logos* in the sense of assertion" (77). The last word is especially striking: what could be less true of the Platonic dialogues than that they present a philosophy of assertion. What, in the end, has changed of Heidegger's interpretation of Plato?[43]

Heidegger's still prevailing critical attitude toward Plato is stunningly summed up when he turns, however briefly, to the question of why Plato used myths such as the myth of Er, his answer to the question he indicated earlier we are not prepared to answer, that of the "basic character of myth in general and its relation to Plato's metaphysics" (92). "People have often been puzzled by the occurrence of myths in the Platonic dialogues. The reason they turn up from time to time is that Plato is indeed prepared to abandon the primordial thinking in favor of the later so-called 'metaphysics,' but precisely this incipient metaphysical thinking still has to preserve a recollection of the primordial thinking. Hence the story" (98). It is hard not to hear a note of condescension in this passage. Poor, poor Plato. He *wanted* to leave behind myth and mythical thinking and turn to hard-nosed metaphysics, but the poor guy couldn't yet bring himself to do so! That, presumably, remains for Aristotle, the "more clear" thinker than Plato.[44]

So despite signs of an incipient recognition of the problem of reading Plato as a Platonist and despite the imaginative interpretation of phrases from the myth of Er, Heidegger still remains wedded to his earlier doctrinal reading of Plato as the founder of metaphysics. But might it be that his sensitivity to the dialogues is exhibited in the late works in a much different way, not in a repudiation of his earlier critiques of Plato—perhaps for whatever reasons Heidegger could not bring himself to do that—but in another way, in the highest compliment of imitation, in Heidegger's turn several times in his late works to the dialogue form? Perhaps with an examination of his own late use of the dialogue form in his "Dialogue with a Japanese" and *Gelassenheit*, Heidegger exhibits his recognition of the power of the Platonic dialogue. Let us turn, then, to an examination of those Heideggerian dialogues.

HEIDEGGER'S DIALOGUES

I have argued in this book that when Plato chose to present philosophy in the form of dialogue, he did so not as a literary flourish, some irresistible urge to indulge in a quasi-poetic genre deriving from his youthful engagement with poetry. Rather, he did so as an exhibition of a certain conception of philosophy; philosophy is itself essentially dialogical, and therefore is best presented as such. It is notable that such was the depth of Plato's commitment to this dialogical conception of philosophy that his entire corpus was written in this single form. The later tradition, including, as we have seen, Heidegger, transmuted that conception and that presentation into a collection of supposed "doctrines,"—the "theory of ideas," "Plato's metaphysics," "theory of recollection," "theory of the ideal state," "earlier epistemology," and so on—notwithstanding that no such "theories" or doctrines are ever presented as such in the dialogues. I have argued strongly for the poverty of that reading of Platonism, and specifically for the poverty of Heidegger's own doctrinal reading.

Not surprisingly, the dialogue form has appealed to later philosophers in the Western tradition, from Aristotle to Augustine to Berkeley and Hume, among others, though it should be noted that none saw fit to present their entire written corpus in this form, as Plato had. In these later cases, the dialogue form was an occasional genre, tried once or twice by each of them. In no case, it is fair to say, did the later philosopher's effort at dialogue become regarded as the *magnum opus* of the philosopher in question. Nor did the subsequent dialogues ever succeed in attaining the dramatic and interpretive complexity of the originals. In each case, the voice of one participant is clearly the authoritative voice of the author, and the setting and cast of characters never plays the deep and complex role that it does in Plato's dialogues. In short, in each case, and unlike the Platonic dialogues, the dialogue *could* have been presented as a treatise without significant loss of meaning, and it is therefore no surprise that the authors returned to the treatise form for their other works.

At first glance, the case of Martin Heidegger would seem to be similar. Here is a writer who has written in a variety of writing genres, including on at least two occasions dialogues: the 1959 "Dialogue on Language," supposedly the report of a 1953–54 visit to Heidegger by the Japanese Professor Tezuka, and, also in 1959, the "Conversation on *Gelassenheit*," reported as an account of a conversation in 1944–45 among a teacher, a scholar, and a scientist.[45] But Heidegger has written in many writing styles, from treatises such as *Being and Time*, to his published lectures, to his many shorter essays, to the quasi-poetic *Aus der Erfahrung des Denkens*. This wide variety is in itself instructive; it attests to the fact that Heidegger was thoughtful about his choice of writing genre, that he did not, as it were, automatically choose the dominant philosophical writing style, and therefore it suggests that his choice of dialogue on these two occasions must have been self-conscious and carefully meditated. Though we can hardly expect him in just these two efforts to achieve the gold standard of dialogue writing set by the Greek master, we surely can fruitfully consider Heidegger's choice of dialogue in these two cases, examine how and how successfully he employs that genre, and consider whether, while hardly mentioning Plato's name therein, these dialogues perhaps embody an unsaid recognition of their own of what Plato was attempting in his dialogues.

After a brief discussion of the "Dialogue on Language," I shall focus on the *Gelassenheit* dialogue, which, in respect to Heidegger's use of the characteristics available to the dialogue form, is a far richer work. In both cases, I shall address what is said in the dialogue; that is, the actual propositional content, only in so far as it is germane to or reflected in dimensions of the dialogue form itself. That is, my intent here is to address primarily Heidegger's use of the dialogue form itself rather than the specific content of each dialogue, although a certain overlap between form and content will be inevitable. I turn first to a discussion of the "Dialogue on Language."

That discussion can be brief because Heidegger's use of the rich possibilities offered by the dialogue form is utterly spare in this instance. In a note, Heidegger reports that it originated in 1953–54 on the occasion of a visit from Professor Tezuka of the Imperial University, Tokyo.[46] Does this suggest that in fact Heidegger made no use of the specific literary possibilities of the dialogue form at all, that this was nothing but a report of the actual conversation, as from a stenographer? Hardly! Plato's *Apology* also takes its origin from an historical event, but only the most naïve interpreter would take that core philosophic text as nothing but a report of the actual trial. And in any case, Heidegger here clearly does employ at least some of the dramatic possibilities of the dialogue genre, however sparsely. Let us see how.

To be sure, Heidegger makes next to no use here of the possibilities of dramatic background offered by the dialogue form. There is no indication at the beginning of context, of the specific location of the dialogue, the time of day, or even the set of events that occasioned the visit. The dialogue simply begins with the "Japanese" reminding "the inquirer" that a Count Shuzo Kuki studied with him for a number of years. That brings us to the two persona of the dialogue.

The visitor is referred to only as "the Japanese" in the dialogue itself. Only the note at the end informs us of his real name. The other character is called simply "inquirer" (*Fragender*), though he is obviously Heidegger himself, since his own works are regularly referred to as such. So the dialogue is between these two, presumably alone, with next to no indication or employment of dramatic location, time, or circumstance.

Still, there are a few moments when the possibilities of dramatic dialogue are engaged. There is a dim hint that they may be walking (*US*, 113; *OWL*, 23) though given the context, that they are "walking toward the danger" of their own dialogue, the walking may be metaphorical. On one occasion, we are told that "The Japanese closes his eyes, lowers his head, and sinks into a long reflection. The inquirer waits until his guest resumes the conversation." (*US*, 114; *OWL*, 23). This, alas, is the dramatic climax of the dialogue, although a more successful and sustained one might be the prolonged hesitation the Japanese has in mentioning the Japanese word he has in mind for the essence of language, and the corresponding agitation of the inquirer anxious to hear it, all of which culminates in the Japanese, "after further hesitation," finally uttering the words *koto ba* (*US*, 142; *OWL*, 45). There is also a passing reference to the dialogue having to come to an end soon, since the Japanese has to leave tomorrow for Florence. The latter suggests that he stay an extra day (*US*, 134; *OWL*, 39).

Two other incidents of the dialogue deserve note. First, toward the end, the very notion of dialogue itself is invoked. The inquirer has repudiated his earlier (that is, in Heidegger's previous works) discussions of the hermeneutic circle and the very effort to speak *about* language in favor of an effort to speak *from* language in an authentic saying. He comments that "A speaking *from* language could only be a dialogue" (*US*, 150; *OWL*, 51). After developing his notion of a dialogue as the genuine saying of and from language, the Japanese speculates that "In this sense, then, even Plato's Dialogues would not be dialogues?" and the inquirer retorts that he will leave that open to question (*US*, 151; *OWL*, 52). Whatever else we make of this passage, it is clear that the dialogue genre itself is being invoked as the paradigm of "authentic saying." Hence, Heidegger's own dialogue is presumably intended as an exhibition of that whereof it speaks. In particular, we need to wonder how, if the Japanese' speculation that Plato's dialogues do not constitute a genuine speaking from language is warranted, Heidegger's dialogue(s) overcomes that weakness.

Second, occasionally throughout the dialogue but especially toward the end, the two speakers begin to engage in a tendency that often does occur in intense and deep conversations: they begin to finish each other's sentences. This occurs a number of times but is perhaps most dramatic in the very last lines of the dialogue, which goes:

J: How are we to think that?

I: As the gathering of what endures. . . .

J: . . . which, as you said recently, endures as what grants endurance. . . .

I: . . . and stays the Same as the message. . . .

J: . . . which needs us as messengers.

I shall want to say more about this tendency when I turn to *Gelassenheit*, where it is used, I believe, with heightened effect. But even in the "Dialogue on Language," its presence is noteworthy, symbolic at very least that at this point the subjective barriers between the speakers have withered away, that it is now the matter for thought and not individuated egos that are carrying the conversation, perhaps even that here "language speaks." Is this perhaps a hint at the event of "speaking from language" that may be missing from the Platonic dialogues?[47]

Judged by the Olympian standards of the Platonic dialogues, Heidegger's dramatic use of the dialogue form in this work is rather thin. By those standards, of course, so is everyone else's. Little is done with the location, which often plays such an important role in Plato's dialogues. The characters remain largely undeveloped, and there is little dramatic action between them. In sum, this dialogue in the end does read largely as a report of a conversation, with precious little dramatic embellishment. One can well imagine Heidegger writing an essay of equal length about the relation between his own efforts to speak "from" language and the Japanese understanding of language, without significant loss of content or impact.

The same could not be said, I want now to argue, of Heidegger's other dialogue, *Gelassenheit*. Here some of the possibilities special to the dialogue form, including location and dramatic action, are utilized to powerful effect; in this case, the dialogue actually works as dialogue; not, to be sure, with the complexity of the Platonic dialogues, but nevertheless, here elements are captured that genuinely add to the power of the thought.

Begin with the cast of cast of characters. There are three, a teacher (*Lehrer*), scholar (*Gelehrter*), and scientist (*Forscher*). It is instructive that the three are not given individual names, but identified only by type. One is reminded of the Eleatic Stranger of the *Sophist* and *Statesman*. This is consistently maintained throughout the dialogue; the three do conform to their respective types, though there is next to no personality development beyond the type. The scholar is the one who regularly reminds the others of scholarly references: to Kant (*G*, 29ff; *R*, 58ff), to Meister Eckhart (*G*, 34; *R*, 61), to the etymology of *Gegnet* (*G*, 39ff; *R*, 66), to Heraclitus's fragment 122 (*G*, 68; *R*, 88), to the distinction between the ontic and ontological (*G*, 53; *R*, 76), and even to *Being and Time* (*G*, 59; *R*, 81). The scientist is the strongest exemplar of that representative thinking, or calculative thinking (*rechnende Denken*) that they are trying to get beyond. Consequently, he again and again has the most difficulty comprehending the sense of *Gelassenheit* and its related notions: willing not to will, waiting, *Gegnet*. An instructive passage in this regard occurs early in the dialogue, shortly after the notion of *Gelassenheit* has been introduced. The scientist, puzzled, laments,

Scientist: With the best of will, I cannot re-present to myself this nature of thinking.

Teacher: Precisely because this will of yours and your mode of thinking as re-presenting prevent it.

Scientist: But then, what in the world am I to do?

Scholar: I am asking myself that too.

Teacher: We are to do nothing but wait.

Scholar: That is poor consolation.

Teacher: Poor or not, we should not await consolation—something we would still be doing if we became disconsolate.

Scientist: Then what are we to wait for? And where are we to wait? I hardly know anymore who and where I am.

Teacher: None of us knows that, as soon as we stop fooling ourselves." (*G*, 34–35; *R*, 62)

To be sure, the scientist begins to catch on as the dialogue ensues, but not without difficulty. Later, after being helped along by the others, especially the teacher, the scientist comments, "I can follow, after a fashion, all that we have said now about releasement, that-which-regions, and regioning; all the same, I can re-present nothing of it to myself" (*R*, 74).[48] In each case, the scientist's difficulties are not to be understood as somehow personal, the difficulties of this particular individual, but as difficulties of his type. The scientist as scientist, that is, as foremost exemplar and paragon of that representative thinking that has distinguished the West, will have the most difficulty getting beyond that kind of thinking.

He is helped primarily, though not exclusively, by the teacher, the third participant who is indeed the teacher of the others. As the longer passage quoted above nicely demonstrates, the teacher regularly leads the others in the most fruitful directions. He has the strongest sense of where they are trying to go, yet at the same time, best understands the limits of their efforts to do so. He is thus "wise" not in the sense of having full advance knowledge of what they are trying to attain, but more in the Socratic sense of "knowing what he knows and what he does not know." One is tempted to identify the teacher as Heidegger himself, though this is not nearly so explicit as with the inquirer in the "Dialogue on Language."

This dialogue, like the "Dialogue on Language," purports to be based on an actual event. A note by Heidegger says that it "was taken from a conversation written down in 1944–45 between a scientist, a scholar, and a teacher" (*G*, 72; *R*, 58). Again, this in no way suggests that we need treat it as a mere recording of the actual conversation. Since, as the date indicates (1944–45), Heidegger cannot remember the exact date of the conversation, it is hardly likely that he recalls the exact words that were spoken. Moreover, one has to wonder, if this is indeed an actual record of the conversation, how, toward the very end of World War II, in Germany, these three found the leisure to take a quiet and peaceful evening walk under the stars and away from the town. Were this an actual event, one would expect their conversation to be interrupted by bombs or machine-gun fire. Whatever the historical basis of the conversation, then, the dialogue as it is written can be taken largely as a creation of Heidegger's own.

Beginning, I want to reiterate, with the characters as identified. Were this an actual recorded conversation, one would surely expect these guys to know each other's names. Yet they are identified only as teacher, scholar, scientist. Clearly, then, what Heidegger wants us to know about them, the impact their characters are intended to have, is focused on the specific types they represent, not on the idiosyncratic personalities of each. These are not Euthyphros, Critos, or Thrasymachus's with specific personalities and idiosyncracies, but generic types: teacher, scholar, scientist. That is how we are to think of them.

This dialogue also makes use of a number of dramatic features missing from the "Dialogue on Language." Specifically, it employs particular locations, times and actions, all of which, as we shall see, bear on the content of the dialogue. As the subtitle of the dialogue indicates, the conversation supposedly takes place on a country path (*Feldweggesprach*). Early on, we are reminded that at that point the three are "far from human habitation" (*G*, 31; *R*, 60), and toward the end, the scientist comments that there is a certain urgency about the scholar's introducing the Heraclitean word he is reluctant to utter, since "we again near human habitation," and so the conversation must end (*G*, 68; *R*, 87). All three factors of location, that the conversation occurs on a country path, that it begins, or rather, we are introduced into the conversation, far from human habitation, and that the conversation must end as they approach the town, have both internally specific and larger general significance on which I wish to comment.

Take first the fact that the dialogue begins far from human habitation. This can be connected specifically to the first issue raised in the dialogue as the reader enters the discussion. The opening line of the dialogue is uttered by the scientist: "Toward the last you stated that the question concerning man's nature is not a question about man." This leads to the first central point of the dialogue, the mysterious observation that at least with certain things, such as "man" and thinking, we best gain access to them by looking *away* from them. Commensurate with the need to look away from human being in order to understand its nature, the dialogue begins away from human habitation.[49]

In a parallel way, the fact that the dialogue ends as they again approach human habitation is connected to one of the closing points of the dialogue. The introduction of Heraclitus's one-word fragment, *Anchibasie*, takes place as part of an effort to gain a sense of the notion of *das Gegnet*, "that-which-regions," as "the nearness of distance and the distance of nearness . . ." (*G*, 66; *R*, 86ff.). Commensurate with that difficult notion, they near the town and the conversation must end, that is, as they near the town the "distance" of their conversation abides.

In addition to the specific references of the beginning and ending locations, there is a larger, more general issue raised by the fact that the dialogue on *Gelassenheit* begins away from the town, takes place on a field-path, and must end as they reapproach the city. In the public "Memorial Address" in Heidegger's home town of Messkirch that precedes the dialogue, Heidegger develops in a simplified way the notion of *Gelassenheit*, "releasement," in terms of the notion of "openness to the mystery" and, crucially, by drawing a distinction between two kinds of thinking, "calculative thinking"(*rechnende Denken*) and "meditative thinking" (*besinnliche Nachdenken*) (*G*, 13; *R*, 46). Calculative thinking is the kind of technological reckoning that has dominated Western thought, indeed become its paradigm, and which Heidegger associates with the dominance of technology and various forms of civilization (air travel, radio, television, etc.). Meditative thinking is the other kind of thinking that is in danger of being lost by the very technological dominance that has given us the sway of calculative thinking. In drawing out this difference, Heidegger clearly associates the dominance of calculative thinking with technology and the danger of forgetting meditative thinking with the loss of a sense of "rootedness" brought about by technology itself (*G*, 16; *R*, 48–49). That invites the obvious conclusion that meditative thinking requires somehow an abandonment of technology and the civilization it has spawned in favor of a return to some sort of more primitive, peasant-like existence where meditative thinking might once again flourish. However, in a movement familiar to readers of Heidegger, having invited this conclusion he takes steps to counter it:

> Still, we can do otherwise. We can use technological devices, and yet with proper use also keep ourselves so free of them, that we may let go of them any time. We can use technical devices as they ought to be used, and let them alone as something which does not affect our inner and real core. We can affirm the unavoidable use of technical devices, and also deny them the right to dominate us, and so to warp, confuse, and lay waste our nature. (*G*, 22–23; *R*, 54)

This is easier said than done. It is surely easier to imagine the preservation of meditative thinking while ensconced in ones simple hut in the *Schwarzwald* than amidst the hustle and bustle of a technologically dominated city. The task of living in the midst of all this technology, living with it in the sense of employing it in our daily lives, yet not being dominated by it, is an achievement few of us, I suspect, have been able to attain. Indeed, many of us who do want to preserve something like this meditative thinking do so precisely by seeking retreats *away* from the dominance of technological civilization, small country places, out of the way, with few technological amenities. Even, apparently, as Heidegger did.

This problematic is repeated again and again in Heidegger's thought. On the one hand, he laments the dominance of technological living and thinking, laments what is lost therein, and does so in such a way as to invite a supposed return to a more primitive, simpler situation. On the other, he recognizes immediately that such a return is neither plausible nor possible. The alternative solution is not always so clear. Two other examples will suffice.

The first is the famous interpretation of van Gogh's painting of shoes, which Heidegger, in *The Origin of a Work of Art*, controversially understands as a painting of *peasant* shoes. Here he presents a powerful evocation of the simple but thoughtful life of the peasant woman whose shoes these supposedly are. It reads in part:

> From the dark opening of the worn insides of the shoes the toilsome tread of the worker stares forth. In the stiffly rugged heaviness of the shoes there is the accumulated tenacity of her slow trudge through the far-spreading and ever-uniform furrows of the field swept by the raw wind. On the leather lie the dampness and richness of the soil. Under the soles slides the loneliness of the field-path as evening falls. In the shoes vibrates the silent call of the earth, its quiet gift of the ripening grain and its unexplained self-refusal in the fallow desolation of the wintry field. This equipment is pervaded by uncomplaining anxiety as to the certainty of bread, the wordless joy of having once more withstood want, the trembling before the impending childbed and shivering at the surrounding menace of death. This equipment belongs to the *earth*, and it is protected in the *world* of the peasant woman. From out of this protected belonging the equipment itself rises to it resting-within-itself.[50]

Heidegger immediately warns us against taking his interpretation as a subjective projection on the painting (35–36), though that is precisely what it is in the judgment of many subsequent readers. More importantly for our point, a few pages later he acknowledges that there can be no returning to the life of that peasant woman, nor to the world evoked by the Greek temple at Paestum, nor other older works. "The world of the work that stands there has perished. World-withdrawal and world-decay can never be undone" (41). So there can be no question of returning to the world evoked by his interpretation of the van Gogh shoes, however appealingly authentic Heidegger portrays it.

The second example of a similar movement occurs in the 1954 (presented in lecture form in 1951) "Building Dwelling Thinking."[51] Here Heidegger is concerned to develop the notion and possibility of what he calls "dwelling," emphasizing how increasingly rare genuine dwelling is in a world now more and more dominated by technological culture. As an example of genuine dwelling, Heidegger again evokes peasant life:

> Let us think for awhile of a farmhouse in the Black Forest, which was built some two hundred years ago by the dwelling of peasants. Here the self-sufficiency of the power to let earth and heaven, divinities and mortals enter *in simple oneness* into things, ordered the house. It placed the farm on the wind-sheltered mountain slope looking south, among the meadows close to the spring. It gave it the wide overhanging shingle roof whose proper slope bears up under the burden of snow, and which, reaching deep down, shields the chambers against the storms of the long winter nights. It did not forget the alter corner behind the community table; it made room in its chamber for the hallowed places of childbed and the tree of the dead—for that is what they call a coffin there: the *totenbaum*—and in this way it designed for the different generations under one roof the character of their journey through time. A craft which, itself sprung from dwelling, still uses its tools and frames as things, built the farmhouse. (160)

So in order to genuinely dwell we must return to the life of simple peasants. Heidegger anticipates and immediately counters this easy inference. "Our reference to the Black Forest farm in no way means that we should or could go back to building such houses; rather, it illustrates by a dwelling that *has been* how *it* was able to build" (160). Fine, we are inclined to reply, but if a return to the simple life of Heidegger's favorite peasant examples is inappropriate and in any case impossible, just how can one dwell in Heidegger's authentic sense if one lives not in peasant farmhouses but in modern city apartments or in a suburb near a shopping mall? To the best of my knowledge, Heidegger nowhere gives a full answer. One is tempted to conclude that he does not genuinely believe it is possible. Yet it surely is a powerful question for any of us at once moved by Heidegger's evocation of dwelling yet inescapably located in technological culture.

This problematic is dramatically highlighted by the setting of the dialogue on *Gelassenheit*. The three participants want to engage in a different kind of thinking, "releasement," a nonrepresentational "willing not to will" that leaves behind the willful representational thinking characteristic of the age of technology. To do so, appropriately enough, they walk outside of the town, "far from human habitation" and the technological culture embodied there. Or is the situation more radical? Is it perhaps that they *must* carry on this conversation away from human habitation, that ensconced within technological culture such "released" thinking simply has no chance? Is the *Feldweg* on which this dialogue takes place one more Heideggerian indication of the unlikeliness, perhaps the impossibility, that such a thinking as *Gelassenheit* can take place within fully modern, and that means fully technological, culture? In this light, the scientist's remark toward the end of the dialogue already cited takes on greater poignancy: they are again nearing human habitation, and so their authentic dialogue, their "released" thinking, *must* end.

I turn next to another dramatic element in the setting of this dialogue, the time of day in which it occurs. The walk along the field path must have begun in the evening, for as we, the readers, are introduced into the already begun discussion, night has set in. There are only three references to the night time in which the dialogue takes place, one at the beginning, and two toward the end, but all are significant. The first reference occurs after only a page or two of the dialogue we read. The scientist has just had his first breakthrough in his effort to understand the different kind of thinking toward which they are tentatively moving: "You want a non-willing in the sense of a renouncing of willing, so that through this we may release, or at least prepare to release, ourselves to the sought-for essence of a thinking that is not a willing" (*G*, 31; *R*, 59–60). After the teacher and scholar hesitantly congratulate him, he responds,

> Scientist: That I succeeded in this was not my doing but that of the night having set in, which without forcing compels concentration.
>
> Scholar: It leaves us time for meditating by slowing down our pace.
>
> Teacher: That is why we are still far from human habitation. (*G*, 31; *R*, 60)

The night compels concentration by slowing things down, thus allowing for the inauguration of meditation. The hustle and bustle of human habitation, we see again, is inimical to the kind of slow, highly concentrated, nonwillful mediation required for *Gelassenheit*. The night, which literally slows us down and compels concentration so that we may see, joined with the field path away from human habitation, is an apt symbol of the different kind of thinking they seek.

Much later, as their conversation nears an end, the scholar has occasion to invoke a poem of a friend, "In-dwelling," that he hopes will sustain their thinking. The teacher comments,

> Teacher: The in-dwelling in releasement to that-which-regions would then be the real nature of the spontaneity of thinking.
>
> Scholar: And, following the quoted lines, thinking would be commemoration, akin to what is noble.
>
> Teacher: In-dwelling in releasement to that-which-regions would be noble-mindedness itself.
>
> Scientist: It seems to me that this unbelievable night entices you both to exult.
>
> Teacher: So it does, if you mean exulting in waiting, through which we become more waitful and more void.
>
> Scholar: Apparently emptier, but richer in contingencies."
> (*G*, 60–61; *R*, 82)

The night leads us to become more waitful, more attentive, more empty but richer in contingencies. I take that to mean that in the darkness of night our concentration must become more focused, less predisposed to everyday expectations, more open to whatever will happen. Again, this waitful focus, this responsive openness as one might call it, is an apt image of that thinking which is *Gelassenheit*. To put it another Heideggerian way, night brings home to us more forcefully the element of concealing that is always present in every revealing, the *lethe* in every *aletheia*. Night forces on us the awareness of concealing.

The last reference in the dialogue to night is the most dramatic, for it occurs in the very last lines, as their exultation reaches its height. As the end nears, they have decided provisionally to accept a revised reading of Heraclitus Fragment 122, *Anchibasie*, as "moving into nearness." (*In-die-Nahe-gehen*). The scholar comments,

Scholar: *Anchibasie:* 'moving-into-nearness.' The word could rather, so it seems to me now, be the name for our walk today along this country path.

Teacher: Which guided us deep into the night. . . .

Scientist: . . . that gleams ever more splendidly . . .

Scholar: . . . and overwhelms the stars. . . .

Teacher: . . . because it nears their distances in the heavens . . .

Scientist: . . . at least for the naïve observer, although not for the exact scientist.

Teacher: Ever to the child in man, night neighbors the stars.

Scholar: She binds together without seam or edge or thread.

Scientist: She neighbors; because she works only with nearness.

Scholar: If she ever works rather than rests. . . .

Teacher: . . . while wondering upon the depths of the height."
(*G,* 70–71; *R,* 89–90)

In a lovely image, the teacher suggests that night "nears the distances" of the stars in the heavens. That is, strange as it seems, night, the darkness in which seeing becomes more concentrated and more difficult, in which more is hidden, makes visible, brings near, the stars. Just as we have to go into the darkness of night in order to see the stars, so we must move into the realm of the concealed in order to experience the concealed as concealed, and so to experience the fullness of truth itself as *aletheia.* This is what *Gelassenheit* calls for. And night accomplishes this neighboring of the stars without work even as *Ereignis* gives what is. That is, we see at the end that night is Heidegger's image of *Ereignis,* which has been reticently under discussion throughout the dialogue in the long discussions of horizon and that-which-regions. Like *Ereignis* night gives us to see what is to be seen, while bringing home most forcefully the hiddenness of the hidden.

The passage from *Gelassenheit* just quoted comes only five lines from the end of the dialogue. After the teacher finishes the sentence above with ". . . while wondering upon the depths of the height," the dialogue comes to an end as follows:

Scholar: Then wonder can open what is locked?

Scientist: By way of waiting. . . .

Teacher: . . . if this is released. . . .

Scholar: . . . and human nature remains *appropriated* (*ge-eignet bleibt*) to that. . . .

Teacher: . . . from whence we are called. (*G*, 71; *R*, 90)

We note here a final affirmation that *Ereignis* has all along been at stake in the dialogue. However, these last lines culminate the dialogue in another sense that is the final point I would like to make. Increasingly, as the dialogue develops and especially in the final pages, the three characters begin to finish each other's sentences, as nicely instantiated in the passage quoted above. We noted earlier a similar tendency in the "Dialogue on Language." What is the significance of this dramatic feature of the dialogue?

Earlier in the dialogue (*G*, 46; *R*, 71ff.) there is an occasion when they begin to wonder which of them had introduced the term "releasement" (*Gelassenheit*). But they realize quickly that in genuine conversations such as these, who says what is not the matter at stake. What counts is the saying. The scientist concludes the point, "So let's not quarrel over who first introduced the name, releasement, let us consider only what it is we name by it" (*G*, 47; *R*, 72).[52] As soon becomes clear, there is good reason for this conviction. For part of what such thinking as releasement entails is precisely the overcoming of that subject-object dichotomy and the willful subject implied by it, that would make it matter which individual could take credit for saying this or that. A few pages later, this issue becomes thematic:

Scientist: Earlier, we began by illuminating the relation between the ego and the object by way of the factual relation of thought in the physical sciences to nature. The relation between the ego and the object, the often mentioned subject-object relation, which I took to be the most general, is apparently only an historical variation of the relation of man to the thing, so far as things can become objects. . . .

Teacher: . . . even have become objects before they attained their nature as things.

Scholar: The same is true of the corresponding historical change of the human being to an ego . . .

Teacher: . . . which likewise emerged before the nature of man could return to itself . . .

Scientist: . . . providing we do not regard the coining of man into the *animal rationale* as final. . . .

Scholar: . . . which would hardly be possible after today's conversation." (*G*, 55; *R*, 77–78)

So clearly, the kind of speaking and thinking that would constitute *Gelassenheit* would be a speaking and thinking in which, as we say, our egos would no longer be involved, in which what counts and only what counts is the matter for thought, not who says it. A perfectly appropriate symbol of this experience, indeed, perhaps its *telos* is when the matter for thought so takes over the conversation that individual identities are submerged, and the characters finish each other's sentences. And that is precisely what happens, increasingly in the dialogue as the movement toward *Gelassenheit* intensifies, and culminating at the very end, in the quoted passage.[53]

I have tried to suggest a number of ways in which Heidegger's dialogue, *Gelassenheit*, works as dialogue, ways in which Heidegger employs the possibilities of the genre in order to enhance and exhibit what is explicitly said. One of the things the dramatic possibilities of the dialogue form can do, as Plato knew so well, is to evoke, to call forth in a necessarily oblique presence, what is best left unarticulated or even what cannot be explicitly said. What cannot be explicitly said nevertheless can *happen* in a dialogue or can be recognized *as missing*, or can be ironically problematized by a certain disparity between word and deed . In Heidegger's earlier "Dialogue on Language," as was pointed out, Heidegger leaves open the question of whether Plato's dialogues were genuine dialogues in the sense he and the Japanese are developing. I close this study of Heidegger's reading of Plato by re-opening that question in perhaps a more positive vein. Could it be that Plato's dialogues *remain* the model of dialogue for Heidegger and the rest of us, that in the complexity of the drama of his dialogues Plato was trying to allow to happen what cannot be explicitly theorized, and that Heidegger's dialogues attain to genuine dialogue just insofar as they follow in the path blazed by the Greek?

If so, Heidegger's apparent failure or refusal to reconsider his earlier, doctrinal reading of the Platonic dialogues in the light of the movement of his own later thinking becomes at once more puzzling and more disappointing. For everything about Heidegger's later thinking, especially as embodied in these dialogues, points to a movement of thought wherein he *should* have found in the Platonic dialogues a tremendous and positive stimulus precisely to his own thoughtful development toward a poetic thinking that does not reduce a thinker's work to a set of doctrines, said or unsaid. Everything points to a rich dialogue between Heidegger and the Platonic dialogues; it is a loss to us all that Heidegger never apparently allowed that dialogue genuinely to take place.

Chapter Two

Derrida's Plato

"I asked a hundred painters and a hundred poets
how to paint sunlight
on the face of life
Their answers were ambiguous and ingenuous
as if they were all guarding trade secrets
Whereas it seems to me
all you have to do
is conceive of the whole world
and all humanity
as a kind of art work
a site-specific art work
an art project of the god of light
the whole earth and all that's in it
to be painted with light

And the first thing you have to do
is paint out postmodern painting"

—Lawrence Ferlinghetti,
"Instructions to Painters & Poets"
in *How to Paint Sunlight.*

"Thus, at least, spoke Zarathustra. We have refrained from substituting Nietzsche's name for his, as if, from one ghost to another, it never came down to the same one."

—Derrida, *Politics of Friendship*, 288.

As is clear from my discussion of Heidegger's interpretations of Plato just completed, my most general objection to Heidegger's reading of Plato is his failure to take with adequate seriousness the philosophic significance of the dialogue form, his failure genuinely to integrate that significance into his interpretation of Plato's philosophy. As the present chapter will demonstrate, my problems with Derrida's often rich interpretations of passages from this or that dialogue center on the same failure. Nevertheless, since Derrida is a very different thinker from Heidegger, let me introduce the problematic of the dialogue form in this chapter in a somewhat different way than I did in the case of Heidegger, one that I hope will appropriately prepare us for Derrida's readings of Plato.

How shall we write if we call ourselves philosophers? As professional philosophers today, we hardly need think about that any more. For what I will call the treatise format, writing discursively in the first person (singular or plural) has become so deeply canonical for writers of philosophy that, quite literally, we do not need to think about it when we decide to write. We need think, to be sure, about the specific content, perhaps about the specific style of writing—will we be formal? Informal? Playful or serious? As direct as possible or strategically allusive? But the content of our writing and its style will be framed within a treatise format, because that is the way, the almost exclusive way, that philosophic writing has been done for over two millennia, since Aristotle at least. So dominant has this writing format become in philosophy that we have largely forgotten that there might be other, very different ways of writing philosophically. A sure sign of this forgetting is that now, when confronted occasionally by those other ways of philosophic writing—and most of all by the dialogues of Plato—we simply read them as if they, too, were treatises, concealed treatises, perhaps, but treatises nonetheless. *Die Schreibvergessenheit!* Almost all of us today, including those who write about the dominance of the treatise format, as I am doing, write in the shadow of this forgetfulness.

But this forgetfulness, this literally thoughtless decision that we all make to write our philosophic works in the treatise format, is not without warrant. It presupposes a certain conception of philosophy itself, and so of philosophic writing, that we have all more or less accepted. Or even if some of us have dared to call that conception of philosophy into question, we have not yet dared to change our writing format accordingly. So we need to ask, what is that underlying conception of philosophy that makes the treatise format so utterly, deeply, unproblematically appropriate for philosophic writing?

Suppose, first, that every person who calls herself a philosopher has certain philosophic positions. My philosophic position in this chapter is, or will be, that Derrida reads Plato's dialogues, always reads Plato's dialogues, inappropriately. Derrida has positions that involve a certain interpretation of language, an interpretation that leads to a strategy of reading and thinking that he calls "deconstruction," and that subsequently involves the deconstruction of texts of many of the canonical writers in the history of philosophy, certainly including Plato. Virtually all philosophers who write today write to express their positions. So, first, I, Derrida, we, have philosophic positions. Even if, as some of us including Derrida insist, those positions are not asserted dogmatically but ventured tentatively, questioningly, playfully, they are, for the time at least, our positions.

Second, for whatever the reasons, I, you, Derrida, decide not to keep that position to ourselves. We decide to express that position publicly; our philosophic position is one that we desire to assert. We decide to assert it more publicly, in principle, than just to a small group of friends. We decide not just to speak our philosophic position but to write it.

Third, we assert it in writing, not just for the sake of asserting it but to persuade others, our readers, of our position. That persuasion may have varying degrees of strength. In the strong cases, we may want to prove our position. Or we may want to refute the position of someone else. In the weaker cases, we may hold back from claiming proofs, but want only to be suggestive, to be thought-provoking, to raise questions in a plausible way. One way or another, we assert, prove, refute, suggest, call into question, in the most persuasive way we can.

Could there be a better format by which to assert, prove, refute, suggest, or call into question a philosophic position than the treatise? The crucial characteristic of the treatise format, in this light, is its first person orientation. *I* write what *I* think about this or that, and I do so in the most persuasive way I can. To be sure, some exceedingly confident philosophers have claimed to speak not in the first person but in the third, to articulate "the view from nowhere," to state "what is the case," to gain access to "the way the world is." But as soon as someone disagrees with them, this claim is revealed for what it is: a first person claim emboldened to make a pretense at third person objective truths. This gesture already inherent in the treatise format toward a certain subjectivism, even by those writing treatises denying subjectivism, is surely one worth pursuing at another time. For now, the point we need to recognize is that once we decide that this is what philosophy is, that we have a philosophy, one that we want to assert, prove, refute, suggest, or call into question, it virtually follows that the treatise format will become the paradigm of philosophic writing. And so it has.

In this light, let us consider or reconsider Plato's decision to write dialogues as his way of philosophic writing. If we assume, as we all seem to do, that Plato, like us, had philosophic positions that he wanted to assert as persuasively as possible—those positions that have come to be called, but never once by Plato, "Plato's metaphysics," "Plato's early epistemology," "Plato's moral theory," "Plato's late ontology," "Plato's theory of forms," etc.—and that the reason he wrote was, like us, to assert those views as persuasively as possible, then his choice of the dialogue form in which to present those positions represents, we must conclude, an astonishing lapse in judgment, not to say an act of obtuseness.[1] For precisely what is lost in the dialogue form is what makes the treatise format so singularly appropriate for the assertion of philosophical positions: the first person format that enables us to identify, even if through a glass darkly, the position that the author wants to assert as his own. In a desperate effort to avoid the attribution of such obtuseness to Plato, and in a desperate effort to rope the dialogues into the same philosophical standpoint as the treatises we write, we impose on the dialogues the same interpretive assumptions that we with good reason apply to treatises: since Plato must have been doing what we all do, asserting his philosophic views as persuasively as possible, and since no character named "Plato" ever does so, it must be that the main character in any given dialogue is "Plato's mouthpiece." Socrates, Timaeus, the Eleatic Stranger, the Athenian Stranger, speak for Plato. Their assertions are Plato's assertions. Their questions are Plato's questions. Their refutations are Plato's refutations. Decisively, their flaws are Plato's flaws. The dialogues, in the end, are indeed concealed treatises, expressing, though with often maddening obscurity, Plato's philosophical positions. We impose this interpretive assumption on the dialogues despite the fact that Plato never once suggests anything like it and in fact, in one of the few writings of his (controversially his) that do speak in the first person, his famous seventh letter, he explicitly denies it.[2]

What would it mean to avoid this massive interpretive assumption, one now grounded in a two-millennial tradition of philosophical treatise writing—that Plato, though for bizarre reasons of his own he chose to write dialogues, is nevertheless in the end doing the same thing as we who write treatises, articulating his own philosophic positions, and so can be read accordingly? We might dare such a thought experiment by comparing the situation Plato faced when he wrote with our own, and taking seriously the utterly different situation he encountered. For Plato surely did not have a two-millennial tradition of philosophical treatise writing in front of him. He had, instead, something like a two-*hundred* year tradition of writing by those who called themselves philosophers, and moreover, one that presented him with an astonishingly rich palette of writing formats from which to choose. He had, to be sure, the "concerning nature" treatises of a number of what we now called presocratic writers, including Thales, Anaximander, Anaximenes, and Anaxagoras. So the treatise format was an option, as it were, from the beginning. But he also had the philosophic poems of Parmenides and Empedocles, the aphorisms of Heraclitus and Democritus, not to mention the plays of the great tragedians and comedians.

The difference between Plato's situation and ours has a number of important consequences. It means, first, that Plato simply could not have had the choice of writing format virtually made for him, so that he would write treatises without further ado. Which is to say, his decision to write dialogues had to be a much more thoughtful, self-conscious decision than the one most of us make when we decide to write, a decision that had to include a thoughtful reflection on just what he was trying to accomplish in his philosophic writings.

Second and decisively, it means that the question of why Plato wrote dialogues instead of, say, treatises, becomes especially pertinent (by contrast, say, to the question as to why most of us in philosophy write treatises, the answer to which would be something like, "because that is what we've been taught to do, it's what everyone does in philosophy, it's what we have to do if we want to get published in philosophic journals," etc.). We can begin with a point already intimated, that if Plato wrote dialogues because he had a certain set of philosophic positions of his own that he wanted to articulate as clearly and persuasively as possible, and he believed that the best way to present those views clearly and persuasively was the dialogue, then he made an exceedingly poor choice of writing format indeed. But that is unlikely on the face of it. If that had been his intention, he already knew very well, from the examples of Thales, or Anaximander, or Anaxagoras among others, that the treatise form would have been the appropriate writing style. His choice of the dialogue form thus implies that his guiding intention could not have been to express his own philosophic positions clearly and persuasively. So the question becomes, what then were Plato's intentions in writing dialogues, or if one wants to avoid the language of intentionality, what is it that happens in the Platonic dialogue, if not primarily the articulation of Plato's views?

Before making some suggestions on this, I want to remind the reader of an important qualification. I am not here siding with the extreme esoteric interpretive position that Plato's views are entirely absent from the dialogues he wrote. Thirty-some dialogues, some of them long and complicated, in which not a single view of the author shines forth? That is unlikely indeed. But I am saying that the expression of his views could not have been the guiding intention of his writing dialogues, from which it follows, crucially, that discovering what we take to be Plato's views in the dialogues should not be our guiding intention in reading and thinking about the dialogues. At least, if we want to be true to the dialogues themselves. Another way to put this point would be to say that if you want an example of writing that has largely freed itself from the so-called "metaphysics of subjectivity," (before there was such a thing), you could hardly find a better example than the Platonic dialogues. The implications for the endless chatter about "Plato's metaphysics," "Plato's moral theory," or "Plato's theory of forms," should be clear.

So the obvious question is, why then did Plato write dialogues? What is going on philosophically there if not primarily the expression of the author's views? I have written at length on this both earlier in this book and elsewhere,[3] and will therefore here only mention briefly some suggestions. In any case, the crucial point for the question of Derrida's reading of Plato will be the negative one already made, that the guiding point of the dialogues cannot have been the expression of Plato's own views, and that we read Plato inappropriately if we see in the dialogues primarily vehicles for the expression of those "Platonic" positions, on, say writing, or the knora, or friendship, or the forms, or metaphysics.

Imagine, once again, that we were in something like the cultural situation faced by Plato. The two-hundred year old tradition of philosophy up until then had been, as has been aptly suggested, a history of heresy. One presocratic philosopher after another had been exiled— or worse—from his city as a danger to the health of his city—most famously Heraclitus and Pythagoras. Plato's own teacher, Socrates, had been in Plato's early manhood put to death for impiety and corruption. In a way that we can hardly imagine today, philosophy was regarded as a very serious danger, and it was altogether controversial whether philosophers should be allowed to conduct themselves free of the constraints of political orthodoxy. Should we save the city or save philosophy? The answer to that question held very widely was, save the city, constrain the philosophers.

Suppose that Plato, writing in that cultural milieu, wanted, plausibly enough, to save philosophy. It is by no means self-evident that the best way to do so would be to write a treatise, perhaps even a manifesto, defending philosophy against the charges made against it. For that he may have suffered the same fate as many of his predecessors, a likelihood that later made the always more prudent Aristotle leave Athens, "lest Athens sin twice against philosophy." What he did instead was to write imitations of philosophy, the dialogues that we know, imitations that portrayed philosophy, again and again in very different ways, as a great benefit to individuals and the city, indeed, as the one thing needful. They are also imitations that portrayed what it would be like, in various situations and with various people, to live philosophically. This is at least part of the meaning of the remark cited earlier in the Seventh Letter, that Plato had never written his philosophy. The dialogues are not his or anyone's philosophy; they are imitations of philosophy. Moreover, these imitations are written in such a way that they are again and again invitations to philosophy as well. They invite the reader into philosophic issues and philosophic questioning. This is nowhere more evident than in the so-called aporia dialogues, those that end with the question at hand unresolved, so that the reader must continue the dialogue himself. It is a dreary mark of our own philosophic obsession with people's philosophic positions discussed earlier that when most of us read these *aporia* dialogues, instead of accepting the invitation to keep on thinking the issue through and out of the dialogue, we obsessively look within its lines for the hidden clue to Plato's view. But it is not just those dialogues or those aporetic endings that invite us into philosophy. At each step along the way, we are invited to ask ourselves whether we, too, would answer Socrates' questions as Lysis does, or Menexenus, or Crito, or Phaedrus, or Glaucon, or Adeimantus. The supposition that Plato would answer, or wanted us to answer, as his often quite flawed characters do, is yet another sorry wonder of the history of Platonic scholarship. Why in the world should we suppose that Plato wanted his thoughtful readers to respond exactly the way a 16 year-old boy would, or the way an old and unphilosophical businessman would, or the way a moderately intelligent dilettante would, or the way an arrogant sophist would? Yet that is the supposition of almost all orthodox Platonic interpretation.

The dialogues, then, function as imitations of and invitations to philosophy.

The philosophy which is imitated and to which we are invited is deeply, deeply interrogative. Socrates' famous procedure of questioning and *aporia* as his philosophic stance (the recognition that he is not wise and so must question after wisdom, not claim to know) are only the most obvious manifestations of the deeply interrogative character of the philosophy exhibited in the dialogues. This point for our purposes might be put quasi-grammatically. Earlier, I spoke of the conception of philosophy held by most of us as that of having a philosophic position that we espouse, prove, assert, or suggest. We might say that for us, assertion is the fundamental philosophic speech-act, and assertions are best made in the form of propositions. For making assertions and uttering propositions clearly and persuasively, there is simply no better format than the treatise. But suppose that, with the Platonic dialogues, you hold that philosophy, one might say the life of philosophy, is not so much assertive (of this position or that) as interrogative. If so, then the fundamental speech-act of philosophy is no longer the assertive proposition but the question. And it is hardly so obvious that the best way of portraying the interrogative character of philosophy is through treatises composed exclusively or predominantly of questions. Not that it need be impossible, but simply that Plato's choice of the dialogue form to best portray the deeply interrogative character of philosophy was surely a plausible one, as the same choice by which to assert his own philosophic positions would not have been. So we are invited to ask, what would it mean to read the Platonic dialogues in such a way that our fundamental orientation was toward what the fundamental *questions* being raised were, and what it would mean for us to enter deeply and fully into that life of questioning?[4]

Let us turn, then, to Derrida's reading of Plato. Derrida has a strategy by which he reads Plato, the same one by which he reads most other authors. That strategy has been named by him and has come to be called "deconstruction." Derrida explicitly denies that this deconstructive strategy of reading can be called a "method," presumably because that word carries much too strong connotations of a formal procedure that can be simply imposed on any text, whereas part of Derrida's insistence is that deconstruction seeks to discover the play of meanings "without end" that operate within a text, rather than any definitive meaning intended or not intended by the author. So deconstruction is not a rigid, step-by-step method after the naïve model of a scientific method. Still, in a much looser sense, there is a way of deconstructive reading, and so I have adopted from Derrida the term "strategy" to signify this way of reading, which does have, if not a rigid lock-step method, a set of procedures that constitute the deconstructive strategy. I want to cite a number of these procedural strategies, particularly as they apply to Derrida's readings of Plato.

A given text will contain a number of asserted theses, the central theses of the text, presumably though not necessarily the ones intended by the author. In the strong cases, the author will believe that he or she is asserting those theses unequivocally, that, to use the famous Cartesian phrase, the theses are asserted clearly and distinctly. But, deconstruction asserts, that is not the way either of writing or of language. At play in any text, even, presumably, the supposedly most clear and distinct ones, are an indefinitely large set of other meanings from the obvious or predominantly asserted ones, meanings often on the "margins" of the given text, meanings that *differ from* and at the same time are *deferred by*, put off by or even denied by, the predominant meanings. Hence the famous deconstructive notion of *differance*, that play of meanings that differ from and are deferred by the apparent or dominant meaning. A deconstructive reading thus intends to destabilize, to call into question, the claimed univocal assertions of a given text, to show that instead of a single or obvious thesis, the text, any text, contains a "play of meanings without end." Deconstruction is thus an invitation to become sensitive to the instability, the fluidity, and so the nonfoundational or nonessential character of any writing or indeed of any language, and so of any text.

For these reasons, deconstructive readings are very different from most previous readings of texts. In those more usual readings, one's guiding task as careful reader is to identify the central thesis or theses, then concentrate ones attention on those theses, analyzing them, commenting on them, elucidating them, criticizing them, so that the central meaning of a given text can be clarified, perhaps definitively. Characteristically, these elucidations of the central meanings of texts claim to gain access to the intention of the author—what Kant intended, what Hegel was getting at, what Plato said. Deconstructive readings also begin by identifying the central theses, but not to concentrate one's interpretive energy on them. Instead, deconstructive readings identify the central set of meanings in order precisely to pass on to those other, often marginal, different and deferred meanings that constitute the *differance* of a given text.

Consequently, deconstructive readings are warranted in not concentrating their attention on the central or obvious claims of a text. This explains an otherwise puzzling characteristic of deconstructive readings, certainly including Derrida's. They do not give full interpretations of entire texts, from beginning to end, taking into account the entire text as a whole. They do not, we can now see, because their strategy does not require it. Thus Derrida can raise the question of "Plato's Pharmacy" with little or no attention to the context of eros that takes up the first two thirds of the *Phaedrus*. He can turn directly to the *khora* passage in the *Timaeus* without dwelling on the text that leads up to that discussion, including the very particular character of the man who is supposedly telling the tale. He can make a reference to the *Lysis* or *Menexenus*, now here, now there, without grounding the reference in the dialogue as a whole. Interested in the margins, interested in the different and deferred meanings of a text, a deconstructive reading, having identified the central or guiding claims, can pass over their horizon to the play of differential meanings at the margins. Thus Derrida, unlike Heidegger, would seem to have a clear theoretical justification for not rendering interpretations of entire works but selecting particular passages out of context: the deconstructive strategy he espouses.

I want to turn now to a brief examination of some of the presuppositions of Derrida's deconstructive strategy, for, perhaps contrary to his own convictions, I think it does have presuppositions. First, in order to identify a marginal meaning as marginal, the difference between the asserted or intended meaning and the marginal meaning must be visible. Again, a differential meaning must be different from the more obviously stated or intended meaning and so must be distinguishable as such. So in order for a given text to be deconstructable, it must contain an intended or central thesis that does place other meanings on the margins, which does allow for other, less obvious meanings to differ from it and be deferred by it, to be at work within it in ways that destabilize its implicit claim to univocity. Deconstructive readings are thus appropriate for any text that has a set of central or intended meanings, identifiable as such, and from which the play of other, marginal meanings can be differentiated.

But what if the text in question contains no author's assertions to deconstruct? What if there is no set of manifestly central theses that marginalize other meanings? What if the very point of the text in question is to set into play a host of meanings, of theses, of questions, to play off against each other in a dialogue without conclusion and without end? We are at last ready to turn directly to Derrida's reading of Plato.

I hope that my earlier discussion of Plato's strategy of writing, the dialogue form, has made at least plausible the notion that Plato simply did not regard as his guiding intention the persuasive presentation of his own philosophic positions. The dialogues, as imitations of philosophic situations and invitations to philosophy, invite us not to determine Plato's view but to enter thoughtfully into the philosophic situations and philosophic questions portrayed and to think through and out of them. We want then to ask, what will it mean to install the strategies of deconstruction into a text with no authoritative claims to deconstruct? Let us look at the way Derrida does so.

Derrida obviously reads the Platonic dialogues as deconstructable. That is, he believes that they do contain a set of guiding, intended, central claims, those that have come to be called "Platonism." His deconstructive readings, from "Plato's Pharmacy" on, seek to elicit from those dialogues that set of marginal, differential meanings that undercut, destabilize, render problematic the guiding claims that constitute Platonism. This means, following the deconstructive logic that we have just set out, that Derrida is warranted in not giving full interpretations of entire dialogues from beginning to end, but rather going, more or less directly, to those marginal meanings that deconstruct the presumed central themes. Thus in "Plato's Pharmacy," the multivocal meaning of the term *pharmakon* as it is employed several times by Socrates in the *Phaedrus* offers the basis for a deconstructive reading that discovers meanings of *logos* at work in the text that destabilize the central, supposedly "Platonic" teaching (we shall address the latter issue presently). Addressing the *Timaeus*, Derrida can turn more or less directly to the *khora* passage to show how that "marginal" discussion—it only takes up a page or two of the text—is a classic instance of *differance*, in that, as an unarticulable third intelligible only by the use of metaphors and a "bastard logic," it exhibits a different and deferred meaning from the dualism of Platonism, one that upsets, destabilizes, the central Platonic teaching of the dialogue (again, more of the latter later). In *Politics of Friendship*, Derrida can refer now to this passage in the *Lysis*, now to that in the *Menexenus*, without reference to either dramatic or philosophic context.

He can do so, again, because he assumes that the Platonic dialogues are deconstructable, and he holds that they are so, as we saw, by assuming that there is a central teaching, which can be deconstructed by marginal, differential meanings in the text, the central teaching that constitutes Platonism. But how does he get this assumption?

Certainly not from anything that Plato himself ever tells us. As I indicated in my earlier discussion of Plato's writing strategy, not only does no character in any dialogue give the slightest indication that he (or she, in the crucial cases of Diotima and Aspasia) is speaking for Plato, not only is there never a character called Plato who speaks in the author's name (though interestingly, Plato is mentioned as present but silent in the *Apology,* and as absent from the *Phaedo*), but in the case of the two instances we have where Plato (or the anonymous letter writer who understood the dialogues so well) comments on his writing in his own name, he explicitly denies that his philosophy is presented in his writings. So if not from Plato, whence come the clues to what constitutes Platonism in the Platonic dialogues?

Alas, Derrida takes his cues from the very assumptions about Plato's writing that I called into question earlier in the chapter. First, he seems to assume that, since these dialogues are, after all, philosophic writings, they *must* be written with the intent of presenting Plato's philosophic position. But given the complexity of the dialogue form and the absence of a character called "Plato," where is the Platonic teaching contained? Well, a character called "Socrates" does most of the talking in most of the dialogues, so Derrida assumes, with scholars as diverse as Heidegger and Gregory Vlastos, that whatever Socrates says is what Plato believes. Platonism, then, is whatever Socrates asserts.

Except, of course, when Socrates is silent or nearly silent, as he is in dialogues such as the *Timaeus, Sophist, and Statesman.* If Derrida and his fellow interpreters had stuck consistently to their interpretive guns and declared that in those dialogues where Socrates is silent we are not presented with Plato's positions, it would at least be an interesting and controversial suggestion. But instead, if another character speaks more than Socrates, then what that character says is Plato's position in that dialogue. So in the *Timaeus,* Timaeus speaks for Plato; in the *Sophist and Statesman,* the Eleatic stranger speaks for Plato. And so on.[5] When we notice, as we must because it is unmistakable, that the "teaching" of a Timaeus, or an Eleatic Stranger, is utterly different from and often contradictory to the supposed teaching of Socrates, indeed, when we notice that Socrates himself contradicts himself from dialogue to dialogue, we are forced by our adherence to the assumption that Plato must be asserting his own positions through these mouthpieces into what can only be described as wildly speculative hypotheses about Plato's development, the early Plato, the mature Plato, etc.

In this light, Derrida's very insightful remark about the relation of Nietzsche to his character, Zarathustra in *Politics of Friendship* that I quoted at the beginning of this chapter becomes especially poignant. "Thus, at least, spoke Zarathustra. We have refrained from substituting Nietzsche's name for his, as if, from one ghost to another, it never came down to the same one" (288). Derrida here sees what so very few interpreters of *Thus Spoke Zarathustra* notice, that given the dramatic context of that work, given the manifest way that Zarathustra's thinking and self-understanding develops, changes, contradicts itself, suffers defeats, is revealed as foolish, etc., what Zarathustra says at any given moment simply cannot be taken without further ado as "Nietzsche's teaching." Would that Derrida had addressed the problematic of the Platonic dialogues with the same sensitivity! But instead, we get from this ingenious and sensitive reader of literary texts a disappointingly orthodox interpretive principle for the Platonic dialogues.

One sees this in a striking way if one looks at the citations with which Derrida begins chapter 6 of *Politics of Friendship*, entitled "Oath, Conjuration, Fraternization, or the 'Armed' Question." The citations read simply as follows:

> Following its meaning in German (as in so many other languages), 'friend' is originally only the person to whom a genealogical bond unites. Originally the friend is but the friend of blood, the consanguine parent or again the 'parent by alliance' through marriage, oath of fraternity, adoption or other corresponding institutions.
>
> Carl Schmitt

> If, then, you two are friendly to each other, by some tie of nature (*phusei pe oikeioi*) you belong to each other.
>
> Plato[6]

Carl Schmitt writes in the first person. His writing style and rhetoric is such that one can plausibly assume that if he said the above sentences, then he believes them. But then, Derrida implicitly makes precisely the same assumption with the citation from Plato. A character, somewhere in some dialogue, says the above, so it can be signed "Plato." And presumably regarded as a dimension of Platonism.[7] There is, the quotations implicitly assume, no interesting difference in attributability between a treatise by Schmitt and a dialogue of Plato. Similarly, in the chapter entitled "The Phantom Friend Returning" of the same text, calling into question a passage from Schmitt, Derrida says, "Plato does say, in fact, that the Greeks, where there is a disagreement between themselves, consider it an internal discord, since it is quasi-familial, but they never bestow on it the name of war" (90). "Plato," of course, says no such thing. Socrates says it, to very specific people, within a very specific dramatic context, in the midst of the construction "in speech" of a city that he later admits will never exist in any case.[8] Perhaps most strikingly of all, toward the end of the book and moving toward his conclusion, Derrida says, "The remaining question—about which it can be asked what is left once these questions have finished ringing out—is one whose novelty we will keep in the very form which Plato gave it in *Lysis,* at the moment of his leave-taking following his failure: not 'what is friendship?' but who is the friend?" (293–294). It is not, of course Plato who leaves or Plato who fails at the end of the *Lysis*: it is Socrates who leaves having *apparently* failed, and whether we decide that he does indeed fail would depend on a host of interpretive decisions based on a most careful reading of the entire dialogue: at what does Socrates fail? He fails to arrive at an irrefutable definition of friendship. Is that what he was really trying to do with the two boys? Or were his intentions far more multiple and complicated than that? Then what about Plato? Does *he* fail? At what? Are we really to assume, as Derrida apparently does, that Plato, like his Socrates, really wants to finish the *Lysis* with a sustainable definition of friendship, but, having tried, has to end the dialogue by admitting his failure? That assumes in an almost self-refuting way all the interpretive assumptions I called into question earlier, assumptions that, alas, Derrida seems to assume unquestioningly.

Passages such as the ones cited above, where Derrida assumes that what Socrates says is what Plato believes, abound in this text, as they do throughout Derrida's writings.[9] In fact, I know of no passage where Derrida matches his astute remark on Zarathustra and Nietzsche with a similarly astute indication of his recognition of the problematic of the relation of Plato to his character, Socrates, nor for that matter, to any other character in the dialogues. One might be tempted to suggest the intriguing and puzzling *The Post Card: From Socrates to Freud and Beyond* as an exception. But that work, which juxtaposes speculations on a most curious post card of Plato standing behind Socrates who is writing, with letters from Derrida (presumably to his wife) and reflections on all sorts of other things as well, does not focus on the problematic of the relation between the *Platonic* Socrates, that is, the Socrates of the dialogues, and Plato himself. Instead, it focuses, first, on the possible interpretations—some of them hilariously ribald—of the post card, and to an extent, the implications for the relations between the historical Socrates and the historical Plato. Perhaps the most interesting, if tangential remark that touches on Plato's actual texts is Derrida's suggestion, again derived from speculations about the post card, that "Plato must have hated Socrates (or Bettina), hated him as one can hate whoever teaches you hatred, injustice, jealousy, resentment, bad conscience. As one can hate more than anyone else. Whence the vengeful plot that is called Platonism, and that insatiable mob."[10] But this intriguing if wild suggestion is never sustained by a careful look at the dialogues.

Why should it not occur to such a sensitive reader of texts as Derrida that there was exhibited in the Platonic dialogues an immense problematic of what counts as Plato's view, indeed, a problematic of the whole issue of the dialogue as a vehicle for philosophy? One can only speculate, but my speculation is that Derrida's *unorthodox* deconstructive readings of the dialogues *require*, in order to begin the strategy of deconstruction, the *orthodox* assumptions about Platonism that Derrida makes. As we have seen, a given remark, metaphor, or issue can only be marginal to Plato's view, can only constitute a *différance* to Platonism, if what counts as Plato's view is taken as visible from the start. To get the beginning that allows the deconstructions to begin, Derrida needs to assume that *there is* Platonism in the Platonic dialogues.

Or does he? What if one point of presenting an image of philosophy that includes the differences among personalities, differences of time, place, existential situation, in short, all of the limitations and possibilities that confront us every time we in fact enter into a philosophic discussion with some specific person, on some specific topic, in some specific circumstances, what if the point is precisely to show that those aspects of the conversation, marginal to the content of the actual discussion, marginal in the precise sense that they offer the context and horizon without which the content is at best abstract and at worst unintelligible, are in fact imperative to a genuine understanding of the intellectual content itself? What if, then, one point of the dialogue form in which Plato wrote is to exhibit that what might appear marginal to the intellectual content of a given discussion is not marginal (in the negative sense of unimportant) at all but central (in the sense of a *sine qua non*) to any genuine understanding of the intellectual content itself? What if the point is to call into question the very distinction between the marginal and the central, to treat that very distinction, as it were, *sous rature*? To exhibit that any genuine understanding of a given philosophical issue must take into account that which appears tangential, marginal, incidental?[11] If so, then the only way to fulfill that recognition is to read the dialogue as a whole, taking it into account as a whole, from beginning to end, not assuming in advance what is marginal and what not. We should do this not in order to fully understand Plato's doctrine of this or that, but as true to the recognition that the dialogues are imitations of philosophy. As imitations, they give us opportunities, unprecedented opportunities, to practice what it would mean to be philosophical about our lives. Thinking through a Platonic dialogue as a whole, without prior decisions as to what is marginal and what central, would then be practice for thinking through our lives philosophically as a whole, thinking about the role of the marginal in our lives and how those margins play into, and so are determinative of, what we might suppose is central. Such thinking would be practice for being philosophical.

Reading the dialogue as a whole, and so calling into question the distinction between the marginal and the central, might be said to vitiate the very need for deconstructive readings of the dialogues. A reading of the dialogue as a whole, already attentive to the margins and how they play out with the apparently central intellectual issue, would make a *rereading* that is attentive almost exclusively to the margins only a partial repetition of a genuine reading.

In other works, Derrida claims explicitly that justice and democracy are undeconstructable.[12] Presumably, they are undeconstructable because, as always "to come," (justice to come, democracy to come), never realized at a given moment, they are never here, present, to be deconstructed. I wonder if, for related reasons, the Platonic dialogues, read in their totality, are not the first writings that are undeconstructable, undeconstructable because the putative central thesis, that would be deconstructed is also not there, present, to be deconstructed. Such a recognition would lead us to a radical rethinking of the so-called "metaphysics of presence" that supposedly begins with Plato.

If so, Derrida's deconstructive readings of Plato can be helpful in that they show us what has too often been ignored by more orthodox interpreters of Plato, that the supposed margins of the dialogues are crucial to any genuine understanding of what is going on therein. What Derrida's readings do not do is call into question what I will call the "metaphysical" distinction between the marginal and the central itself, a calling into question that would lead us, and Derrida, to read the dialogues not just at the margins, and certainly not just for what we regard as central, but as a whole, a whole of a most peculiar sort, in that each dialogue is a whole that is never completed, never fulfilled, and so an image, an imitation, of life itself, an imitation that invites us to reflect on human life in its unending, uncompletable wholeness, its central issues and its margins, both, together, in a unity without closure. One way to put my larger point, then, would be to suggest that there is a much greater kinship between what is happening in the dialogues and Derrida's own deconstructive strategy than Derrida perhaps acknowledges. Perhaps the dialogues are not so much *texts to be deconstructed* as *deconstructive happenings* themselves. To elicit this more fully, let us turn in some detail to Derrida's own most detailed studies of texts—or rather, of passages in texts—of Plato: the section of *Disseminations* entitled "Plato's Pharmacy," and the study of the *knora* passage in the *Timaeus,* in *On the Name.*

"PLATO'S PHARMACY"

One way to put the most general objection I have been developing to Derrida's reading of the Platonic dialogues is to call it a problem of attribution. As my introductory section has just indicated, Derrida, in order to begin his deconstructive project, seems to need to attribute to a text a given claim, which claim, it can then be demonstrated by the language of the text itself, will be deconstructed, destabilized and even undercut, by the marginal, differential meanings at play within the text. That central claim is then attributed to an author, in this case, Plato, despite occasional denials in passing that there even *is,* in the strict sense, a text or an author ("In a word, we do not believe that there exists, in all rigor, a Platonic text, closed upon itself, complete with its inside and outside." [PP, 130]). So "Plato" holds this or that "position," which can then be deconstructed within the margins of the Platonic texts themselves. The position, or set of positions, that Derrida attributes to Plato, is, not surprisingly, Platonism in its various guises. This includes, among others, dualism, an urge to system, the founding of metaphysics, and decisively for what Derrida develops in "Plato's Pharmacy," an urge for univocity in language and a corresponding distaste for, indeed flight from, multivocity, the very play of meanings that Derrida argues is inherent in language itself. Thus, to cite only a few instances of these attributions, early in the text, having developed the claim of a kind of patriarchal position vis-á-vis language in Plato, "the permanence of a Platonic schema that assigns the origin and power of speech, precisely of *logos,* to the paternal position," Derrida adds, "But the fact that 'Platonism,' which sets up the whole of Western metaphysics in its conceptuality, should not escape the generality of this structural constraint, and even illustrates it with incomparable subtlety and force, stands out as all the more significant" (PP, 76). One must note in passing that the attribution of such "paternalism" to Plato is radically destabilized by the constant appeal on the Platonic Socrates' part to *women* as the source of his philosophical inspiration (Diotima, Aspasia, his midwife mother, Phaenarate, to name only the most obvious references to the crucial role of the "feminine" in philosophy as it is portrayed in the dialogues).[13] Presumably, Derrida would recognize this regular appeal to the feminine in philosophy only as an unintended *differance* within Platonism, but why not recognize it as precisely the intention of the author? We shall examine the reasons at greater length presently.

Later, having developed, presumably again as an unintended (by Plato) *differance* within the dialogues, the crucial ambiguity of the term *pharmakon*, (it can mean both "poison" and "medicine"), Derrida clearly reveals his assumption that Plato is a dualist: "It is precisely this ambiguity that Plato, through the mouth of the King, attempts to master, to dominate by inserting its definition into simple, clear-cut oppositions: good and evil, inside and outside, true and false, essence and appearance" (PP. 103. It should be noted here that not only is Socrates "Plato's mouthpiece," so is the King within the myth of Theuth.) A bit later this set of dualisms is augmented by that between *mneme and hypomnesis*, which "opposition will appear to us to form a system with all the great structural oppositions of Platonism" (PP, 111).

The crucial element of Platonism that gets deconstructed within this essay, however, is the presumed urge—or demand—of Plato for univocity within language. In reference to the ambiguity he has elicited in the word *pharmakon*, Derrida says,

> On the one hand, Plato decides in favor of a logic that does not tolerate such passages between opposing senses of the same word, all the more so since such a passage would reveal itself to be something quite different from simple confusion, alternation, or the dialectic of opposites. And yet, on the other hand, the *pharmakon*, if our reading confirms itself, constitutes the original medium of that decision, the element that precedes it, comprehends it, goes beyond it, can never be reduced to it, and is not separated from it by a single word (or signifying apparatus), operating within the Greek and Platonic text. (PP, 99)

So Plato is the great metaphysical asserter of the ideal of a perfectly univocal language, which ideal gets unintentionally undercut by the very language of the dialogues, by the play of *differance* within them.

As I argued in my earlier remarks on Derrida's general strategy, I find this attribution of the doctrines of Platonism to *Plato* within the dialogues altogether problematic, especially considering the very nature of the dialogue form itself as employed by Plato. I find no reason not to hold that it was *Plato's intention* precisely to set into play these destabilizing, contending, even contradictory positions for the consideration, the provocation, of the thoughtful reader. Indeed, it is precisely out of the consideration of these variations and contradictions that certain directions of thinking might emerge that might constitute something like the direction that Plato wanted the thoughtful reader to take. Such directions, it is important to emphasize, would precisely *not* be fully contained in the explicit speeches or positions of this or that person within the dialogue, certainly including Socrates. But Derrida's deconstructive strategy seems committed to denying the relevance of anything like authorial intentions. Let us examine that conviction in some detail.

> Up to this point in the dialogue, one can say that the *pharmakon* and the grapheme have been beckoning to each other from afar, indirectly sending back to each other, and, as if by chance, appearing and disappearing together on the same line, for yet uncertain reasons, with an effectiveness that is quite discrete and *perhaps after all unintentional.* But in order to lift this doubt and on the supposition that the categories of the voluntary and the involuntary still have some absolute pertinence in a reading—*which we don't for a minute believe,* at least not on the textual level on which we are now advancing—let us proceed to the last phase of the dialogue, to the point where Theuth appears on the scene. (PP, 73; my emphasis)

Somewhat later in the text, the essential point is repeated:

> Plato does not make a show of the chain of significations we are trying progressively to dig up. If there were any sense in asking such a question, which we don't believe, it would be impossible to say to what extent he manipulates it voluntarily or consciously, and at what point he is subject to constraints weighing upon his discourse from 'language . . .' Yet all these significations nonetheless appear, and more precisely, all these words appear in the text of 'Plato.' Only the chain is concealed, and, to an inappreciable extent, *concealed from the author himself, if any such thing exists.* (PP, 129; my emphasis)

From the beginning of the text to the end, as exemplified in the quotes above, Derrida explicitly and implicitly denies alternatively that Plato was conscious of the ambiguities and differential meanings at work in his text and that the question of intention is even a relevant issue. The two claims are obviously not the same. The irrelevance of the issue of intentionality would seem to follow from the deconstructive principles set out earlier.[14] Since *differance*, the play of meanings without end, is a characteristic of language as language, the difference between those plays of meaning that a given author might intentionally put into the text and those plays of meanings that simply occur as a function of language, quite independent of the author's intentions, would be beside the point. Though some authors, indeed many in the philosophical tradition, might try to write without ambiguity or univocally, and so without such plays of meanings, others might intentionally write in such ambiguities. In any case, so the thesis would go, any language *will have* such differential meanings, intended or unintended by the author. But whether a given play of meaning, as in the case of the *pharmakon* that Derrida is here addressing, is intended or not by the author becomes an issue precisely when the question of attribution is raised, as it is by Derrida in the above passages and throughout the text whenever he attributes this or that view to "Plato." This is why Derrida vacillates between claiming that the issue of intentionality is irrelevant and claiming that Plato was *not conscious* of this or that play of meanings within his texts.

Regarding the claim that the meanings of texts will always go beyond the intentions of its author, there can be no disagreement between Derrida and the Platonic Socrates. One of his objections to writing that he relates to Phaedrus is precisely that a written text immediately becomes out of the hands of its author and susceptible of all sorts of interpretations that the author may not intend. Indeed, one main problem with written speech is that it cannot answer questions asked of it but maintains a solemn silence (*Phaedrus*, 275d–e). The implication regarding the superiority of spoken language is that the speaker, present and alive, at least has a chance of clearing up misconceptions before they become common currency. But a moment's reflection on our own conversations attests that this is hardly a guarantee, indeed at best a pious hope. Not only does Plato have Socrates explicitly articulate this recognition in the *Phaedrus*, he exhibits that recognition by writing in the dialogue form, one of whose special features is that by having Socrates speak to different characters in different ways and with very different degrees of understanding (consider Phaedrus, Lysis, Theaetetus, and Euthyphro as examples), he gives us concrete instances of the different readings that Socrates' words are given, as well as the different words that Socrates must use with different people. Indeed, in the light of our consideration of these features of the dialogue form, is there a more complete recognition of the multivalence of language in all of philosophy than the Platonic dialogues? So we can conclude that the recognition of the multivalence of language, always beyond a speaker's intention, is an insight at work in the dialogues and shared by Derrida. On this, one might tentatively venture, Plato and Derrida seem to agree.

The question of Plato's control of his language, how much of this play of meaning he intended, is another matter. Again, despite Derrida's occasional claims about its irrelevance, it becomes an issue when he begins attributing certain views to Plato and explicitly denying that Plato was conscious of others. Having acknowledged, with Derrida and the Platonic Socrates, that there is an element of language that always goes beyond the intent of its author, it does not follow either that the author has no control over what happens in the text or that she only has control over the manifest content or presumed intended meaning. I take it as self-evident that different authors, depending on the kind of writing they do, the importance they give to their writing, even their level of genius, will have different levels of control over their language. So the question becomes, to what extent are we warranted in assuming that Plato, this particular writer, exhibited a level of control over his language sufficient to call into question Derrida's denial of that control to Plato, or at least to argue that his control went beyond the manifest meaning of this or that speech?

For it is clear that Derrida regularly claims that Plato did not have the sort of control that would go beyond manifest meaning. Perhaps the most remarkable example of this is that throughout the text he takes the critique of writing, which Plato has his Socrates (who in fact never did write anything that we know of) articulate through the imaginary voice of the King in the Theuth myth, as *Plato's* critique of writing. "Plato, through the mouth of the King. . . ." (PP, 103), etc. By making this assumption, Derrida misses the absolutely crucial difference between Plato and Socrates, that Socrates, apparently, took the criticisms of writing with sufficient seriousness that he never wrote, whereas Plato writes this very critique in his dialogue. If we appreciate this irony, we will be led immediately to wonder whether Plato might not have regarded his choice of the dialogue form as somehow answering the charges against writing that he himself writes.[15] But this assumes that Plato had a degree of control of his writing that Derrida will not allow. For Derrida, Plato "never comes to grips with the writing he uses. His intentions are always apparently didactic and analogical" (PP, 159). I submit that to the contrary, and as I have tried to show, Plato very much came to grips with the writing format he employs, in such a way that Derrida's regular attribution of unconscious and unintended meanings within the dialogues misses precisely the significance of what Plato was trying to "give us to think."

But we might return to an aspect of the general formulation of deconstruction and ask, since, after all, in one of its formulations the question of authorship simply does not matter to the deconstructive project, what does it matter that Derrida, despite that claim, regularly attributes this or that doctrine to Plato, other than to cause a certain tension in his position? It matters very much, both on a specific and a more general level. On the specific level, it matters because we, all of us including Derrida, are trying to understand what is happening philosophically in the dialogues, and Derrida has claimed to know what is happening therein, and what is happening, he says, is the espousal of a certain set of doctrines that we have come to know as Platonism. I argue that such a claim can be made only on the basis of a misreading of the philosophical intent of the dialogues, that they are not intended primarily to be didactic and doctrinal, but precisely to *raise the kind of provocations* that Derrida thinks are the unconscious and unintended result of his own deconstructive analyses. So the specific problem is a misreading and subsequent misinterpretation of the dialogues. Second and more broadly, this doctrinal reading—and deconstruction—becomes part of an account for Derrida—as we saw earlier it did for Heidegger—of an interpretation of the entire history of metaphysics, a history of which, we are told again and again by Derrida, Plato inaugurates. If my criticisms of Derrida's interpretation are valid, and if my own interpretation of the dialogue form is more plausible, then this problematizes the entire broad interpretation, by no means confined to Derrida, of the history of metaphysics as beginning with Plato. If I am right, Plato's dialogues problematize that history, in effect, before it happens.

There are a number of other specific problems with Derrida's reading of Plato in "Plato's Pharmacy" that I could address, but I close our study of this text with a consideration of an issue that is at once decisive to the problem I have just addressed and points the way to the need to study Derrida's *Khora* essay. One crucial point of Derrida's deconstruction of the term *pharmakon* and its cognates is to show that, despite Plato's own efforts (according to Derrida) to present a metaphysical and univocally formulated dualism, nevertheless, despite that intention, the *differance* within the text, exemplified by the *pharmakon*, destabilizes and undercuts that univocal metaphysical claim insofar as the ambivalence of the term means not only that it is not and cannot be univocal, but that it cannot even be comprehended within the metaphysical categories that Plato—again, according to Derrida—is trying to espouse: subject/object, being/nonbeing, presence/absence. Thus, having developed this nonmetaphysical status of the differential *pharmakon* as a "supplement" to any metaphysical position, Derrida comments, "Why is the surrogate or supplement dangerous? It is not, so to speak, dangerous in itself, in that aspect of it that can present itself as a thing, as a being-present. In that case it would be reassuring. But here, the supplement *is* not, is not a being *(on)*. It is nevertheless not a simple nonbeing *(me on)*, either. Its slidings slip it out of the simple alternative presence/absence. *That* is the danger" (PP, 109; Derrida's emphasis). Once again the issue of attribution becomes crucial. It is important to recognize that Derrida is characterizing this supplement to Plato's metaphysics as a result of the deconstruction of that metaphysics, as an unintended *differance* of the very language in which it is stated that undercuts its stability. Later, in a long but crucial passage, Derrida well sums up the effect of this destabilizing *differance*.

> Philosophy thus opposes to its other this transmutation of the drug into a remedy, of the poison into a counterpoison. Such an operation would not be possible if the *pharmako-logos* did not already harbor within itself that complicity of contrary values, and if the *pharmakon* in general were not, prior to any distinction-making, that which, presenting itself as a poison, may turn out to be a cure, may retrospectively reveal itself in the truth of its curative power. The 'essence' of the *pharmakon* lies in the way in which, having no stable essence, no 'proper' characteristics, it is not, in any sense (metaphysical, physical, chemical, alchemical) of the word, a *substance*. The *pharmakon* has no ideal identity; it is aneidetic, firstly because it is not monoeidetic (in the sense in which the *Phaedo* speaks of the *eidos* as something simple, noncomposite: *monoeides*). This 'medicine' is not a simple thing. But neither is it composite, a sensible or empirical *suntheton* partaking of several simple substances. It is rather the prior medium in which differentiation in general is produced, along with the opposition between the *eidos* and its other (PP, 125–126; Derrida's emphasis).

As such a nonsubstantial being that does not fit into the metaphysical dichotomies of being and non-being, presence and absence, etc., the *pharmakon* undercuts, presumably in spite of himself, Plato's efforts to set up that set of dualisms that will become Platonism. For Derrida, this deconstructive force of *pharmakon* in Plato exemplifies precisely the deconstructive element of *logos*, of language itself. The *pharmakon* is thus illustrative of the way in which *logos*, the very language that Plato uses, will not allow him to successfully articulate the univocal metaphysical dualism that he (again, according to Derrida) wishes to promulgate. The inherently ambivalent status of *pharmakon*, its refusal to submit to anything like univocal meaning, means that *pharmakon* is *différance* itself: "The *pharmakon* is the movement, the locus, and the play: (the production of) difference. It is the *différance* of difference. It holds in reserve, in its undecided shadow and vigil, the opposites and the differends that the process of discrimination will come to carve out" (PP, 127).

It is important to see, before moving on, how important the question of attribution is to Derrida's interpretation, despite his occasional claims to the contrary. On his view, Plato wants to assert an unequivocal metaphysical dualism. He doesn't *like* things like ambiguity, destabilization, plays of meaning. However, *in spite of Plato*, as it were, his very own language works precisely to destabilize that dualism, to set into play an unending series of meanings that undercut anything like univocity. The question is, how many times must Plato install into his texts precisely these destabilizing intermediaries that undercut any possible clean dualisms before it will begin to occur to us that that is precisely what he intends? He does so in the case of the *pharmakon* and the *logos* it exemplifies. But he also does it with Diotima's crucial discussion of eros in the *Symposium*, which, we are told, is characterized precisely by this intermediary status: it is *in between* (*metaxu*) good and evil, knowledge and ignorance, beauty and ugliness, and crucially, the mortal and the divine (*Symposium*, 201e–203a). In so far as the divine makes reference to the Forms, and the mortal to phenomena, we see clearly here how eros undercuts anything like a metaphysical dualism. But Plato also undercuts this dualism with Socrates' altogether mysterious remarks about the Idea of the Good, in the *Republic*, which, we are told, is not Being (which would make it fit nicely within the supposedly Platonic Being/becoming dualism) but is "beyond being," and beyond intelligibility as well (*Republic*, 509 aff.) No less striking is Plato's accomplishing of the same movement in the *Timaeus*, where he has his Timaeus first develop an account of the cosmos that does assert a dualism, but then have to "begin again" with a more adequate account, whose distinguishing characteristic is precisely to insert an intermediary between the dualism of Forms and phenomena, the equally mysterious *khora*, accessible only by a "bastard reasoning," and articulated by Timaeus only in terms of the metaphors of the "nurse of all becoming" and the "receptacle" (*Timaeus*, 48–53). Should it not occur to us, after noticing that Plato again and again has his characters' attempts to assert a dualism undercut by some mysterious intermediary not reducible to either pole but playing ambiguously between them, that Plato wants the thoughtful reader to notice that this always happens, perhaps always *must* happen? That, just as Derrida wants to suggest *against* Platonism, language, even the language of metaphysics, always introduces us into a realm of precariousness, of destabilization, of, in one of Derrida's favorite expressions, "a play of meanings without end?"

Derrida addresses the famous passage on *Khora* in the *Timaeus* at some length, in a later article that becomes part of the book, *On the Name*,[16] although still within the set of assumptions we have already seen, that the presence of the *khora* represents the presence of an unintended *differance* within Plato's intended dualism. Let us turn to that essay in somewhat greater detail.

KHORA

For the reasons we have set out in our general discussion of deconstruction, Derrida feels justified in turning more or less directly to the famous section of the *Timaeus*, beginning almost in the exact middle of the dialogue at around 48a, where the *khora* is introduced, without paying extensive attention to the dramatic context of the dialogue in which it is set. For the reasons I have set out in contrast to that strategy, let us begin instead by pointing briefly to just some of the background existential issues in the context of which the *Timaeus*, and so the *Khora*, takes place. This is obviously no time for a full interpretation of that complex dialogue; instead, I shall here only cite some of the most striking contextual elements in terms of which the *khora* eventually gets introduced, and in the light of which, I would argue, it must be understood.[17]

Let us begin with the question of beginnings.[18] The *Timaeus* is striking in the number of beginnings it makes, the number of failed beginnings, incomplete beginnings, new beginnings, that it contains. Socrates begins by counting: "One, two three,—but where, my dear Timaeus, is the fourth of our guests of yesterday, our hosts of today" (17a). After Socrates charges those present with what he desires from them, Critias begins a story of ancient Athens that he supposedly will complete later. Timaeus then begins his cosmology, but soon indicates that he has only explained the world's body before accounting for its soul, which is in the reverse order, and so has to begin again with an account of the world's soul (35ff.) Then, at 48a, he has to make a new beginning in order to explain the workings of "necessity" and introduce the *khora*. One might say that the *Timaeus*, as an account of origins, is all about beginnings; but then the various and disjointed beginnings of the *Timaeus* would correspond to the *disorderly* motions discussed within its pages. How would the *khora* fit into—or disrupt—this pre-occupation with beginnings?

Let us try another beginning, beginning with the title character, Timaeus. This dialogue is a perfect example of how important it is to consider the cast of characters, the character types they represent and what that might signify for the meaning of the dialogue. Timaeus is a well-known Pythagorean, from Locri, itself a center of Pythagorean-ism. Not surprisingly, therefore, the account he gives of the structure of the cosmos is shot through with Pythagoreanism. Most obviously, this includes the tendency to mathematicize the universe, to under-stand its structure in terms of geometric forms. But it also includes other elements of Pythagorean doctrine, certainly including its rein-carnation teaching and notorious misogyny, exemplified in the claim, made toward the end of the dialogue, that men who are cowards are changed into women in the next life (91a), not to mention the hilarious account of hysteria at 91c.[19]

Doctrinal interpreters of the dialogues usually take all this as Platonic doctrine, and thus as an indication of the influence of Pythagoreanism on Plato. But one might consider it in another way. Pythagoreanism was, after all, an important intellectual movement in Greece (as its more sophisticated modern version is now). Plato no doubt took its claims seriously. It hardly follows that he accepts all or even its fundamental teachings. Perhaps he is asking, suppose the Pythagoreans are right and the world really is mathematical through and through? What would a Pythagorean, mathematical account of the structure of the universe actually look like? How far could one take it? And what, crucially, would be its limits? In this sense, espe-cially given what actually happens in the dialogue, Plato's project here could be seen as a critique in the Kantian sense, an examination of the possibilities, but also of the limits, of a mathematical account of the whole. Or even, more harshly but with some plausibility given what later happens in the dialogue, as a kind of reductio ad absurdam of such an effort.

One might then ask, what is the internal evidence that the *Timaeus* might be an examination of the limits of Pythagorean, mathematically oriented accounts of the cosmos (as well as its possibilities) rather than simply Plato's straightforward espousal of this view? First, it is impor-tant to recognize that one of the great appeals of mathematical ac-counts—both then and now—is the precision and certainty that mathematics can paradigmatically exhibit. And to be sure, those sec-tions of the account that are mathematical, the elaborate accounts of the solids, etc., do exhibit these qualities. Yet this very dialogue, which most thoroughly mathematicizes the universe, is literally shot through with warnings that this can at best only be a "likely story." I count at least 14 different times when we are warned that we are here talking about only "likely" or "probable" accounts.[20] Built into the rhetoric of the dialogue, then, seems to be a limit on the very possibility of mathematically precise accounts of the structure of the universe.[21]

The dialogue begins in what would seem a paradigmatic Pythagorean way, by counting. "One, two, three,—but where, my dear Timaeus, is the fourth of our guests of yesterday, our hosts of today?" (*Timaeus* 17a). Does not this opening sentence itself point to another limit of mathematical accounts? From simply counting, we *cannot tell* who the fourth, missing person is (and we are never told—a source of unending speculation by interpreters of this dialogue). Mathematics, and in particular that fundamental mathematical act of counting, does not delineate or identify individuals as individuals. It is incapable of doing so. Consequently, a mathematical account of things can at best be a general or abstract account, at best an impersonal account. Is it not for this very reason that so many mythical and quasi-mythical elements must be introduced into the account (the demiurge, the receptacle, the "nurse and mother of all becoming," [Timaeus 49ff.] etc.), to fill out the abstractions that the mathematical sections can present? Indeed, yet another crucial indication that this dialogue is a critique of Pythagorean mathematical accounts is the apparent necessity, which arises again and again, to augment the mathematical sections with these more poetic, metaphoric, and mythical elements.

The very distinction between *mythos* and *logos* is in fact very much in play in the *Timaeus*. In a most striking contrast, Critias' opening tale, supposedly of ancient Athens, is introduced by him explicitly as a *logos* and *not* as a *mythos*, although it is manifestly mythic through and through (*Timaeus*, 20 eff.; this claim is underscored, perhaps ironically, by Socrates at the conclusion of Critias' introductory story, when he comments that he is especially pleased that the story is "not a myth but a true logos" [26e]). Whereas Timaeus' cosmology, with its mathematization of the universe, is explicitly acknowledged by Timaeus to be a "likely myth" (29d), though he *also* characterizes it as a *logos* (27c). So the overtly political discourse of Critias is characterized as a logos in contrast to a myth, while the supposedly mathematical cosmology of Timaeus is admittedly a myth, as well as a logos. Are we not invited by these puzzling remarks and especially by the ambiguity of Timaeus's speech to reflect on the connection, perhaps the necessary interaction, of myth and logos? Are we not especially invited to wonder what the admission of the necessarily mythical dimension of Timaeus's

Pythagorean cosmology implies for any claim to give a pure, mathematical logos of the origins of the cosmos? Is not Plato inviting us to consider, then, the *necessary* interplay of logos and mythos? If so, so much for univocal metaphysical accounts of the whole; so much for Platonism.

There is another beginning to the *Timaeus* that surely must be considered in any adequate interpretation of the dialogue. At 17b, Socrates begins a most curious summary of his discourse of "yesterday," a summation, apparently, of the *Republic*. But it is a bizarre summary indeed. What is included in this summary are for the most part those aspects that made the "city in speech" least possible and least desirable: the radical one person one job principle, the notion of a philosophical guardian perfectly just but wanting no possessions, the community of wives and children, "noble lies" concerning marriage contracts, parentage, and the secret movement of "hybrids" between classes.

This is an utterly inaccurate summary both in terms of what it includes and what it excludes. At 18a, Socrates says that the guardians will guard against attacks "from within and without" the city. Yet the rhetoric of the *Republic* assumes that everyone *within* the city will be perfectly just, accepting of their status in the hierarchy of the city, doing their job and not interfering with others, and therefore not *needing* to be guarded; only outsiders must be guarded against. Perhaps more importantly, nothing is said in this summary of what most consider the absolutely most important things discussed in the *Republic*: the education of the philosopher-rulers, the Ideas, the Idea of the Good, the sun, divided line, and cave analogies.

Yet when Socrates asks Timaeus whether anything has been left out, Timaeus replies, "Not at all, Socrates, this is just what you said" (19a). What are we to make of this utter lack of precision by this devotee of Pythagorean mathematics? At very least, we must wonder about his enthusiastic acceptance of this amazingly inaccurate summary of the *Republic*. Could someone who does this really be Plato's mouthpiece in the dialogue? Could he really be spouting Platonic doctrine? Platonism?

There is another dimension to this summary that becomes clearer when Socrates finishes it and makes his request to the others present, after which Critias launches into his (unfinished) account of ancient Athens, to which, he says, he will return after Timaeus finishes his account of the cosmos (27aff). This means that this mathematicized account of the cosmos is decisively framed by the political. Will this not affect both what is said by Timaeus and its significance? Would we not have to take into account this deeply political framework in any interpretation we would give of Timaeus' speech and of the *khora* in particular? Yet Derrida does not do so.[22]

At 19b, Socrates indicates how he would like his hosts to entertain him today. He wants the city that was constructed in speech yesterday to be put into action today. This is a strikingly odd request. "Yesterday," at the end of Book IX, Socrates and Glaucon explicitly agreed that it *does not matter* whether such a city could really exist or not, since the real issue is establishing the realm of justice within the individual soul (*Republic,* 592b). Why, with these people here today, is he indulging in the pretense that it might really be put into action? And in any case, when Critias actually begins and tells his story, it is not of the city in speech of yesterday but of ancient Athens. So in fact, Socrates never does get what he requests. No less odd is the characterization of the city in action that Socrates requests. "In action," apparently, means "at war" (19c). He wants to see the city at war. If nothing else, this underlines the deeply political framework within which the *Timaeus* takes place, and which Derrida for the most part ignores.

At last, Timaeus begins the first of his several beginnings (27 dff.). This first beginning, which features the strong distinction between being and becoming (27d) as well as the introduction of the Demiurge (28c), is deeply teleological. At 34c, however, Timaeus acknowledges that they have begun in a disorderly way, accounting for the body of the cosmos before its soul, whereas the soul of course precedes the body. So he begins again with an account of the world soul. Then, at 48a, yet again recognizing the incompleteness of the earlier beginnings, he must begin again in such a way as to take into account the role of *necessity (anangke)*. It is within this third Timaean beginning that the mysterious *khora* is introduced, which becomes the theme of Derrida's essay to which we can presently turn.

I have here barely touched upon the many important issues and themes in the context of which Plato has placed the cosmology (and the chorology) of the *Timaeus.* But I hope I have said enough to make persuasive my claim that any adequate interpretation of the strange and difficult *khora* passage must place it within the context of these issues and interpret it within that framework. The Platonic dialogues, I argue, simply are not the sorts of texts that can be adequately interpreted by leaping in here or there, whether to a passage that is claimed to be central or marginal. Let us turn to Derrida's *Khora* essay.

Derrida can, against the interpretive strategy that I have been defending, pass over all the existential details discussed above and leap directly to the *khora* passage because he believes that *khora* constitutes the deconstructive moment in Platonism, the *differance* of any Platonic dualism or doctrine of eternal essences. This is testimony to the agility of his deconstructive strategy, since it is not all clear at first just how anyone could construe *khora* as *marginal* to the *Timaeus*. Not only does it occur almost in the exact center of the text (a point that Derrida explicitly notes), but almost no one would be tempted to pass over the *khora* as marginal to the core teaching of the text. It has long been regarded as a central problem of interpreting the *Timaeus*, as Derrida again acknowledges. And it is utterly implausible that Plato was unaware of its problematic centrality, given the fact that he has Timaeus introduce it as part of a necessary new beginning. To the contrary, I would argue that it is clearly Plato's explicit intention to *make* the *khora* problematic for the relatively clean dualism of Being/ becoming that Timaeus has up to that point espoused. Precisely in the deconstructive sense, *khora* differs from and is deferred by that dualism, at least until the middle of the dialogue.

Indeed, what the *khora* *is* marginal to, what it does deconstruct, that of which it does constitute the *differance*, is exactly the straightforward dualism of eternal Being and ever-changing becoming with which Timaeus begins his first beginning, and which Derrida persists in identifying as Platonism. But is it at all plausible that this deconstructive moment takes place, as it were, in spite of Plato, that he was unaware of, or at least could not control, the way it undercuts the dualism of Timaeus's first beginning? This would only make any sense at all on the interpretive assumption that the dialogues are in fact vehicles for the espousal of Platonic doctrines, and that the Platonic doctrine being espoused in the *Timaeus* is not the *khora* teaching but the less complicated dualism of Being and Becoming. But I have been calling into question the first of these assumptions from the beginning, and the second, I submit, is implausible on the face of it. Why should we take Plato to be espousing a doctrine that he explicitly, not subtly or in the margins but explicitly, contradicts? I shall therefore argue in this section that Derrida is surely right that the *khora* does deconstruct and undercut any straightforward dualism. He is wrong, however, in his implication that Plato is unaware of this, that this is, in effect, an example of the multivocal character of language running away from the author's intentions; he is wrong, second, in assuming that the dualism that the *khora* so decisively undercuts is Plato's doctrine, though he is right that it later becomes a simplified version of what comes to be called Platonism.[23]

Consider, then, the effect, taken together, of the three crucial notions of *khora*, the Idea of the Good, and eros, three notions that no one could consider marginal to the Platonic dialogues. All three of these crucial notions undercut the clean dualism that constitutes Platonism, but each does so in a distinctive way. *Khora*, as Derrida shows so well in this essay, stands outside any possible dualism, and explicitly outside the "Platonic" dualism of Being and becoming that Timaues introduces in his first beginning. The Idea of the good, on the other hand, is, Socrates tells us, *beyond* Being (*Republic* 509b), and so in another way undercuts the Being/becoming dualism. Eros, on yet another hand, is characterized regularly as *in the middle* (*metaxu*) between the divine (Being) and mortal (becoming), and so in yet a third way undercuts the assertion of a straightforward dualism. How many times, in how many different ways, must Plato do this before we begin to get the point to which he is provoking us? Contrary, then, to the standard attribution of dualism to Plato shared by Derrida, it would be more true to say that Plato in his dialogues *never* allows dualism to be presented without being undercut, that he never allows the unchallenged and unproblematized assertion of the dualism that becomes associated with his name. As John Sallis cautiously but well puts the point:

> If one were to take metaphysics to be constituted precisely by the governance of the twofold, then the chorology could be said to bring both the founding of metaphysics and its displacement, both at once. Originating metaphysics would have been exposing it to the abyss, to the abysmal *khora*, which is both origin and abyss, both at the same time. Then one could say—with the requisite reservations—that the beginning of metaphysics will have been already the end of metaphysics. (*Chorology*, 123)

Derrida shows in detail and depth the remarkable extent to which the *khora* undercuts dualisms. Not only does it undercut explicitly the metaphysical dualism of Being/becoming asserted earlier by Timaeus, it also undercuts the linguistic dualism of *mythos* and *logos* that we have seen is very much at work in this dialogue. For, as we shall presently see, the language in which the *khora* is articulated is clearly not a *logos* in the technical sense of a demonstration, yet it is no less clearly not a myth either:

> It is perhaps because its scope goes beyond or falls short of the polarity of metaphorical sense versus proper sense that the thought of the *khora* exceeds the polarity, no doubt analogous, of the *mythos* and the *logos*. Such at least would be the question that we should like here to put to the test

of a reading. The consequence which we would envisage would be the following: with these two polarities, the thought of the *khora* would trouble the very order of polarity, of polarity in general, whether dialectical or not. Giving place to oppositions, it would itself not submit to any reversal. (*Khora*, 92)

Troubling these polarities, the *khora* also undercuts the crucial polarities of metaphysics. It is not a subject or a substance. It is neither an eternal essence, nor does it participate in an essence.

"*Khora* is not a subject. It is not the subject. Nor the support. . . . But if Timaeus names it as receptacle (*dekhomenon*) or place (*khora*) these names do not designate an essence, the stable being of an *eidos*, since *khora* is neither of the order of the *eidos* nor of the order of mimemes, that is, of images of the *eidos* which come to imprint themselves in it—which thus *is not* and does not belong to the two known or recognized genera of being." (95; Derrida's emphasis)

Perhaps most perplexingly but most importantly of all, this means that our usual approach to interpreting difficult passages such as the *khora*, to try to "clear it up," is at once impossible and inappropriate (94). Those gestures, entirely appropriate for things that come to be or for Being, are, it is suggested by the dialogue, simply not even possible with regard to *Khora*. Whatever the manner of our thinking *khora*, that thinking will not be in the service of the metaphysical goal of "clear and distinct ideas." Plato makes this clear by not only having Timaeus tell us that we can't understand *khora*, but by formulating it in an explicitly contradictory way.

Consider the following passages, all coming close upon one another. First, at 50e, Timaeus says of *khora* that "Wherefore it is right that that which is to receive into itself all forms (*panta gene*) should itself be free of forms (*ektos eidon*)." Yet a few sentences later we are told that "We will not lie if we say that it is some kind of invisible form (*anoraton eidos*) and formless (*amorphon*), receiving everything, participating (*metalambanon*) somehow in a most unfathomable way (*aporotata*) in the intelligible (*noetou*) and (yet) difficult to capture (*dusalototaton*)" (51a9).

Yet a page later we are told,

And there is a third kind (*genos*) the everlasting (*aei*) *khora*, which does not receive (*ou prosdekhomenon*) destruction (N.B.

So it does not receive *everything*), which provides room for everything that comes to be, but itself, with non-sensation, graspable with a kind of bastard (*notho*) reasoning, hardly trustworthy, which we see as in a dream and say that all that is must of necessity be in some place (*topo*) and occupy some *khora*, but that which is neither on the earth nor in heaven to be nothing. (52b)[24]

Given all these reservations, qualifications, and tensions if not contradictions, given, that is, that *khora* cannot be thought within any of the standard polarities (e.g., either with logical consistency or with an appealing myth), what, then, will be the manner of our thinking on *khora*? We could add, or on the Good, which is "beyond" Being and intelligibility, or on eros, which is "in the middle," neither itself a form nor a finite instance of one? Derrida shows that he is acutely aware of the problem:

But what is said about *khora* is that this name does not designate any of the known or recognized or, if you like, received types of existent, *received* by philosophical discourse, that is, by the *ontological logos* that lays down the law in the *Timaeus*[25]: *khora* is neither sensible nor intelligible. There is *khora*; one can even ponder its *physis* and its *dynamis*, or at least ponder these in a preliminary way. But what *there is*, there, is not; and we will come back later to what this *there is* can give us to think, this *there is*, which, by the way, *gives* nothing in giving place or in giving to think, whereby it will be risky to see in it the equivalent of an *es gibt*, of the *es gibt* which remains without a doubt implicated in every negative theology, unless it is the *es gibt* which always summons negative theology in its Christian history. (96; Derrida's emphases)

Derrida is exactly right to raise these issues, for they are indeed issues raised by Plato's having Timaeus need to make this new beginning which includes the *khora*. To respond, Derrida now enters upon a brief discussion of the way in which the problematic of how to speak philosophically culminates in Hegel, in a notion of dialectic that always makes *logos* superior to *mythos*. Since this is precisely the polarity that the *khora* itself undercuts, one might expect Derrida to see in it Plato's own problematizing of this and other polarities. Instead, continuing his deconstructive assumption that Plato was not conscious of all this, Derrida concludes that these polarities are not *imposed* on

Plato but "derives from a certain 'Platonism' " (102). To support this, Derrida quotes Timaeus' summary of his account toward the end of the dialogue.

> First, the programme. The cosmogony of the *Timaeus* runs through the cycle of knowledge on all things. Its encyclopedic end must mark the term, the *telos*, of a *logos* on the subject of everything that is: 'And now at length we may say that our discourse (*logos*) concerning the universe (*peri tou pantos*) has reached its termination.' [92c]. This encyclopedic *logos* is a general ontology, treating of all types of being, it includes a theology, a cosmology, a physiology, a psychology, a zoology. Mortal or immortal, human and divine, visible and invisible things are situated there. (103)[26]

Yet the *khora* would seem to disturb this claim to an encyclopedic *logos*:[27]

> And yet, half-way through the cycle, won't the discourse on *khora* have opened, between the sensible and the intelligible, belonging neither to one nor to the other, hence neither to the cosmos as sensible god nor to the intelligible god, an apparently empty space—even though it is no doubt not *emptiness*? Didn't it name a gaping opening, an abyss, or a chasm? Isn't it starting out from this chasm 'in' it, that the cleavage between the sensible and the intelligible, indeed, between body and soul, can have place and take place? (103)

Derrida concludes that this oversight on Timaeus' part, this failure, in claiming at the end an encyclopedic *logos*, to acknowledge the problematic of the *khora*, is *Plato's* failure. Though he does not explicitly mention that it is Plato's failure, the implication is clear, as in the following conclusion:

> The ontologico-encyclopedic conclusion of the *Timaeus* seems to cover over the open chasm in the middle of the book. What it would thus cover over, closing the gaping mouth of the quasi-banned discourse on *khora*, would perhaps not only be the abyss between the sensible and the intelligible, between being and nothingness, between being and the lesser being, nor even perhaps between being and the exis-

tent, nor yet between *logos* and *mythos,* but between all these couples and another which would not even be *their* other. (104; Derrida's emphases)

It is crucial to note the implicit and undefended move from Timaeus' failure (if indeed it is a failure rather than simply a looser manner of speaking) at the end of the dialogue to acknowledge the problematic of the *khora* to the assumption that it is *Plato's* failure as well. I suggest instead that if it is a failure on Timaeus' part, it is at least as likely that Plato *wanted us to think about* this failure as, perhaps, a failure of *Pythagorean mathematicicm* to, as it were, take account of the unfathomable.

Derrida next turns, for the first time, to the political context of the early parts of the *Timaeus,* in order to point out some fascinating parallels and ironies with regard to those sections and what is later said of the *khora.* This section of the text is full of insights into the ironic parallels between the *khora* and Socrates' own situation as "without place" *(atopos).* Near the end of this discussion, Derrida entertains a possible conclusion that, were he to have stayed with it, would have been penetrating and transforming in its insight:

> In this theatre of irony, where the scenes interlock in a se-ries of receptacles without end and without bottom, how can one isolate a thesis or a theme that could be attributed calmly to the 'philosophy-of-Plato,' indeed to *philosophy* as the Platonic thing? This would be to misrecognize or vio-lently deny the structure of the textual scene, to regard as resolved all the questions of topology in general, including that of the places of rhetoric, and to think one understood what it means to receive, that is, to understand. It's a little early. As always. (119; Derrida's emphasis)

Would that Derrida would have pursued this insight further! It is a fine summation of one of the guiding points I have been making all along, both in regard to Heidegger's and Derrida's reading of Plato. Taken seriously, it would force Derrida to rethink every attribution in his own works, the very ones we have been examining, of something someone says in one dialogue or another to Plato or Platonism. In sum, it would force a revision in his interpretation of just the sort I have been advocating. But alas, in the very next paragraph, beginning the very next sentence, Derrida withdraws this insight, opting once again for an attribution of "Platonism" to the texts of Plato that, in effect, places the responsibility for Platonism squarely in *Plato's* hands. Because this passage is so important, I quote it at length:

> Should one henceforth forbid oneself to speak of the philosophy of Plato, of the ontology of Plato, or even of Platonism? Not at all, and there would undoubtedly be no error of principle in so speaking, merely an inevitable *abstraction*. *Platonism* would mean, in these conditions, the thesis or theme which one has extracted by artifice, misprision, and abstraction from the text, torn out of the written fiction of 'Plato.' Once this abstraction has been supercharged and deployed, it will be extended over all the folds of the text, of its ruses, overdeterminations, and reserves, which the abstraction will come to cover up and dissimulate. This will be called Platonism or the philosophy of Plato, which is neither arbitrary nor illegitimate, since a certain force of thetic abstraction at work in the heterogeneous text of Plato can recommend one to do so. . . . 'Platonism' is thus certainly one of the effects of the text signed by Plato, for a long time, and for necessary reasons, the dominant effect, but this effect is always turned back against the text. (119–120; Derrida's emphases)

Despite the qualification in the last clause of the above quote, it is clear that Derrida is advocating the legitimacy of what he himself acknowledges is the abstracting of this or that doctrine from the text of Plato and naming them Platonism. But *is* it legitimate to do so, and under what conditions? Let us return to our earlier discussions about Plato's choice of the dialogue form. If he had chosen, as he might have, to write treatises espousing his doctrines, there would be no question of the legitimacy of abstracting those doctrines and giving them the name Platonism. Even if, as most writers of dialogues subsequent to him, he had written dialogues in which one character obviously and consistently espoused the doctrines of the author, one could affirm the legitimacy of what Derrida espouses. If, that is, Plato had chosen the treatise form or a dialogue form that was manifestly a concealed treatise, there would be warrant, even retrospectively, for considering that he, too, was primarily interested in getting across a doctrine that he wanted people to accept. But he did not! Quite to the contrary, by writing dialogues of the exceedingly complex sort that he did, dialogues where it is next to impossible to say with any confidence just what view the author wishes to espouse, Plato, I want to suggest, *removed himself in advance* from the philosophic controversy over doctrines that became the history of philosophy. He quite clearly wanted to do something else, something of the sort that I have been arguing the dialogues accomplish. Consequently, the attribution to him of that set of doctrines under the name of "Platonism" constitutes not a legitimate drawing out of the content of the dialogues, as Derrida wants to suggest, but an illegitimate imposition on those texts of a set of assumptions that derive from treatises and which we can take Plato to be rejecting in his decision to write dialogues.

Moving toward his conclusion, Derrida reiterates and extends the point he has elicited, that the *khora*, in its mysterious non-essence, problematizes how to speak about it, and so, he concludes, problematizes how philosophy is to speak about itself:

> The discourse on *khora* thus plays for philosophy a role analogous to the role which *khora* 'herself' plays for that which philosophy speaks of, namely, the cosmos formed or given form according to the paradigm. Nevertheless, it is from this cosmos that the proper—but necessarily inadequate—figures will be taken for describing *khora*: receptacle, imprint-bearer, mother, or nurse. These figures are not even true figures. Philosophy cannot speak directly, whether in the mode of vigilance or of truth (true or probably), about what these figures approach. The dream is between the two, neither one nor the other. *Philosophy cannot speak philosophically* of that which looks like its 'mother,' its 'nurse,' its 'receptacle,' or its 'imprint-bearer.' As such, it speaks only of the father and the son, as if the father engendered it all on his own. (126; my emphasis)

"Philosophy cannot speak philosophically" (126) about its origins. We need to ask here, according to what conception of philosophy and philosophic speaking? Plato's? To be sure, we now have a long, Aristotelian, tradition wherein philosophy is warranted in speaking of the ground of other disciplines, their "first principles," in speech that is not itself an instantiation of that discipline. So we have "philosophy of . . ." science, art, religion, etc. But on this conception, the project of speaking about the nature of philosophy itself is not something different from philosophy but simply an instantiation of what it always already been. There is thus something circular, and at the same time unfathomable, mysterious, about philosophy's effort to bespeak itself.

But to decide whether, *for Plato*, "philosophy cannot speak philosophically" (126) about itself and its origins, we would have to determine first just what philosophy and especially speaking philosophically entails in and out of the dialogues, and that, I have been arguing throughout this book, is an immensely difficult task, by no means reducible to a set of arguments abstracted from this or that speech for this or that doctrine. The dialogues, to say it once again, are not a conglomeration of arguments for this or that doctrine that can then be assigned to Platonism. They certainly do not present a set of arguments for what philosophy itself is and how to speak philosophically. But they are, instead and as I have argued, an *exhibition* of that whereof they speak, an exhibition of what it would be like to philosophize, to speak philosophically. But according to a tradition now almost a century old, that speech which does not so much prove or present arguments for, but instead exhibits, makes visible, the matter for thought is called "phenomenology." Are not the dialogues, then, something like "Plato's phenomenologies"?

I want to close by underlining the great sympathy I have with Derrida's strategy of deconstruction, despite my criticisms within this chapter. Many of the issues and questions Derrida elicits from the dialogues through his deconstructive readings are just the ones that I think should be elicited and that I would want to elicit. For that reason, I think there is much to learn from his reading. But I also think that the issues and questions that he elicits are some of the very ones that *Plato himself* wants us to elicit; at very least, they are the ones called *for* by what is happening in the dialogues themselves. Thus, in so far as deconstructive readings assume or imply that what is discovered is unintended by the author, I begin my disagreement with Derrida's reading. To put it another way, deconstructive readings (without the judgments about what Plato did and did not intend) would seem to be exactly what Plato wanted, given the way he wrote the dialogues. Derrida comes "this close" to seeing all this. Perhaps he comes "this close," as well, to seeing the implications of this position, that he would have to rethink his own regular attribution of this or that position to "Platonism," indeed, that he would have to rethink the entire project of what it would mean to deconstruct dialogues that are perhaps undeconstructible, and so what it would mean to deconstruct Platonism. Perhaps, understandably, he recoils from that spectre. But I have tried to make plausible that we, thinking with and after Derrida, need to begin that rethinking.

Chapter Three

Irigaray's Plato

L uce Irigaray is one of France's leading feminist philosophers. Her
substantial oeuvre has had an important impact on Continental
thinking, not only within feminist circles, but with the psychoanalytic
community, the postmodern movement, as well as those interested in
the history of philosophy, on which she has commented often and in
depth. Although references to and comments upon Plato occur regularly throughout Irigaray's work, in two of her works she addresses
aspects of Plato in great depth, and it is on those that I shall concentrate in this chapter. These are her 1974 work, *Speculum of the Other
Woman*,[1] which contains a complicated interpretation of the cave analogy in the *Republic* in a long chapter entitled "Plato's Hystera," and
her 1984 book, *An Ethics of Sexual Difference*,[2] which contains an important chapter entitled "Sorcerer Love: A Reading of Plato, *Symposium*,
Diotima's Speech." I shall begin with the earlier work.

"PLATO'S HYSTERA"

I want to begin, however, with a passage from an interview among
four feminist philosophers, Pheng Cheah and Elizabeth Grosz, editors

of *Diacritics*, who are interviewing Judith Butler and Drucilla Cornell ("The Future of Sexual Difference: An interview with Judith Butler and Drucilla Cornell," *Diacritics* 28.1: 19–42, Spring 1998, p. 19. The entire issue is devoted to Irigaray). The passage I quote is Judith Butler's first remark, answering Elizabeth Grosz's question about the influence of Irigaray on her own thinking. I quote it because it succinctly formulates a slew of problems raised in reading Irigaray's *Speculum*.

> I think that probably early on, when I started working on French feminism as a graduate student in the early '80s, I was not interested in her at all because she seemed to me to be an essentialist and that was a term we used quite easily then, when we thought we knew what it meant. In the late '80s, I started to rethink my objections to her on that basis and found that she was, among the feminist theorists I had read, perhaps the most versed in philosophy and that her engagement with philosophy was a curious mixture of both loyalty and aggression. And it became very interesting to me when I started thinking about her whole practice of critical mimesis—what she was doing when she was reading Freud, what was she doing when she was reading Plato—and I read *Speculum* again and again, frightened by its anger, compelled by the closeness of the reading, confused by the mimetism of the text. Was she enslaved to these texts, was she displacing them radically, was she perhaps in the bind of being in both positions at the same time? And I realized that whatever the feminine was for her, it was not a substance, not a spiritual reality that might be isolated, but it had something to do with this strange practice of reading, one in which she was reading texts that she was not authorized to read, texts from which she was as a woman explicitly excluded or explicitly demeaned, and that she would read them anyway. And then the question is: what would it mean to read from a position of radical deauthorization in order to expose the contingent authority of the text? That struck me as a feminist critical practice, a critical reading practice that I could learn from, and from that point on, highly influenced by both Drucilla's [Cornell] work and Naomi Schor's work, I started to read her quite thoroughly.

Let me begin by raising a very general issue. The cave analogy that Irigaray addresses is, obviously, an *analogy*. Alternatively, we may say that it is a *metaphor*. Now whenever any author employs analogy or metaphor, we are immediately presented with a problem. The analogy is an analogy because we are supposed to see certain similarities between the analogy and its object, of what it is intended to be an analogy. But "supposed to see" and "intended" already invoke the *intention* of the *author*. That is, the author employs, invents the analogy because she feels that it is an effective or dramatic way of showing a certain similarity to the matter under discussion. The first point, then, is that it is very difficult to make any sense of the meaning of an analogy without invoking the intention of the author. It goes without saying that the author's intention may not be the ultimate or final word on the meaning of the analogy. But it is hard to see how we can begin to think about the meaning of an analogy without at least *considering* the intention of the author. Surely we have to ask of any analogy, "what did the author intend us to see as similar to the matter at issue in this analogy?" That may not be the end, but it is surely the beginning, of our interpretation.

But second, an analogy, by being an analogy, is not an identity. Which is to say, an analogy, by being an analogy, will always have possible meanings, nuances, etc., which are not similar to the matter at issue, at least in the eyes (i.e., the intention) of the author. So a seemingly natural first step in our reading of any analogy is to ask, what are the features of the analogy that are analogous to the matter at issue, and which not? And the initial version of this question would seem to be, what are the similarities that *the author intended* by this analogy, and which not? Typically, any similarities that might be pointed out that the author did not intend are dismissed as irrelevant. The author, if present, might simply say, "that's not what I had in mind by the analogy."

We might even go further. We might point out aspects of the analogy that the author did not have in mind, but, when they are pointed out, the author agrees—or would agree if alive—that they are appropriate even though he did not originally intend them. They fit with the point of the intended analogy. Or we might point out a dimension of the analogy that would be problematic to the author's intended use, even contradictory to it. The author might typically parry that dimension with the familiar cliché "that's where the analogy breaks down." Again, in the simple, or perhaps naïve cases, the author here is *authoritative*.

Now this simple situation, this well-established hermeneutics of analogy, one might say these rules or even laws of analogy, are deeply disrupted by the strategies of deconstruction. According to these laws, the task of the reader is first to interpret the text in question, which in the case of analogy means gaining access to the meaning of the analogy intended by the author. But for deconstruction, interpretation in this sense is not the issue. According to deconstruction, as we have seen, language, any language, any text, is subject to a play of meanings, marginal to the manifest meaning and so beyond the possible intention of any author, meanings that embody *differance*, that is, which carry meanings that are different from the manifest, presumably intended meaning, and at the same time deferred by that manifest meaning.

Analogy would seem to play perfectly into the deconstructive strategy. Who cares what the author intended and whether a meaning at play in the analogy was intended by the author or not? *Language* is at play here, and so there will be a "play of meanings without end," waiting for the deconstructive reader to elicit them. What counts are not what particular dimensions to the analogy the author intended, but instead what is at play in the language of the analogy.

Now Irigaray has been deeply influenced by Derridean deconstruction. Her reading of the cave analogy clearly intends to elicit meanings quite unintended by Plato, meanings not just deferred by Plato's intended meanings but even suppressed by them, meanings that carry with them a feminist project, a feminist critique of the very meanings Plato presumably intended. Or not. So as we read Irigaray's own reading of the cave analogy, one of our eyes should be on the extent to which she is employing the strategies of deconstruction.

A second profound influence on Irigaray has been Lacanian psychoanalysis. Irigaray, as is well known, was a participant in Lacan's school, the Ecole freudienne, from which she was summarily dismissed when *Speculum of the Other Woman* was published. For our purposes, the dimension of Lacanian psychoanalysis that is especially important to understanding this text is that Lacan saw the major theater in which the Freudian psychoanalytic categories played themselves out to be *language.* To put this too simply, a Lacanian psychoanalyst applies the strategies of Freud not directly to the psyche, or the inner self of the patient, but to the *language* the patient uses. It is language that is the locus, the theater, in which the drama of Freudian psychoanalysis is played out.

It is again easily seen how Irigaray takes this Lacanian conviction and engages it in a feminist psychoanalytic reading of Plato and the other thinkers from the Western canon—Hegel, Plotinus, Freud, Nietzsche, etc.—whom she addresses. So we need to watch how these two influences, deconstruction, and Lacanian psychoanalysis, are at play in Irigaray's reading of Plato.

One dimension of Irigaray's reading of the cave is certainly a deconstructive one. Plato *thinks* he is developing the analogy to express one particular set of meanings: as an image of our education, as an image of the pain and struggle involved in the movement of revelation, etc. But at work in this analogy, presumably unintended by Plato, is a deeply masculinist standpoint, even in his construal of knowledge, a masculinist standpoint that actively *suppresses* the feminine. Irigaray brings Lacanian and Derridean tools to bear in the service of revealing this marginal, violently masculinist dimension to the text, the details of which we shall turn to presently.

Now this particular dimension to her reading can presumably be evaluated in the general way that any deconstructive reading would be evaluated. Does it make its case well? Does it show, with adequate attention to the language, that the meanings claimed really are marginally, deconstructively at play in the text? In principle, then, this dimension of Irigaray's reading can be read and assessed in a relatively standard deconstructive way.

But that is not all Irigaray is doing, and here things get much, much more complex. For she is doing something else in her writing, something inseparable from the very particular style in which she writes. In addition to deconstructing the writings she examines, almost all of which are part of the male canon of Western philosophy, she is also trying, in effect, to *rewrite* them from a feminist perspective. In a sense, this is an even more positive strategy than the deconstructive one. She wants to rethink and rewrite these canonical texts in a feminist way, give a different reading in a different language of what a feminist "take" on these texts would look like. Consequently, in addition to understanding and evaluating the deconstructive dimension to her project, we need also to understand this more positive project, and then, ask ourselves how, by what standards, we are to thoughtfully evaluate it.

The first characteristic of this new language is that by the standards of the canonical one it is very obscure. As Elizabeth Weed puts it in "The Question of Style," "Her rhetorical techniques are various and wily, and she does not hesitate to mystify, to mislead."[3] In a striking passage earlier in *Speculum*, Irigaray herself acknowledges the point, and at least limns the reason why:

> The (re)productive power of the mother, the sex of the woman, are both at stake in the proliferation of systems, those houses of ill fame for the subject, of fetish-words, sign-objects, whose certified truths seek to palliate the risk

that values may be recast into/by the other. But no clear univocal utterance, can in fact, pay off this mortgage since all are already trapped in the same credit structure. All can be recuperated when issued by the signifying order in place. It is still better to speak only in riddles, allusions, hints, parables. Even if asked to clarify a few points. Even if people plead that they just don't understand. After all, they never have understood. So why not double the misprision to the limits of exasperation? Until the ear tunes into another music, the voice starts to sing again, and (re)production no longer inevitably amounts to the same and returns to the same forms, with minor variations. (*Speculum*, 143)

To speak clearly, that is, according to the canons of Western, and therefore masculinist, thought, is to be trapped into the very misogynist symbolic system she is trying to undercut. So a new, different, and by the old standards, unclear language is called for.

But the point is not just to write in an obscure or mystifying way to irritate masculinist readers. Rather, in a strategy that often has brought her intense criticism from other feminists, she addresses in depth the male canonical figures of the tradition, not just addresses them but cites them, quotes them in enormous length. Yet some feminists have asked, in effect, "Why dwell upon and cite endlessly the very male figures we are trying to replace? Better to write *about* women, including the forgotten women in the tradition, *for* women." So goes one charge of some feminists against her strategy.

This criticism would miss Irigaray's point. Irigarayian citation is not at all reverential or even accurate. Rather, in her own term, her citations are *mimetic*. She *mimes* the canonical writers, seeming to repeat their words endlessly but doing so in a way that subtly undercuts them, brings out the marginal, deferred meanings that are always biased in a masculinist way. That is, this is not the invention of a new vocabulary or syntax. Rather, since women have always had to, only been allowed to, *repeat* what men say, Irigaray will *mime* this very repetition by seeming to continue to do so. She repeats, imitates, canonical authors, but in such a way as to undercut the pretension of the males she cites. In this sense, she does not merely, in deconstructive fashion, identify the *différance* in the texts she examines; her writing *becomes* the *différance* of the very texts she cites mimetically. As Elizabeth Weed puts it,

Faced with her inevitable implication in the logic she aims to expose, Irigaray takes a homeopathic approach to the

problem. If there is no metadiscourse, and if women especially can only repeat, then repetition it will be. Reading
Irigaray's work of two decades, it becomes evident that her
mimetic reading-writing practice is generalized throughout,
that hers is a radical citationality. When she takes on the
critical texts of the Western canon, it is those texts—Freud,
Nietzsche, Marx, Hegel, Plato, and so on—that supply the
language, that is to say the conceptual economies of her
writing. She always cites, usually without attribution, and
often ventriloquizes. For her, taking on a writer means more
than intertextuality; it means inhabiting his text. She does
not write on Heidegger, she writes Heidegger. ("The Question of Style," 83–84)

Judith Butler, in "Bodies that Matter," (in *Engaging Irigaray*), makes
a similar point. Speaking of Irigaray's reading of Plato, she says, "If
the task is not a loyal or proper reading of Plato, then perhaps it is a
kind of overreading that mimes and exposes the speculative excess in
Plato" (150). Later in the article, she generalizes this:

Irigaray's response to this exclusion of the feminine from
the economy of representation is effectively to say, Fine, I
don't want to be in your economy anyway, and I'll show
you what this unintelligible receptacle can do to your system; I will not be a poor copy in your system, but I will
resemble you nevertheless by *miming* the textual passages
through which you construct your system and showing that
what cannot enter it is already inside it (as its necessary
outside), and I will mime and repeat the gestures of your
operation until this emergence of the outside within the
system calls into question its systematic closure and its
pretension to be self-grounding. . . . *This is citation, not as
enslavement or simple reiteration of the original, but as an insub-
ordination that appears to take place within the very terms of the
original, and that calls into question the power of origination that
Plato appears to claim for himself.* Her miming has the effect
of repeating the origin only to displace that origin *as an*
origin. (157–158; Butler's emphasis)

The point is, because woman's voice has never been heard in
philosophy, the task is not to now outshout the men, as it were, but to
mime their words in such a way as to allow to emerge the hidden,

unstated, or illegible voice that is the very condition for the canon's being the *masculine* voice that it is. Again, Butler puts the point well: "How can one read a text for what does *not* occur within its own terms, but that nevertheless constitutes the illegible condition of its own legibility?" (150). That is, for Irigaray, the masculine discourse of philosophy becomes masculine precisely by the exclusion, the silencing, of the feminine. Her reading of the cave, I believe, is intended as an exhibition of this very point.[4]

With this general sense of Irigaray's project, let us turn now to Irigaray's chapter on the cave analogy, "Plato's Hystera." Despite the obscurity of the individual sentences, it is not difficult to fathom the general drift of her rereading. The cave is intended as an image of our education, of our beginning by taking mere images as real and our painful transition to looking at the true objects of knowledge, the forms that are "out" of the cave, and finally at the sun, the source of all being and truth. But reformulating the terms of the cave slightly, an utterly different dimension is revealed: the cave is the womb, the wall behind which the figures carry images, a diaphram, the passage out, virtually ignored in the explicit analogy, the vagina. Escape from the cave is therefore escape from the mother, or being reborn. Leaving behind the cave is leaving behind the maternal origin in favor or the "man's" world of the light and the sun. (And as for returning to the cave, well, the less said the better.) The world outside the cave is thus entirely a *man's* world, exemplified by the fact that only the male pronoun is used throughout and the clear association of the sun/Good as the "father" of all that is. Irigaray emphasizes that in characterizing the sun as the father, and in saying that it is the sun that is the source of the being and intelligibility of all that is, the feminine source, the womb of the cave, from which we really do come, is ignored, suppressed in its own originating function. The intelligible world outside the cave, the "true" world that is the world of philosophy, is thus a homo-generated male world that has suppressed the feminine. And so is inaugurated the history of Western metaphysics as masculinist through and through, as a thoroughgoing suppression of the feminine.

Crucial to this mimetic deconstruction is Irigaray's emphasis on the constant use of the metaphor of sight, of light, as the appropriate metaphor for knowledge, and the masculinist bias inherent in this metaphor. Where does this association come from? It has at least three important sources. The association of sight with metaphysics, as the paradigm of knowing, comes most directly from the enlightenment emphasis on vision as the key to knowing, on light as the source of freedom. Clearly, the proximate roots of this are at play in the cave analogy. How does this get associated with the masculine? Aside from a look at the history of philosophy as, with precious few exceptions, the history of *male* philosophy, the most direct source of the association of sight with the masculine is Freud. For Freud, it is the *sight* of the mother's or sister's lack of a penis that first puts the horrific thought into the young male that he too might lose his, and so generates the whole Oedipal complex that, one might say, gets psychoanalysis started. Moreover, as is well known, in sexual relations themselves, sight is typically more important to male sexual experience than to the female's, which is more oriented toward touch. Finally, Derrida, before Irigaray, has explicitly associated sight with that male-oriented history of metaphysics that he calls "phallogocentricism."

So Irigaray is hardly inventing the association of sight with male experience. But she certainly develops it in striking directions. As she plays out the cave analogy, the emphasis on light, on seeing correctly as the paradigm of knowing, on the sun/good as the source of all that is, signifies the utter dominance of masculine experience, the suppression of the feminine, indeed, in claiming the sun as the sole source of what is, the pretense of an entirely male generated cosmos. Cathryn Vasseleu puts this succinctly:

> Irigaray argues that the drama of concealment and unconcealment which is played out in philosophy's metaphoric labyrinth is an elaborate concealment of a maternal origin which is refractory to metaphysical conception. According to Irigaray, the fantasy which heliocentricism upholds is a masculine re-origination, or the appearance of giving birth to oneself—grasped self-reflexively through the mediation of light.[5]

This is in fact an exceedingly complex issue. As I have argued earlier, the Greeks were very aware of the significance of the various metaphors for knowing (sight, touch, hearing) and selected one to predominate according to a definite conception of what the metaphor was to entail. Thus, Heraclitus emphasized the hearing metaphor: "Listening not to me but to the Logos, it is wise to believe that all is one" (Fr. 50). The hearing metaphor fits well with the important notion of *attunement* in Heraclitus, the notion that gaining access to the ever-becoming *logos* was more like listening to a speech as it develops than like looking at a permanently present object. For Plato, as the cave analogy surely demonstrates, the predominant metaphor is sight. The force of the sight metaphor is that in seeing (at least as the Greeks understood it), the object seen is left alone, literally left untouched. That is, the sight metaphor underscores the possibility of knowing things as they are in themselves. Seeing things does not change them, distort them, control them. This is in explicit contrast to the metaphor of grasping, more prevalent in Aristotle, where the force of the metaphor takes on the implication of control, mastery. In this sense, as the Greeks understood it, the sight metaphor might be said to be less aggressive, less macho. It is important to recognize, of course, that no Greek philosopher that I know used one of these metaphors to the entire exclusion of the others. All were invoked in appropriate contexts. The issue is one of prevalence, not of exclusive presence or absence.

For Irigaray and much of the feminist tradition, these metaphors take on very different meanings. For them, the sight metaphor connotes a certain distance, lack of involvement, even disinterest, a certain coldness and self-control, all associated with the masculine, as we have seen. Whereas touch connotes greater intimacy, deeper communication, more of a union with the thing known, and so with the feminine. Just as with the Greeks, Irigaray is not proposing to simply replace the masculinist sight metaphor with an exclusive use of the feminine metaphor of touch. Rather, as Vasseleu argues, she is calling instead for a radical rethinking of each in the light of the other, a mutual implication of each in the other: "In criticizing 'photology' [the dominance of the light metaphor and its masculinist bias] Irigaray is not simply replacing it with a touch metaphor more congenial to women, but calling for a radical rethinking of each in the light of the other. A mutual implication of the one in the other" (*Textures of Light*, 17–18).

What is at work here in this stark contrast in the meaning of the metaphors? That sight is the prevalent metaphor in the cave analogy, and for that matter in the dialogues as a whole, is indisputable. What is more controversial is the meaning, the significance of those metaphors. Is Irigaray's association of sight with masculinist distance and suppression of the feminine a mimetic presentation of a *differance* in the Platonic text, something at play in spite of the author, as she no doubt intends? Or is it an *imposition*, a much later imposition possible only after the advent of Freud and the history of metaphysics, an imposition that therefore was not only not intended by Plato, but not even plausibly at play in that early text? Has the sight metaphor for knowing always and in every culture signified a masculinist suppression of the feminine? And how would we adjudicate such questions?

Suppose we could show that in another way, the feminine was always in play in the dialogues, in play not marginally, unintended by the author, but in play explicitly as a dimension of life inseparable from the stance of philosophy itself? Suppose we could show that not just in the mimetic deconstructive way that Irigaray tries to elicit, but instead quite explicitly, the dialogues present a conception of the nature of philosophy itself as, literally, androgynous, a "discrete mixture of masculinity and femininity," to borrow a phrase from that noted feminist, Allan Bloom?[6] That will be a long story, but it is just what I hope to at least present in outline in the discussion soon to follow on Irigaray's interpretation of the *Symposium*. But if it can be done, what will be the effect on the force of Irigaray's interpetation? At least this, I want to suggest. As Irigaray presents it, her feminist mimetic deconstruction of Plato's cave analogy undercuts the overt, masculinist standpoint that determines the subsequent history of Western metaphysics. But if Plato can be shown quite intentionally to *include* the feminine in his very conception of philosophy, then, first, Irigaray's claim that the feminine is suppressed in Plato would have to be called into question; second, her insistence that the feminine needs to be reintroduced would have to be understood as part of Plato's explicit intention; and third, the subsequent history of philosophy, which may indeed be construed as largely if not exclusively masculinist, would have to be understood as a thorough misreading of the Platonic project. And that would make for a very different history of philosophy than most postmodern thinkers would allow. But before we turn to Irigaray's interpretation of the *Symposium* in order to make that argument, let us first look at some of the specific details of her reading of the cave analogy in *Speculum* that may be problematic.

We can begin with the most obviously problematic dimension of her reading. Irigaray, like Heidegger, like Derrida, feels warranted in leaping into the cave analogy without reference to context. No reference to the characters, the dramatic situation, even what has been said earlier in the dialogue. We begin, almost in imitation of the cave dwellers themselves, in the cave. For all the reasons I have developed so far, I think this undercuts her interpretation—insofar as it is an interpretation—from the start. The most extreme example of this in Irigaray's book, indeed, perhaps in the history of Platonic scholarship, is the remarkable section of *Speculum* entitled "On the Index of Plato's Works: Woman." This is a compilation, which by its lack of qualification intimates completeness though it is surely not complete, of the various references to "woman" in the dialogues (by my count, she lists thirty-eight). Each citation not only fails to give the context, but even fails to name who is speaking. Presumably, following Derrida and Heidegger, anyone who speaks in the dialogues speaks for Plato. I need not repeat my objections to this interpretive principle. This strategy is continued throughout her interpretation of the cave, where she not only takes whatever Socrates says as Plato's view, but also whatever is said by Phaedrus (319), Agathon (319), and Timaeus (322). So all the deep problems of attribution that we have seen in Heidegger and Derrida are repeated by Irigaray in her reading of the cave. It never occurs to her to consider the possibility that Plato might be putting forward the cave analogy not as a doctrine that he believes but as a provocation to thoughtfulness, to be considered for what it reveals and what it conceals, even as Irigaray herself is doing.

Second, one of the recurring themes that Irigaray emphasizes in her reading of the cave is that of sameness. The force of her emphasis is to suggest that Plato is opposed to, refuses, suppresses otherness in favor of a near obsession with sameness. This affirmation of sameness and refusal of the other, or the suppression of difference, is characteristic, in the sort of critique that thinkers like Irigaray espouse, of Western metaphysics in its entirety, and its origin in Plato can be thus taken as one more confirmation that he is indeed the father of the metaphysical tradition that postmodern thinkers are trying to undercut, if not overcome.

Irigaray finds sameness affirmed and otherness denied in myriad ways throughout the cave analogy, indeed by implication, throughout Plato's writings. The central "same" is, of course, the Idea. All instances are made intelligible as "the same" through their participation in the same Idea. "These 'inters' [the "interventions" and interactions of people and things in the cave] can be calculated or combined as proportions of a more or less correct relation to the sameness (of the Idea); . . . copies, that is, of the same, the identical, the one, the permanent, the unalterable, the undecomposable. The Being" (*Speculum* 262). This foundation in the Idea makes sameness that toward which (Platonic) philosophers, indeed humans, always strive:

> [This] underlies the whole Socratic dialectic: nothing can be named as 'beings' except those same things which all the same men see in the same way in a setup that does not allow them to see other things and which they will designate by the same names, on the basis of the conversation between them. Whichever way up you turn these premises, you always come back to *sameness*. (263; Irigaray's emphasis).

Moreover, the sameness thus imposed by this Platonic "metaphysics" certainly includes the sameness of the *masculine* experience of things and the corresponding exclusion of the other, the feminine. Or at very least, the other feminine is dialectically incorporated into the masculine as, after all, in the most important respects, the same. In an excursion into the *Phaedrus* and the discussion therein of the lover seeing the beloved as possessed by the God, Irigaray comments, "This 'God' will, often, take for himself the face of a *young boy*, closest equivalent in this life to absolute beauty. As that has been defined in philosophy, of course. Where one never gets away from the search for sameness." (322; Irigaray's emphasis). Thus, in regard to the homoerotic attraction of men to each other, "The only men who love each other are, in truth, those who are impatient to find the same over and over again" (327). Anything that appears as other, certainly including the feminine, gets transformed into the same: "And no alteration is imaginable given that the principle of the Other is here included in the definition of self-identity and submits to the cause of Sameness alone" (333). Thus the philosopher seeks endlessly the Same: "Whereas what is needed is, simply, to stick with the repetition of the same, for that repetition finds its representative basis in the image of the like and its speculative model in God—who, throughout all eternity, has not, and will not, suffer the slightest alteration" (336).

Now this radical affirmation of sameness and denial of otherness is, of course, a possible view to hold—one thinks of the standard but altogether problematic interpretation of Parmenides. But why does Irigaray take it as the view being espoused by Plato? Why especially by a reader who, as we shall see presently, is a careful reader of the *Symposium* and the discussion therein of eros? How could Irigaray not remember that the very first thing Socrates shows Agathon when their discussion begins is that eros is always *of* something and of something *other* than the lover, which the lover *does not have* (*Symposium* 199 c,ff.)? That is, eros, so definitive of human experience, *just is an orientation toward otherness*. This is even shown by Diotima in her myth of eros's parentage. Quietly contradicting Pausanias's earlier assertion that the parentage of the "noble eros" was of the male only (and thus, one could say, of sameness), Diotima insists that eros is the child of the heterosexual couple, Poros and Penia (*Symposium* 203 b,ff.). Eros, thus, is *the offspring of otherness*. To be sure, the strong affirmation of otherness inherent in eros is in tension with the emphasis on sameness that Irigaray finds in the cave analogy and elsewhere. So which is Plato's teaching? Are we to say, with the developmentalists, that he kept changing his mind? Or that one position is the unintended *differance* to the other? Or does it not make more sense to say that Plato is presenting us in this tension with the provocation, the problematic, of how we are to make sense of the necessary co-presence of sameness and otherness in coherent existence? There is no evidence, in any case, that Plato wants us to reduce otherness—and quite especially the otherness of the feminine—to sameness, as we shall see when we turn in detail to Irigaray's interpretation of Diotima's speech.

The final issue I want to raise regarding Irigaray's interpretation of the cave will enable us to turn to her later essay on the *Symposium*. As we have seen, one strong thread of her interpretation is that the cave, representing the womb, gets left behind according to the story, as the men go up and out into the real world. That is to say, the *feminine* gets left behind—indeed, suppressed in regard to its originating function—in favor of what Irigaray notes is the deeply *masculine* world outside the cave, culminating in the image of the sun/good as father. Suppose this is correct, that the cave analogy does imply (though only imply) that the real world of intelligibility is assumed to be a masculine one.[7] To be sure, that is an implication that Glaucon seems to accept when, at the end of Book VII, he sums up the results of what he has learned. Speaking of the philosopher-rulers who are the ones who will be lead out of the cave into the intelligible realm so that they can rule with genuine knowledge, Glaucon comments in summation, "Just like a sculptor, Socrates, he said, you have produced ruling men who are wholly fair" (*Republic*, 540c). But Socrates immediately and explicitly *corrects* any supposition that the rulers, and the intelligible realm into which they are introduced and access to which qualifies them as rulers, will be limited to the masculine. "And ruling women, too, Glaucon, I said. Don't suppose that what I have said applies any more to men than to women, all those who are born among them with adequate natures" (540c). The clear implication is that if one were, with Glaucon and Irigaray, to interpret the intelligible realm as a peculiarly masculine one, it would be a *misinterpretation*. To understand why, we must turn to the *Symposium*, and to Irigaray's later interpretation thereof.

IRIGARAY'S INTERPRETATION OF THE *SYMPOSIUM*

In the section of *An Ethics of Sexual Difference* entitled "Love of the Other," long after her study of Diotima in Plato's *Symposium*, Irigaray has occasion to refer to some earlier research she had done on the language of "certain groups of neurotics," (she adds in parenthesis, "and which of us is not neurotic?") from the standpoint of sexual difference. The results she draws are these:

"The typical sentence produced by a male, once all substitutions have been allowed for, is:

I wonder if I am loved or *I tell myself that perhaps I am loved.*

The typical sentence produced by a woman is:

Do you love me?"[8]

We are not told of the empirical evidence for these findings, or of their relative strength. Nevertheless, in the immediate context, Irigaray goes on to note the "wariness of a doubt" that pervades the male response, as well as its self-absorption and exclusion of the other. A page or two later, however, she takes note of a further difference: "For example, negative expressions are much more frequent with men, and interrogative expressions with women" (136, 129). It is this latter theme with which I will begin our study of Irigaray's reading of the *Symposium*, the notion that there is something distinctively "female" about the linguistic act of questioning. In accord with that intuition, I shall want to suggest that precisely insofar as Socratic/Platonic philosophy is fundamentally aporetic, and so insofar as its fundamental speech act is not assertive but interrogative, it will be imperative for Plato not only to introduce women into his dialogues and therefore into what had been in that epoch an almost exclusively male discourse, but to transform philosophy itself into an activity that embodies both the male and the female, an activity that I have called, in the spirit of Aristophanes' speech in the *Symposium, androgynous.*

I begin, however, by reminding the reader once more of our earlier discussions of the significance of Plato's choice of the dialogue form, and in particular, of the difference between that form and the treatise format that has since Plato become the dominant one for philosophic writing. Recall that one crucial issue in that discussion was that the treatise format was particularly suited for a certain conception of philosophy, one which Plato was obviously rejecting by not writing treatises. Specifically, the treatise format is particularly suitable for expressing ones own philosophy, where "ones own philosophy" signifies a set of propositions about this or that issue which the author thinks are true and for which there is sufficient and compelling evidence that can be adduced. That is to say, the treatise format is particularly appropriate for making assertions about this or that. Of course it is possible to ask questions within this format. It is no doubt even possible to write a fundamentally interrogative essay (although I believe it is rarely done in philosophy, even now and by those who claim to do so). Nevertheless, it remains the case that the task for which the philosophical treatise seems maximally suited is that of asserting ones philosophical views.

This enables us to see something important about the basic character of philosophical discourse subsequent to Plato. To wit, it has been characterized, most fundamentally, by the linguistic act of assertion, the assertion of the author's philosophical views about this or that, or his (I use the masculine pronoun with malice aforethought) proofs of what he believes to be true, or his refutations of the views of others. Asserting, proving, refuting, these become the basic intent of post-Platonic, and quite especially of modern philosophy, and it is therefore no wonder that modern philosophy has so predominantly adopted that writing format so singularly appropriate for the tasks of asserting, proving, refuting: the essay. Thus Descartes, in his quest for the achievement of indubitable certainty, employs this genre, the *Meditations* being, in his hand, only a variant on the theme; Spinoza even formats his most famous work as a set of geometric proofs; Kant and Hegel both indicate at the ends of their best known books that the task of philosophy is now more or less complete. Even a twentieth-century thinker like Heidegger, who loves to entitle his books with questions and who insists throughout his career that his guiding philosophical light is the *question* of being, remains in the end the most assertive of philosophers. Those relatively few philosophers since Plato who have written dialogues—one thinks of Augustine, Berkeley, Hume, Heidegger—write dialogues that are really hidden treatises, where one character manifestly represents the views of the author[9] (though I have qualified this judgment earlier in the case of Heidegger).

Irigaray's supposition cited earlier (itself asserted in a philosophic treatise, of however an unusual sort) becomes especially pointed in the light of these considerations. What if there is something characteristically feminine about the linguistic act of questioning? If so, can there then be any doubt that there is a complicity between the relative absence of women in the history of philosophy, the predominance of assertion as the characteristic philosophic speech act, and the near hegemony of the essay format in philosophy?

Or can it be surprising that Irigaray herself turns so often to Plato? Plato, who, in exact contrast to the subsequent philosophic tradition, makes not the assertion of his own views but the sustaining of philosophical questioning his basic philosophic task, who accordingly writes in a genre especially appropriate for the raising and development of questions, and who introduces women and the feminine at decisive moments into his texts in a culture by no means amenable to such feminine inflections in philosophy?

Yet Irigaray is decidedly guarded in her embrace of Plato, here in *An Ethics of Sexual Difference* and even more so, as we have seen, in the earlier and more angry *Speculum of the Other Woman*. We need to understand both the appeal of Plato's writing to Irigaray's feminist philosophic stance as well as her hesitations concerning the extent of Plato's avoidance of a masculinist philosophic standpoint.

In the opening lecture of the series that becomes *Difference*, "Sexual Difference,"and just preceding the essay entitled "Sorcerer Love: A Reading of Plato, *Symposium*, 'Diotima's Speech,'" Irigaray indicates the basic theme of the essays to follow:

> We must reexamine our own history thoroughly to understand why this sexual difference has not had its chance to develop, either empirically or transcendentally. Why it has failed to have its own ethics, aesthetic, logic, religion, or the micro- and macrocosmic realization of its coming into being or its destiny.

> It is surely a question of the dissociation of body and soul, of sexuality and spirituality, of the lack of a passage for the spirit, for the god, between the inside and the outside, the outside and the inside, and of their distribution between the sexes in the sexual act. Everything is constructed in such a way that these realities remain separate, even opposed to one another. So that they neither mix, marry, nor form an alliance. (14–15: 21)

Given this project and this conviction, the initial appeal of Diotima's account of eros, as presented by Socrates in the *Symposium*, is clear. One of the first issues Irigaray raises in her reading of Diotima's speech is precisely the function of eros as intermediary between various sets of opposites, as that *daimon* which, as Diotima will later say of eros' intermediary function between the mortal and the divine, "binds the two together into a whole" (*Symposium*, 202e). This intermediary function of love is just what will be needed if there is to be a genuine ethics of sexual difference. But first, we must follow the order of Irigaray's reading by taking up, at least in a preliminary fashion, the very introduction of the character of Diotima into the *Symposium* by Socrates.

In her opening comment on the presence of Diotima (20, 27), Irigaray notes both that Socrates does introduce a woman into this heretofore exclusively male party, yet that, in qualification, she is not actually present but has her words reported by Socrates. Irigaray comments, "And Diotima is not the only example of a woman whose wisdom, especially about love, is reported in her absence by a man" (20, 27). Indeed. Nor is Diotima the only woman whom Socrates introduces in the dialogues as his teacher. In the *Menexenus*, Socrates in a similar way reports that he learned what he knows about rhetoric from his teacher, Aspasia, the famous courtesan of Pericles. Not the least noteworthy characteristic of the Platonic Socrates is that in all the dialogues he names only three teachers by name. One, whom he does not follow, is the male philosopher Anaxagoras (*Phaedo*, 97b ff.). The two whom he praises and whom he regards as wise are Diotima and Aspasia. Socrates' two significant teachers are both women, and moreover, women intimately involved with eros; Diotima teaches Socrates about eros, and Aspasia makes erotics her profession.[10] It would be remarkable enough today for a male philosopher to attribute what he has learned to women teachers. All the more so in the society of ancient Athens. That Socrates does so is but the first of many clues that in the Platonic dialogues a revolution is taking place regarding women, not, as some claim, a kind of proto-feminist Plato on social issues, but a revolution regarding the place of the feminine in philosophy.[11] To understand this further, let us return to the person of Diotima, for much more needs to be said about the remarkable presence of this remarkable woman in the *Symposium*.

We should note first that the anti-female bias of ancient Greece is, if anything, accentuated in this dialogue. All of the original participants are men, and men whose sexual preferences, with the intriguing and subtle exception of Aristophanes, are such that they would have even less interest in women than, shall we say, the Athenian man on the street. Partly for this reason, at the suggestion of Eryximachus, who is the lover of Phaedrus, the flute girls (whose services typically included not just musical entertainment but sexual satisfaction of any men at the party who should so desire) are dismissed (*Symposium*, 176e). Women are dismissed at the *Symposium* until Socrates reintroduces them, at least in speech, in the person of Diotima. Given the participants in the banquet, this is hardly surprising. In addition to the erotic relationship of Eryximachus and Phaedrus, Pausanias and Agathon are lovers as well. Both Aristodemus and Apollodorus are called "lovers" of Socrates, though those relationships are presumably less obviously sexual than the others. Later, Alcibiades gives his hilarious "true confession" of his attempt to seduce Socrates (217–220). In sum, Aristophanes is the only member of the party not involved erotically in one way or another with someone else. In the deepest sense, then, this is an exclusively male gathering, and the discourses on love almost always assume male homosexual love as the paradigm of genuine eros.

This dramatic background is necessary in order to appreciate just how striking it is that Socrates should develop his speech on eros to these men by saying, in effect, "I don't know about you guys, but I learned about eros from a woman!" As we shall see and as Irigaray appreciates, not only is Diotima a woman, but her speech incorporates feminine metaphors, feminine insights, and so moderates the exclusively male accounts of eros produced so far.

But Diotima is no ordinary woman, nor is the fact that she is a woman the only trait Socrates finds worthy of mention. She is also a priestess and a stranger. Let us consider each of these characteristics in turn. Diotima is a priestess, who, through her instruction regarding sacrifices, enabled the Athenians to put off the plague for ten years (201d: are we to note that her powers were not so great as to enable her to avoid the plague entirely? Diotima is not omnipotent, as we shall see in her efforts to instruct Socrates on eros). That she is a priestess, as we shall see, is often reflected in her instruction to Socrates: in her regular appeal to religious mythology, in her use of the priestly language of initiation into rites, and especially in what we can call her occasional, not always consistent "otherworldliness." Diotima's speech cannot be understood without remembering that she is a priestess. Decisively, this means that she is *not* a philosopher. Plato does not have Socrates introduce us to "the philosopher Diotima." Now religious inspiration is no doubt related in complex ways to philosophical insight; but the two are not identical. In order to gain access to the genuinely philosophic import of Diotima's speech, we shall have to deconstruct or demythologize her speech at appropriate points to distinguish the religious from the philosophic import. The failure of commentators on Plato, including Irigaray, to do this has caused endless mischief in the interpretation of the *Symposium* in particular and the dialogues more generally. More about this later.

Finally, Diotima is a stranger, the only non-Athenian present at the *Symposium*. This trait is emphasized by Socrates, who regularly refers to Diotima as "O stranger." (e.g., 201e, 204c, 211d). One function, surely, of Diotima's being a stranger is to accentuate, along with her being a woman, her "otherness" from the men present and the positions they represent. It is a signal that something very new, very different, is given voice here, and its difference, its otherness, has very much to do with the feminine. It is surely also a signal that the author of this dialogue is not in the business, consciously or unconsciously, or suppressing the other in favor of the same.

So the first of Diotima's teachings on which Irigaray dwells is the intermediary character of eros, an intermediation that will be

imperative to any possible ethics of sexual difference. Irigaray introduces the issue as follows:

> Diotima's teaching will be very dialectical, but different from
> what we usually call dialectical. In effect, it doesn't use
> opposition to make the first term pass into the second in
> order to achieve a synthesis of the two, as Hegel does. From
> the outset, she establishes an *intermediary* that will never be
> abandoned as a means or a path. Her method, then, is not
> a propaedeutic of the *destruction* or the *destructuration* of the
> two terms in order to establish a synthesis that is neither
> one nor the other. She presents, uncovers, unveils the insis-
> tence of a third term that is already there and that permits
> progression. . . . It is love that both leads the way and is the
> path. A mediator par excellence. (20–21, 27–28).

Eros is an intermediary in at least two decisive senses. First, its
ontological status, as it were, is as a between *(metaxu)*, between various sets of opposites and therefore neither simply the one nor the
other. It is between beauty and ugliness, between good and evil, between ignorance and knowledge, and decisively, between mortal and
divine. Irigaray correctly notes that the young Socrates, and presumably Plato's Greek readers, has considerable trouble comprehending
this intermediary status as between, this interruption of the binary
oppositions that constitute so much of our discursive understanding.

Second, however, this intermediary status of eros is not static; it
is a *daimon*, that *acts* as the mediator between the two sets of opposites, joining them together, as Irigaray emphasizes, without abolish-
ing their difference in a proto-Hegelian synthetic unity. Diotima brings
out this active function in explaining to Socrates the way in which eros
undercuts the apparently irreducible binary of mortal and immortal:

> Then what is love, I replied, a mortal?
>
> Least of all!
>
> But what then?
>
> Just as in the earlier cases, she responded, he is in between
> mortal and immortal.
>
> What is he, then, Diotima?

A great daimon, Socrates. Everything that is daimonic is between god and mortal.

What is its power?

It interprets and conveys things to the gods from human beings and to human beings from the gods—entreaties and sacrifices from the one and from the other commands and gifts in return for the sacrifices. Since it is in the middle it fills in between the two so that it binds the two together into a whole. All prophecy comes through a daimon, and the arts of the priests and of those concerned with sacrifices, rituals, spells, divinations, and magic. God mingles not with human being; on the contrary, every interchange and conversation between gods and human beings is through a daimon, both when we are awake and in our dreams. He who is wise in these things is a daimonic man, but he who is wise and skilled in other arts or crafts is a mere laborer. There are many of these daimons of all sorts, and one of them is love. (*Symposium,* 202d–203a; my translation).

Here is a perfect example of where it is imperative to retranslate the explicitly religious language employed by the priestess Diotima, with its reference to gods, sacrifices, rituals, incantations, etc., into more purely philosophic language. What would it mean, philosophically for Plato to say that eros has access both to the divine and to the mortal, and "binds the two together into a whole."? Everything depends on what, in the end, "the divine" means for Plato, as well as the mortal. Obviously it suggests the question of the relation between the eternal Ideas and their finite instances. This immensely complex but important issue cannot be treated here. But at very least we can note that the passage confirms Irigaray's emphasis that love mediates between two binaries (in this case the divine and mortal), binding them together into a whole, while yet leaving each of them in their integrity as what they are. This is the new dialectic that Irigaray wants to emphasize, and that, again, would have to be at work in any possible ethics of sexual difference.

A crucial consequence of this understanding of eros, and so of the human condition, is that eros, as between mortal and immortal, will never in principle raise the mortal to the level of being simply immortal. The mortal remains mortal. This means that philosophy, as the love of wisdom and so lacking it, will never attain in principle to absolute wisdom. Irigaray sees and emphasizes this: "The mediator is never abolished in an infallible knowledge. Everything is always in movement, in a state of becoming. And the mediator of all this is, among other things, or exemplarily, *love*. Never fulfilled, always becoming" (21, 28).

Here we are at the wellspring of the Platonic Socrates' understanding of philosophy. Philosophy begins with aporia, with the recognition of one's incompleteness and the striving to overcome it (thus far conforming to Aristophanes' understanding of eros earlier in the *Symposium*). Because philosophy is essentially erotic, that is, because we are neither wise nor simply ignorant but in the middle between them, we are condemned to this situation of endless striving after what we are not but would want to be. "Never fulfilled, always becoming." And that means that Platonic/Socratic philosophy is irreducibly interrogative, that its fundamental standpoint must be one of questioning.

To see this, let us look briefly at Socrates' basic philosophic stance, as he develops it in the *Apology* and elsewhere. Socrates' "wisdom" is his self-knowledge, his recognition that he is not wise. He thus regards aporia, this recognition of our *lack* of wisdom as the first sign of "human" wisdom, of self-knowledge. Aporia is thus an achievement over the average everyday human state, that of thinking we know what we do not, and so Socrates' famous elenchus is directed to bringing people *up* to this higher stage of aporia, although the one undergoing the questioning of his beliefs will often misinterpret the experience as destructive. Aporia thus has a triadic existential structure: it is our being as incomplete, that is, as lacking wisdom; second, it is recognizing that lack, and third, it is striving to overcome that lack, an effort that Socrates endlessly makes clear will never be a totalizing success. That is, the state of aporia is about as high an achievement as a human can attain (remember, Socrates is called the wisest of humans), notwithstanding that we will forever desire more, desire completion, desire a totalizing wisdom.

Here the intimacy of the connection of Socrates' philosophic stance of aporia and the account of eros in the *Symposium* becomes clear. To see this, recall the account of eros as presented in Aristophanes' hilarious myth, and which Socrates picks up in more logical form in his refutation of Agathon. Once human beings are split, as Aristophanes recounts it, our existential or ontological situation is changed: we are now incomplete, partial. But we recognize that incompleteness, painfully. Experiencing our incompleteness as such, third, we desire to overcome it by joining together with our original halves so as to become whole, to attain completeness. This incompleteness, recognition thereof, and desire to overcome it, says Aristophanes and later Socrates, is eros. Now, because Aristophanes is Aristophanes, he wants us to think of this situation primarily in terms of personal love, indeed, of sexual union. But Socrates makes clear that this triadic structure of being incomplete, recognizing our situation, and striving to overcome it is far more pervasive a human experience than just sexual desire. Eros is the basic human situation as such.

Incompleteness, recognition thereof, striving to overcome it. The structure of eros is the structure of aporia. Aporia, and so Socratic philosophy, is literally a natural human possibility, a manifestation of our erotic human nature.

What is the basic mode of discourse that will be appropriate to a philosophy understood as aporia? Certainly it will not be assertion, the usual mode of philosophic discourse, exhibited even before Socrates in the various presocratic "Concerning Nature" treatises. Such assertive discourse invites precisely the claim to knowledge that the stance of aporia denies. Instead, the basic mode of discourse for one true to the recognition of aporia will be questioning. For questioning, we can now see, by no means arises out of simple ignorance. Questioning arises out of, is itself an exhibition of, a fundamental *knowledge, self-*knowledge, the recognition of our aporia, or our erotic natures. But this is a curious knowledge indeed, since it is expressed not in assertions (one might parody this as two long lists: "What I know" and "What I don't know"), but through questioning. The exhibition of that self-knowledge that is aporia is questioning. This is why, with utter consistency, the discourse of Socratic/Platonic philosophy is fundamentally interrogative.

Irigaray's provocative suggestion is that Socrates learned all this from Diotima, and learned it precisely under instruction on eros as a young, and we have to say, very peculiar man, whom Plato portrays as understanding so little of erotic things, and who, when he wants to learn of eros, goes, as it were, to a nun.

> Thus she ceaselessly examines Socrates on his positions but without positing authoritative, already constituted truths. Instead, she teaches the renunciation of already established truths. And each time Socrates thinks he can take something as certain, she undoes his certainty. His own, but also all kinds of certainty that are already set in language. All entities, substantives, adverbs, sentences are patiently, and joyously, called into question. (22, 28–29)

If Irigaray is right, and I think she is, then Plato portrays Socrates' philosophic stance as, at the deepest level, indebted to the feminine. Indebted to a feminine proclivity for the question. But not just that.

Irigarary turns next to Diotima's response to the young Socrates' strange question—but a question that we know becomes characteristic of him—"Who are eros' parents?" Diotima replies that eros is the child of Poros (Plenty, Resourcefulness), whose mother is Metis (Invention, sometimes Wisdom) and Penia (Poverty, Lack), and like most children, eros takes after both its parents (and, we can add, more distantly of its grandmother). Irigaray quotes at some length the description Diotima gives of the traits eros inherits from each parent. That heritage would surely seem to be troubling for a feminist reading, but Irigaray does not leave it at that. That the mother of eros is Poverty, Lack, and its father Plenty, would seem to fit all too well with the now traditional association of the feminine with incompleteness and need (Freud's notorious "penis envy" doctrine is hardly the first nor the last such account), and the masculine with energy and power. Yet even granting this problematic, we should also recognize that within the context of the *Symposium*, Diotima's account is a giant step forward, since it corrects the exclusively male geneology of noble eros that Pausanias had insisted upon earlier, and which supported the presumptive male orientation towards eros that had characterized the discussion prior to her introduction (180d–e). However problematic the association of the feminine with lack and incompleteness, at least, thanks to Socrates' Diotima, the feminine is now an essential element in any adequate account of eros. We should note, after all, that *two* women, Eros' mother and paternal grandmother, are mentioned in the geneology, but only one male, the father. And the grandmother, Invention or Wisdom, hardly connotes incompleteness. The very masculine traits inherited from the father, if the myth is to be believed, derive ultimately from a female as well (it would seem that Poros derives his own defining traits primarily from his mother, Metis), again underscoring the strong feminine dimension to this account of eros. If Plato did not want us to consider this, why else would he have mentioned only one grandparent, the mother of the father?

Irigaray, moreover, sees something even more positive in this passage. Precisely insofar as aporia, and so the recognition of our lack or incompleteness, is, as it were, the deep existential structure of Socratic philosophy, the incompleteness dimension, or the inheritance from eros' mother, is really the decisive one as far as the erotic basis of philosophy is concerned. Irigaray only slightly exaggerates when she says,

This [i.e., the account of eros/philosophy developed in the passage] is nothing like the way we usually represent the philosopher: a learned person who is well dressed, has good manners, knows everything, and pedantically instructs us in the corpus of things already coded. The philosopher is nothing like that. He is a sort of barefoot waif, who goes out under the stars seeking an encounter with reality, the embrace, the knowledge or perhaps a shared birth (*connaissance, co-naissance*), of whatever benevolence, beauty, or wisdom might be found there. *He inherits this endless quest from his mother. He is a philosopher through his mother and skilled in art through his father.* But his passion for love, for beauty, for wisdom comes to him from his mother, and from the date that he was conceived. Desired and wanted, moreover, by his mother. (24, 31; my emphasis)

I say that Irigaray slightly, but only slightly, exaggerates here because, as we shall see, not only eros but philosophy itself as conceived and lived out by Socrates and Plato requires the inheritance both of Penia and of Poros, of incompleteness and of what we might call in a Nietzschean key a certain overflowing overfullness, a gift-giving virtue. Nevertheless, her crucial insight into this passage is that not only does eros and philosophy contain a feminine element, but that feminine element is decisive and determining of the very nature of philosophy.

Nevertheless, that the mother is Poverty and the father Plenty still grates from a feminist perspective. Can we therefore reformulate this inheritance, this geneology of eros and philosophy, still remaining true to its positive insight, while mitigating the denigrating association of the feminine component with lack and incompleteness? I believe we can, and I believe the clue to doing so is implicitly present in the teaching of the dialogues themselves.

Return briefly to the point established earlier that the question, or interrogative discourse, is the signature speech act of philosophy as understood by the Platonic Socrates. Suppose we develop a loose phenomenology of questioning. What, phenomenologically, is "happening" when we question? On the one hand, to question is to exhibit a certain *openness* toward that which we question. This is captured in English in the way we speak of holding things "open to question," and in the way we characterize someone who refuses to hold their views open to question as "close-minded." In this sense, the openness of Socratic questioning should be contrasted to the very different, and more closed, stance of *doubt* characteristic of modern and especially Cartesian philosophy. To doubt is to close off in advance. Descartes, unlike Socrates, does not *question* the opinions on which he was raised, thereby allowing for the possibility that there may be something fundamentally worthy in them, but doubts them, rejects them in advance, in order to begin anew and possibly achieve his longed for indubitability. But Socrates' questioning of the opinions of the day requires that he be open to them, to the possibility that they may be partly or even entirely worthy. So we can say that *openness* is a distinctive trait of the stance of questioning.

But questioning cannot be simply openness, else the questioner would merely accept whatever was proffered: openness to this, openness to that. No, to question is at once to *respond* to that to which we have opened ourselves, to respond in and as the questioning. That is, questioning is itself a response, our responding, to that to which we have opened ourselves in questioning. In questioning, we do not merely accept a given view or leave it alone. Within our questioning, we respond to and in the light of the openness we exhibit. Joining this element of responsiveness to that of openness, then, we can say that the stance of questioning, and so the stance of Socratic/Platonic philosophy, is that of responsive openness.[12]

This brief analysis enables us to see just how precarious the stance of questioning as responsive openness always is. Precarious, because it is always in danger of devolving into one or the other of its poles. An excessive openness that loses its responsiveness devolves into a passive acceptance of whatever comes along, of the opinions of the day, of "what's happening." An excessive responsiveness that loses its openness becomes a close-minded, domineering assertiveness. Both are the ever-present dangers into which the stance of questioning can fall.

Just as questioning was shown to be founded in Socrates' philosophic stance of aporia, so its structure as responsive openness can now be connected to the mythical geneology of eros in terms of Poros and Penia. The responsiveness of questioning, clearly enough, is the product of the Poros/Metis-dimension of eros; the energy, power, overflowing character of responsiveness has its origin, albeit not originally, in the "father." But the openness is a function of eros' and philosophy's need; its mythical source is the mother, Penia. Informed by incompleteness, both eros and philosophy must be open to what might fulfill them. Both *need* what is other, and so must be open to the other for its completion. So the responsive-openness of questioning can be shown to be grounded in the incomplete/overfull dimension of eros.

Perhaps not surprisingly, accordingly, responsiveness and open-ness can be gendered according to common gender associations, both in ancient Greece and in our own culture. The responsiveness of ques-tioning, its overfullness, overflowing power, can be associated with Poros, with the masculine qualities Poros embodies.[13] And the open-ness, the receptiveness of questioning, can be connected to the femi-nine qualities associated with the woman, with Penia. But here, I submit, the hierarchical character of most gender associations is largely under-cut. Openness is in no sense less crucial, no less worthy than respon-siveness. The stance of questioning cannot be maintained successfully if either is missing or even significantly diminished. The feminine is at least as significant as the masculine element in questioning, and so in Socratic/Platonic philosophy. Without destroying or denying their difference, philosophy requires their genuine partnership. Not for nothing does Plato have Diotima teach the male Socrates, teach the males present at the *Symposium*, teach us, male and female, this lesson.

Irigaray turns next to the crucial passage at *Symposium* 206 ff, where Diotima asks Socrates whether he knows what the function (ergon) of love is. He does not. Diotima tells him: "This action is giving birth in beauty, both in body and in soul" (206b). Socrates still does not understand. Irigaray comments perceptively on Socrates ut-ter naivete regarding matters of love, this, a young man presumably in the prime of his erotic years: "But Socrates understands nothing of such a clear revelation. He understands nothing about fecundity of body and soul" (25, 32). In an adequate interpretation of this whole speech, we would have to consider in much greater depth the extent to which it contains a quiet but nevertheless stern Platonic criticism of Socrates. Socrates, who seems to know nothing about love out of his own experience, who must learn what he knows of love by sitting at the feet of a priestess, who moreover and as we shall see, seems to entirely, perhaps even exaggeratedly, take on as his own view the priestly otherworldliness that later appears, or risks appearing, in Diotima's speech; so much so that, as Alcibiades later will tell us of the now adult Socrates, his apparent love of handsome youths is only apparent and masks an ironic contempt for all things human (216d-e). We cannot develop this theme at its appropriate length here; but let me just say that no one who carefully reads the *Symposium* with an eye to its critical evaluation of Socrates could ever again regard Socrates simply as "Plato's mouthpiece."[14]

In response to Socrates' continuing ignorance of the function of love to give birth in beauty, Diotima expands with her famous "Every-one is pregnant" speech, the first part of which Irigaray next quotes and comments upon: "The union of a man and woman is, in fact, a generation; this is a thing divine; in a living creature that is mortal, it is an element of immortality, this fecundity and generation" (206c). Irigaray comments perceptively, "This statement of Diotima's never seems to have been heard" (25, 32). How right she is. It may not have been heard by Socrates himself, who, if there is truth in Alcibiades' charge, may not have successfully preserved the recognition of the divine element in human beauty and in the eros between humans. It has certainly not been heard by those subsequent scholars who attribute to Plato a rejection of the "world of appearances," who attribute to him a radical dualism that entails the denigration of the bodily, indeed of the human altogether in favor of the "world of forms," in short, who attribute to Plato the peculiar metaphysical view that comes to be called "Platonism." The question is, as Irigaray now goes on to ask, is it adequately heard by Diotima herself?

Irigaray now embarks on perhaps her central criticism of Diotima's position, at least as it is recounted by Socrates. In her view, this insightful emphasis on the intermediary, daimonic function of eros, this fecundity in the relation of man and woman, this element of the divine therein, gets seriously undercut by the introduction of a new element in Diotima's position, the emphasis on *procreation* as the source of this divine element in love, and so, subsequently, an emphasis on the *procreated object* as the real source of the divine and so the object of our erotic striving.

"Instead of leaving the child to germinate or ripen in the milieu of love and fecundity between man and woman, she seeks a cause for love in the animal world: *procreation*. Diotima's method miscarries here. From this point on, she leads love into a split between mortality and immortality, and love loses its daimonic character. Is this the foundational act of meta-physics?" (27, 33).

Irigaray is surely right that Diotima does proceed to emphasize the importance of the object of procreation as the telos of this quest for immortality on the part of mortal humans. Even human children are part of this; in having children, Diotima suggests, we leave behind something of ourselves after we are gone, and this leaving behind something of our selves, whether of body or soul, constitutes the only kind of immortality available to mortals. This, as Irigaray also correctly sees, means that it "situates the object (of) love outside of the subject: in renown, immortal glory, and so on" (28, 35), and so that in a sense "the stake of love is placed outside the self" (29, 35). It should be noted, however, that the stake of love has always and already been outside the self; the very first point that Socrates makes in his conversation with Agathon, and which he claims Diotima made to him, was that eros is never simply eros, but always eros *of* something (of a brother, of a mother, etc.), and indeed, of something that it lacks (*Symposium* 199c ff.). Love, that is, is intentional in the technical phenomenological sense; it is always directed on an object, and on an object that it lacks. Love, we might say against Aristophanes, is love of *the other*.

Irigaray holds that these two Diotiman positions, love as daimonic intermediary and love as desiring the procreation of an object, are virtually incompatible. With this emphasis on the procreated object, "Love has lost its divinity, its mediumistic, alchemical qualities between couples of opposites. Since love is no longer the intermediary, the child plays this role" (27, 33). And again, "But, if procreation becomes its goal, it risks losing its internal motivation, its 'inner' fecundity, its slow and constant generation, regeneration" (27, 33).

To be sure, there is a certain tension here. I love this woman, but that love is complicated by the fact that I also love the product of our consummated love, our children. I love this student, but I also love the honor and respect I may receive as a fine teacher. I love this man, but I also love the artworks my love for him inspires me to create. Yes, there is this tension in Diotima's account, but I submit that it is a tension true to our phenomenal experience of love. Any love experience is always troubled by this tension, not to mention myriads of others. As Irigaray acknowledges, no sooner does Diotima invoke this emphasis on the procreated object than she returns to the emphasis on the daimonic and constant becoming inherent in eros in her account of the constant regeneration of both the body and the soul, thus establishing a vacillation between these two elements of eros. In invoking this tension, Diotima's method is not "miscarrying here;" she is simply being phenomenologically accurate in her account of the immense complexity and the sometimes painful conflicts of the experience of love.

The question is, does this tension generate the metaphysical dualisms of mortal and immortal, body and soul, which Irigaray sees as the inevitable consequence of the separation of the love relation and the object of love's procreation? It certainly seems to, at least based on the usual reading of the famous "ascent" passage beginning at *Symposium* 210a, to which Irigaray next turns. The usual reading of that passage, from the Renaissance on, interprets it as a movement toward a transcendence of the body, of the human, indeed of the phenomenal world in our ascent toward a vision of "Beauty Itself." And the advocacy of this kind of otherworldly transcendence, with its corresponding depreciation of the bodily and the individual, would seem appropriate coming from a religious priestess, appropriate as well coming from a Socrates who as an adult, according to the Platonic Alcibiades, indulges in the pretense of physical attraction to handsome youths such as Alcibiades himself only playfully and as a mask for his contempt. But is it the view that Plato, the writer of these immensely complex dialogues, wants the thoughtful reader to come away with? I want to suggest that, read with appropriate care, the ascent passage contains a teaching very different from the metaphysical transcendence usually attributed to it, a teaching much more compatible with what Irigaray finds attractive about Diotima's position, though one that remains true to the genuine tensions always present in erotic experience.

Irigaray begins her discussion of the ascent passage with a surprising misreading. "The beings most gifted in wisdom go directly to this end. Most begin by going toward physical beauty and '*must love one single object (physical form of beauty), and thereof must engender fair discourses*" (31, 37; Irigaray's emphasis*). This is not what the text says and is in fact explicitly denied. After expressing skepticism that Socrates will be able to follow the higher mysteries that she is about to invoke (another statement that seems never to have been heard!), Diotima begins most emphatically: "It is necessary [the word is *dei*] for one rightly going into these matters to begin when young by going to beautiful bodies, and at first, if he is rightly led by his guide, to love a single body and therein to generate beautiful speeches. . . ." (210a). As I point out endlessly to my students, Diotima does not say "An appropriate way to begin . . ." or "Most people begin . . ." and she certainly does not allow that egghead intellectuals can skip the bodily stuff and cut right to the intellectual chase. She says that it is *necessary* to begin with the love of a beautiful body. Yet another Diotiman sentence that seems never to have been heard. Why would it be *necessary* for one beginning the movement toward philosophy and insight into beauty, to begin with the love of a beautiful body? Only if the point of the whole journey is to deepen our understanding and appreciation of beauty in all its manifestations, including the physical, would it be necessary to begin with love of bodily beauty. Otherwise, why indeed not skip directly to the beauty of mathematics and begin from there? To skip over the beauty of beautiful bodies is to miss a fundamental manifestation of beauty. This is supported by the subtle and easily overlooked point that at no stage in the ascent does Diotima actually say that we should *leave behind* an earlier stage of the love of beauty as we move to the next. This is no transcendence to another world, leaving behind this one. The most Diotima says, and even the vehemence of this is perhaps attributable to her being a priestess, is that we might "look down" upon an earlier manifestation of beauty and consider it "something small" (210b). So the reason why we *must* begin with the love of a beautiful body, the reason why we do *not* leave behind some manifestations of beauty as we move to others, the reason why, to the extent that we gain insight into "Beauty Itself" we do not somehow stay in that realm and leave behind the phenomenal world, is because the whole point of making the ascent in the first place, the whole point of gaining insight into anything like Beauty Itself, is to deepen our appreciation and understanding of beauty as it appears to us, certainly including its bodily appearances. The point of the Ideas, if indeed Beauty Itself is an Idea, is not to give us another world to understand (a "world of Forms"); it is to help us understand this world, the world in which we live, breathe, and love.[15]

Again, I suggest that Diotima's account is phenomenologically, indeed ethically, accurate here. To love beauty is to appreciate that it appears in many forms and that all of those manifestations are worthy of love. No one, I hope, would recommend to themselves, their friends, or their children that they should find the entire fulfillment of their eros for beauty in the lifelong devotion to one single individual (or a single idea). That insidious ideology is what for all too long kept—and in many cultures still does keep—women locked in their houses finding the only meaning to their lives in devotion to their husbands. Love, the love of beauty, is polymorphous perverse. We find beauty all over the place, and we love it all. That often causes us endless difficulty; but it is the truth.

The most general point of my interpretation is this: Socrates does not speak simply as Plato's mouthpiece, nor does Diotima. Diotima the priestess may speak in language that invites a more otherworldly reading than Plato finally wants us to hold. Socrates himself may, in Plato's view, go too far in that otherworldly direction, thus inviting the legitimate complaint of the Platonic Alcibiades that he does not love the human enough. Perhaps that is why Socrates never wrote, and why Plato did, but wrote dialogues. Perhaps the difference between their two stances hangs on the question of the adequate love of the human, of human embodiment. Perhaps, then, present in what might amount to the critical evaluation of otherworldly positions such as religion (or for that matter Pythagoreanism and what has come to be called idealism) is Plato's call to us to be true to the human, the bodily, the erotic, precisely in the recognition that we will never be entirely satisfied with that, nor for that matter satisfied with anything else. Such is the tragic character of our eros.

For this reason, I think Luce Irigaray is absolutely insightful in the qualified and hesitant way that she concludes her essay on Diotima. "*Perhaps* Diotima is still saying the same thing. But in the second part, her method *runs the risk* of being reduced to the metaphysics that is getting set up. *Unless* what she proposes to contemplate, beauty itself, is seen as that which confounds the opposition between immanence and transcendence. As an always already sensible horizon on the basis of which everything would appear. But one would have to go back over everything to discover it in its enchantment" (33; 39; my emphasis). That, I suggest in closing, is exactly what Plato is trying to tell us to do, or rather, what he is trying to get us to hold ever again open to question. In this sense, Irigaray's much less assertive, more tentative stance in this text, some ten years after her much more aggressive interpretation of Plato in *Speculum*, is itself more questioning, more interrogative, more *Platonic*.

Chapter Four

Cavarero's Plato

Of the interpreters of Plato we have considered so far, Adriana Cavarero is perhaps the one whose interpretations best exhibit the kind of sympathetic reading I have been espousing. My problem with her work is that she renders these sympathetic and imaginative interpretations only very selectively—with regard to certain of the references in the dialogues to women. For the rest of the dialogues, Cavarero too seems content to revert to the kind of doctrinal reading of Plato against which I have been arguing. Let us first look at the strongest part of her readings.

Adriana Cavarero's work on Plato is stimulating and original scholarship. It is scholarship, however, of a most unorthodox sort. Taking what are for the most part the marginal references in the Platonic dialogues to women, Cavarero elicits from them feminist readings that are at once immensely imaginative, provocative, and thought-provoking. These readings suggest fundamentally new ways of thinking, not just about the content of the Platonic dialogues but about that whole tradition, called metaphysics, which, according to Cavarero, those dialogues inaugurated.

In what follows, I shall spend much of my time addressing issues in the one book of Cavarero's on Plato that has been translated into English, *In Spite of Plato*, though I hope that what I say applies implicitly, and sometimes explicitly, to her other, less widely available work.

In that book, her basic strategy is to take four of the many references to women in the dialogues and, as she puts it, "steal" them for a feminist reading of an other possible thinking. Only one of her choices seems obvious: the fourth and last chapter is on Diotima, the famous teacher of Socrates on the nature of eros in the *Symposium*. One might have expected her to address as well the famous treatment of women in Books V–VII of the *Republic*, or perhaps Socrates' mother, Phaenarete, from whom he learns his midwife's calling, or perhaps even Socrates' wife, Xanthippe, so unceremoniously dismissed from the discussion that is about to become the *Phaedo*. These options remind us that although it may be the case that the question of woman does not occupy a sufficiently central thematic place in the dialogues as a whole to satisfy feminist readers, it is surely a much more pervasive theme in the Platonic dialogues than in the vast majority of the canonical works in the western philosophical tradition. The question of woman may not be given a dominant place in the Platonic dialogues, but compared to the tradition both before and after Plato, where the question is for the most part almost entirely forgotten, Plato is an anomaly precisely in the extent to which he does include women and the question of women within the purview of his thinking. This surely in part explains the considerable interest in Plato by feminist philosophers, including Cavarero.

In addition to Diotima, Cavarero chooses as the images of women she will address Penelope, referred to in passing by Socrates in the *Phaedo* (84a–b), the maidservant from Thrace, who famously mocks Thales for falling into a well as reported by Socrates in the *Theaetetus* (174a), and Demeter, the most marginal reference, whose name is made the subject of one of the playful etymologies in the *Cratylus* (404b). In each case, she re-reads these usually marginal references in such a way as to "steal back" these women from the male Plato, give them back their own voice and their own very different standpoint. It is easy to see the influence of deconstruction here. These references to women, with the clear exception of Diotima, are marginal to the "central argument" of the dialogues, and they can be seen as constituting the *différance* to the overt or manifest argument.

In doing so, two themes, both adumbrated in the introduction to the book, serve as what she calls the "axes" of her interpretation: sexual difference, and the primacy of birth. In the case of sexual difference, the fact of women's embodiment and experience cannot be reduced, as it almost always has been, to a supposedly neutral and universal "human" standpoint that is in any case a thinly veiled assumption of *masculine* experience as the norm, as "normal."

> Here [in sexual difference] the revolution in perspective is of a particularly female, feminine sort. It appeals to the basic realism that comes to life when a woman observes her individual embodiment, finding that she cannot negate the sexedness which the neutral/universal noun 'man' neither includes nor describes. (6)

The second axis is borrowed from Hannah Arendt, her emphasis on the category of birth, which Cavarero uses to "bring about a subversive shift in perspective with respect to the patriarchal tradition that has always thrived on the category of death" (6–7). The extent of this subversion in Cavarero's hands proves to be remarkable. One of the most provocative and suggestive dimensions of her book is the extent to which she points out how radical the shift would be, philosophically and culturally, were we to take seriously a renewed emphasis on birth rather than the virtual obsession with death and the finitude it symbolizes that has characterized so much of western metaphysical, patriarchal discourse. I shall develop this point more fully in the discussion of the particular Platonic images of women she addresses.

Using these two axes, Cavarero, as Rosi Braidotti nicely puts it in her introduction,

> questions the patriarchal order by trying to locate the traces of the feminine as a site of male projection but also as a site of feminist reappropriation of alternative figurations for female subjectivity. Of central importance to the whole project is the redefinition of motherhood and the maternal function, which, far from being reduced to a support of patriarchy, is turned into a structuring or foundational site for the empowerment of women. (xvi)

Let us see how this is accomplished in greater detail.

The chapter on Penelope begins from Socrates' passing reference in the *Phaedo*, a negative reference as Cavarero points out, to Penelope's weaving and unweaving her cloth. Cavarero thinks *out* of the dialogue an imaginative reflection on the meaning and significance of Penelope's womanly experience. With the other women in the women's quarters, as Cavarero imagines it, Penelope creates a realm of women's experience in marked contrast to the masculine realm that calls itself "neutral" and "human." Penelope's is a realm whose fundamental orientation is to birth, not to death. In this regard, Cavarero brings out the close connection among a number of positions, all of them grounded in masculinist experience. First, the obsession with death and the morose finitude it symbolizes, and the accompanying forgetting or ignoring of the significance of birth—a birth which, were it given even a symmetrical significance with death, would invoke the ineluctable place of the feminine in all human experience. Both themes are reiterated throughout the book. From at least Parmenides on (44ff.), western philosophy—predominantly male—has focused again and again on the significance of death, culminating, one might say, in Heidegger's famous account in *Being and Time* of "Being-toward-death," which is such a central moment in the occasion of authenticity. Coupled with that obsession with death comes a corresponding ignoring of the significance of birth: "In effect, the philosopher abandons the world of his own birth in order to establish his abode in pure thought, thus carrying out a symbolic matricide in the erasure of his *birth*."[1]

Second, in the face of that obsession with death, philosophy has exhibited a desperate seeking somehow to overcome it, to become immortal.

> Inhabiting the realm of pure thought (which renders the human thinker no longer mortal but eternal), the doctrine of truth [beginning with Parmenides] knows nothing about bodies or about the dead. Thus, inevitably, it does not even recognize birth, which is rooted for all humans in the maternal body. (47; my brackets)

Third, to make metaphysical space for that possibility, a separation of body and soul is drawn, with the human defined as the soul *in contrast to* the body, which thus gets denigrated. "This separation (of soul and body) implies devaluing the body to mere accident. Plato (sic) emphasizes this by attributing to the body the well-known connotations of jail and prison" (27. See also 38, 49). And fourth, these three peculiar obsessions are characterized by philosophy not as the masculine neuroses that they are but as universal, as "the human condition."

> By trivializing the necessary bodily dimension of living, it [i.e. the western philosophy that Cavarero sees inaugurated in the dialogues] now inhibits the symbolic translation of

sexual difference. In other words, a separated and demate-
rialized embodiedness can more easily conceal its sexual
connotation, always marked by difference. Hence the male
gender can easily claim to be neutral and universal. (26)

This transformation of human embodied diversity into a presumed neutral (but in fact male) "man" is an important theme of the
book. "In the idea of man who always immutably is, what is lost and
devalued as mere appearance is the individuality of living humans.
But what is especially hidden is female sexual difference." (52; see also
26, 38, 51, 53, 54, 70). This tendency begins with Parmenides, as
Cavarero sees it, and pervades the western philosophical tradition,
certainly including Plato.

By contrast, Penelope and her women compatriots articulate in
their very lives a much different possibility of human experience, one
which pays attention first and always to birth, which thus does not
separate the human from the bodily, and so does not deny but affirms
sexual difference.

[Penelope] continue(s) to weave the individual whole made
up of body and mind that had already appeared in her *metis*:
the reality where to live is most of all to be born and then,
only at the end, also to die. . . . In the weaving room, these
women neither separate their philosophy from the body to
grant it eternal duration nor entrust their experience of finitude to death in an arrogant desire for immortality. (30)

The second chapter, on "The Maidservant From Thrace," begins
from the reference in the *Theaetetus*, to the maidservant's laughing at
Thales, so concerned with looking at the "things above" that he failed
to pay attention to what was in front of him and fell into a well.
Cavarero dwells on that laughter, a laughter that becomes the laughter
of women at the arrogance of the men who turn their otherworldly
metaphysics into a "neutral" or "universal" condition for humans.
More ominously, perhaps, in this chapter Cavarero brings out the way
in which this otherworldly metaphysics, in its obsession with death,
its separation of body and soul, and especially in its denial of the
significance of birth, contains within it a symbolic matricide. "In effect
the philosopher abandons the world of his own birth in order to establish his abode in pure thought, thus carrying out a symbolic matricide in the erasure of his *birth*" (38). Even Diotima's speech, as we
shall see, participates in this matricide:

The question I already raised regarding Parmenides' goddess becomes an issue in Diotima's case also. What we find
at work in both instances is a subtle and ambiguous strategy requiring that a female voice expound the philosophical discourse of a patriarchal order that excludes women,
ultimately reinforcing the original matricide that disinvests
them. (94)

The third chapter, on Demeter, begins from a seemingly marginal
reference, a playful etymology of Demeter's name in the *Cratylus*.
Cavarero's reflection on Demeter leads her to elicit a new dimension
to the significance of birth. As symbolized in the mythology of Demeter,
a woman's power is not just to *give* birth, but also to *withhold* it, and
this is awesome power indeed. "To put it in more modern terms, the
myth of Demeter reveals a sovereign figure of female subjectivity who
decides, in the concrete singularity of every woman, whether or not to
generate" (64). How this original maternal power devolves into the
maternal as a mere "receptacle" for birth is part of the deplorable
story of the—largely masculinist—history of philosophy. In turn, this
reflection leads her to one of the outstanding instances of the real
challenge of this book, Cavarero's invitation to us to rethink what
have become standard cultural debates from the standpoint of a feminine experience. In this case, the debate concerns the whole question of
control of women's bodies viz-a-viz issues of so-called "abortion rights."
Cavarero suggests with richness and imagination how differently this
debate would have to be construed if it were, for once, thought from the
standpoint and acknowledgement of sexual difference.

In my view this play on the word 'progress' indicates that,
if maternal power has been erased *from the start* and reduced to a reproductive function of the womb, then all
restrictions on invading *bios* are removed; the symbolic order
where living creatures find a secret, protected, maternal
home has been cancelled. This is one of the great many
meanings of the secret of birth: birth is not what cannot be
explained 'scientifically,' but the symbolic figure declared
inviolable by maternal power. (87; Cavarero's emphases)

The final chapter is on Diotima, the priestess from Mantinea who
famously teaches a young Socrates what he says becomes his own
teaching on eros. In addition to further developing the themes already
adumbrated, Cavarero joins with a number of other feminist interpret-

ers of the *Symposium* in seeing the significance of the woman, Diotima as an attempt of a masculine philosophy (and Plato in particular) to *appropriate* feminine experience and insight into a still masculine philosophic enterprise. Two statements of this reading should be noted, however. In the first, more positive one, Cavarero sees in Diotima's presence and speech a recognition on Plato's part that the feminine must be included in a philosophy that would be true:

> Femininity itself belongs structurally to Socrates' and Plato's philosophy. In other words, the works of Plato and Socrates seem marked by a *mimetic* desire for female experience. The pregnant, birth-giving male, like the male who practices midwifery, stands as the emblematic figure of true philosophy." (92; Cavarero's emphasis).

Though this is a basically positive insight on her part, the emphasis on the mimetic character of this recognition is already ominous. Why characterize the Platonic recognition of the necessary presence of the feminine in philosophy as an imitation of the feminine rather than simply the recognition of the significance of the feminine that it is? Put differently, if it is a *mimesis*, then how *could* philosophy acknowledge its feminine dimension in an authentic, nonmimetic way? Accordingly, within a very few pages, the formulation takes on a much more critical tone: the female is in effect *stolen* by a still masculine philosophy to keep it for itself. "In Diotima's speech maternal power is annihilated by offering its language and vocabulary to the power that will triumph over it, and will build its foundations on annihilation itself" (94). There is a danger here of placing philosophy in a "catch 22" situation. If philosophy ignores the feminine/maternal, this testifies to its sexist, misogynist character. But if it endeavors to incorporate the feminine into itself as a necessary component of genuine philosophy, then it is "stealing" the feminine and commiting matricide. How, then, can philosophy *in principle* acknowledge its feminine dimension?

These considerations begin to move us toward a set of criticisms of Cavarero's position. Before doing so, however, it is important to emphasize the power and imaginativeness of the interpretative strategies she employs, even if only selectively. Let me try to point out at least some of the features of that hermeneutic, for they are features I want to affirm as strongly as possible, perhaps even more strongly than Cavarero does.

First and perhaps most strikingly, Cavarero does not make the mistake of so many more orthodox interpreters of Plato and view the dialogues as simply a literary framework, which one may quickly pass over in order to get to the "real" philosophy, the arguments (in the narrow sense) that usually occur in most dialogues. Cavarero's imaginative readings would not be possible without a genuine sensitivity to what might be called the philosophic drama of the dialogues. With the partial, but only partial exception of Diotima, none of the women whom Cavarero takes as her starting point play what more orthodox interpreters would regard as a central role in the "argument" of the dialogue in which they occur. Even in the case of Diotima, whom everyone seems to agree does articulate the central argument of the *Symposium*, how many people make the fact that she is woman, and for that matter a priestess and a stranger, the only non-Athenian in the dialogue, an issue that needs to be fully integrated into the philosophical meaning of the dialogue? For all too many interpreters of that dialogue, Diotima simply speaks for Plato; she might just as well be a male Mantinean Stranger, or Socrates, or for that matter Plato himself. In spite of Plato. In spite of what Plato writes. By contrast, Cavarero's readings could not be purchased without a deep sensitivity to the dramatic aspects of the dialogue form and the philosophic significance thereof. To be sure, Cavarero herself pays special attention to the apparently "passing" references to women, but the principle she engages could and should be generalized: the philosophic richness, the philosophic meaning, of the Platonic dialogues goes way beyond the formal arguments presented therein.

Second, Cavarero's readings exhibit the principle that in reading the dialogues, one must think *out* of them, not limit one's thinking, again, to the content of the explicit arguments within. Another way to put this is to use the apt phrase of Mitchell Miller and say that the dialogues must be read not so much as the purveyors of an intended doctrine, but as provocations to the reader, provocations to thoughtfulness and to philosophy. In this sense, the dialogues must be read as themselves dialogues *between Plato and the reader*, dialogues, therefore, in which a particular reader's response cannot be stipulated or determined in advance, although a writer like Plato, like the Socrates within his dialogues, can certainly point the reader/interlocutor in certain directions.[2] By dwelling on these four women and the issues their presence elicits, Cavarero enters into dialogue with Plato, and that, I want to suggest, is precisely what Plato most wants to happen, what he most of all intends by writing dialogues. We should think not just within but *out of* the dialogue. Enter into dialogue with the dialogue. As Plato intended.

Third and following from this, the dialogues must be read in such a way that no longer is it the case that the primary interpretive aim is to gain access to "Plato's view" of this or that, to "Plato's doctrine," say, of the Forms, or of recollection, or of metaphysics. Indeed, read as Cavarero does, the dialogues are no longer primarily vehicles for the presentation of Plato's or anyone else's doctrine. Rather, again, they are provocations to philosophy, to the imaginative elicitation of philosophic issues worthy of thoughtfulness, of dialogue. *Not* in spite of Plato. Precisely as Plato wrote.

This leads me to the first general criticism of Cavarero's standpoint I would make. When Cavarero focuses on the references to women she chooses and elicits her wonderfully imaginative readings, she follows the hermeneutical principles I have adumbrated in an exemplary way. But when she refers to other aspects of the dialogues, and especially when, as it were, she goes on the attack against Plato, she seems to fall back into precisely the "masculinist," more orthodox reading of Plato against which her fundamental reading of the women she addresses cries out. In these passages, she attributes to Plato precisely that set of doctrines that, I want to suggest, her very reading of the references to women calls into question. Plato is a dualist; he upholds the doctrine of immortality, of Forms, he is "the very father of metaphysics" (Shadow Writing, 7);[3] "the very champion of solitary contemplations" (ibid, 8). Indeed, gaining access to these "doctrines" of Platonism is not especially difficult nor does it require especially imaginative readings, "since, *as we know*, in most of the Dialogues, and certainly in the *Symposium*, it is Plato himself who is speaking through the voice of Socrates" (*In Spite of Plato*, 93; my emphasis).

Do we *know* that? If the philosophically richest way to interpret the various references to women in the dialogues is according to the principles that Cavarero employs, why stop with the references to women? Why not read the entire dialogue, each and every dialogue, according to those principles? What would happen if we ceased holding that whatever Socrates said was Plato's doctrine of this or that, and read the entire dialogue as the kind of provocation to philosophic thoughtfulness that they indeed seem to be?

Cavarero, alas, does not always do so. As we just saw, when she is attacking Plato, she has no qualms about assuming that, as Heidegger earlier put it, "Socrates=Plato" (93). And so does Diotima (91, 92). Moreover, what gets espoused by these figures is unproblematically "Platonism" (22, 25). Still further, Plato is a misogynist (33). Indeed, the implicit feminism that Cavarero herself elicits from the dialogues is there "despite Plato's intentions" (50). And so on.

What I suggest in closing is that the hermeneutical principles that yield under Adriana Cavarero's deft hand such rich readings of the references to women in the dialogues she addresses, should be applied to the dialogues as a whole. If they are, they immensely complicate our reading of the dialogues, to be sure. They yield a Plato far less doctrinal, less metaphysical, less otherworldly, less "Platonic." A Plato, however, far more provocative in the best sense, more open, more interrogative, more relational with the reader, and finally, altogether more friendly to the feminist principles that Adriana Cavarero exemplifies so well, if only selectively.

Chapter Five

Gadamer's Plato

The last Continental philosopher whose interpretation of Plato I shall address is Hans Georg Gadamer. In addressing his work last, I of course take him out of chronological order as well as out of most conceptual orders that one might imagine. After all, as perhaps Heidegger's most important student, one would expect that a discussion of his work would follow immediately upon that of Heidegger himself. But I have chosen to consider Gadamer as the conclusion of the book because he represents for me an extremely important object lesson for a continentally oriented reading of Plato, an object lesson, I believe, that makes a consideration of his Plato interpretations an appropriate conclusion to this book. Let me explain.

One guiding thrust of my book so far has been critical of most of the Continental interpretations of Plato. The basis of my criticisms is in what I hope is an appropriate sense ad hoc. That is, to take first the most relevant contrast, I find it at once more understandable and less interesting that analytically oriented interpreters of Plato have by and large ignored the significance of the dialogue form in which Plato writes and turned more or less directly to what they take to be the "arguments" in the dialogues. That is understandable because one of the guiding principles of most of analytical philosophy has been, to exaggerate only slightly, that *philosophy is argument*. Believing this, it is plausible enough that when they turn to the Platonic dialogues, they would find the "philosophy" there *only* in the arguments—in a quite narrow sense—that occur within the dialogues. However dubious that decision is, however dubious that conception of philosophy might be from the standpoint of this book, it is, it must be said, a plausible inference from this guiding principle of analytic philosophy.

The case is very different with so-called continental philosophy, whose leading spokespersons have taken justifiable pride in their greater sensitivity to existential themes, to the emotional, psychological, lived dimensions of human life, and so, not surprisingly, to the way in which literature can sometimes best portray these elements and issues of life. This greater literary sensitivity manifests itself in any number of ways: in the explicit address of literary works on their part, in their own more literary styles of writing, in their sometimes actually writing works of literature, and certainly, in their sensitivity to the literary dimension of those philosophers—one thinks here of Nietzsche especially—who write their philosophy in a more literary style.

In this light, one might expect these thinkers first and foremost to overcome the analytic prejudice in favor of narrowly construed arguments and philosophical doctrines, to exhibit an appropriate sensitivity to the literary dimension of the dialogue form and in particular to the philosophic significance of that dimension, of Plato's choice to write dialogues. It is their failure, too often at least, to do so that has been perhaps the guiding critical theme of this book. The very thinkers who should exhibit the most sensitivity to the literary dimension of Plato's work have too often fallen back on the analytic principles that in other venues they would strongly reject, and thus have found in the dialogues only or primarily that pile of doctrines that we now know as "Platonism." Is there then, something about the basic convictions of continental philosophy that, just as in the case of analytic philosophy, somehow prevents them from reading the Platonic dialogues with an appropriate dramatic sensitivity? Or can we find among continental philosophers an exemplar of what I have argued is a superior hermeneutic of the Platonic dialogues? Here is where Gadamer is so important; almost from the beginning, I shall argue in this chapter, we have a Continental philosopher who explicitly, even thematically, exhibits in his work on Plato precisely the kind of sensitivity that I have been espousing in this book. I turn to Gadamer, then, as my positive evidence that such a sensitivity to the literary dimension of the Platonic dialogues is not only possible but fully in accord with the guiding principles and themes of continental philosophy.[1]

My consideration of Gadamer's reading of Plato will thus be less critical than the previous chapters, although I will point to what I take to be some of the limits of Gadamer's reading, his occasional failure, as I shall argue, to follow out far enough the implications of his own hermeneutic insights. Nevertheless, Gadamer very much points the way for other thinkers with similar convictions to take further his guiding insights, one might say to radicalize them in an appropriate way. But our first task will be to understand the positive import of Gadamer's reading of Plato and what it calls for.

Perhaps not surprisingly, given his seminal work on hermeneutics in *Truth and Method*, the deepest and most original insights of Gadamer on Plato have to do with the hermeneutic of the dialogue form. I therefore will concentrate my attention on that hermeneutic dimension in my consideration of Gadamer as I have with the other thinkers addressed in this book, connecting that hermeneutic standpoint to some of his guiding insights on the positions taken in specific dialogues, and occasionally noting what I take to be certain discrepancies between his hermeneutical standpoint and the doctrines he occasionally attributes to Plato.

Although Gadamer often and persuasively rejects the developmental interpretation of Plato—that view that explains discrepancies in the apparent teaching of the dialogues as "Plato's development" from one dialogue to another—there is a certain development, or so I shall argue, from Gadamer's own early work on Plato, specifically his 1931 book on the *Philebus, Plato's Dialectical Ethics: Phenomenological Interpretations Relating to the Philebus*,[2] to his later essays. This development is really a working out of the full implications of the hermeneutical principles developed in *Truth and Method* as they are applied to Plato's dialogues. Those principles, as we shall see, are already formulated in the early (1931) *Philebus* book. But in that book, those principles are occasionally in tension with what is at the time the still strong influence of Heidegger's interpretation of Plato on Gadamer. That influence shows itself partly in the technical phenomenological vocabulary I discussed in the Heidegger chapter, but even more in the perhaps too easy way that Gadamer, with Heidegger, appeals to this or that "doctrine" of Plato. I shall argue that this attribution is finally incompatible with Gadamer's own hermeneutics of the dialogue form, and it is precisely this insight that guides his development toward his later, less doctrinal (and in this sense less Heideggerian) readings of Plato. To show this, let us turn first to the *Philebus* book.

In a sense, I hardly even need to develop the tension alluded to above between Gadamer's hermeneutic of the dialogue form and his occasional attribution of this or that doctrine to Plato. Gadamer himself already virtually acknowledges the tension in his 1982 preface to the reprinting of the first edition of the *Philebus* book. Speaking of the tendency to see the dialogues primarily as vehicles for the articulation of Plato's doctrines, Gadamer explicitly contests this reading: "We would be poor readers of Plato if we did not allow his dialogues to lead us to the things, the facts of the matter, themselves, rather than reading them as mere material from which to reconstruct Plato's doctrine of principles" (PDE, xxxiii). Expanding on this point, and quietly preparing for an implicit critique of his teacher, Heidegger's, tendency to criticize Plato from the supposedly "superior" insight of Aristotle, Gadamer adds,

> While fully acknowledging the methodologically primacy that the Aristotelian art of concepts possesses in relation to the interpretation of Plato, phenomenological interpretation leads more and more to an important hermeneutic insight: that literary creations, products of art like the Platonic dialogues, on the one hand, and working papers like the texts that are collected in the *corpus aristotelicum*, on the other, cannot be measured by the same standard and cannot be related to each other at all unless hermeneutic precautions are taken. (PDE, xxxiv)

These later remarks represent pointed, focal crystallizations of points that are already present, but less pointedly and consistently in the 1931 text itself: that the Platonic dialogues are not primarily about the presentation of doctrines, that they have their own appropriate hermeneutic, and that their philosophic power cannot be measured by the standards of what will become the more orthodox philosophical treatise. Let us turn to how these points are already at work in the text itself.

Gadamer announces almost immediately his recognition of the problematic character of the attribution of philosophical doctrines to the dialogues. In the introduction, he qualifies his book's own title with the striking remark that "At the same time, I take it absolutely as a premise that Plato does not teach a philosophical ethics any more than he teaches any other philosophical discipline" (PDE, 2). This is a crucial insight into the dialogues, one that, if its implications are fully acknowledged and followed out, should dispense once and for all with the tendency to understand Plato, as to this day he still almost always is, in terms of his "ethics," "moral theory," "epistemology," and most of all, his "metaphysics."

The reason why the attribution of such philosophical disciplines to the dialogues is problematic is that it ignores what Gadamer takes to be a crucial philosophic significance of the dialogue form, its irreducibly existential dimension. Gadamer, that is, takes with utmost seriousness and depth the notion that has threatened to become a meaningless cliché, that philosophy as Socrates and Plato conceived it must and can only be understood as a *way of life*. Thus, "Plato is a follower of Socrates, and Socrates is the figure through whom Plato expresses his own philosophical intentions, precisely because his literary works repeat, with the explicitness of literature, Socrates' entirely unliterary and undogmatic existence" (PDE, 2). This means that even in so far as there is an abiding tendency within the dialogues to present the theoretical life as an ideal, even that life must be understood as an existential possibility. "The dialogues are comprehended in their own intention only when one understands them as serving to lead the reader toward the *existential* ideal of the philosopher: toward *life* in pure theory" (PDE, 2). This existential dimension becomes one of Gadamer's guiding themes, in many ways the basic principle in terms of which he understands what is said, and more importantly, what happens, in the dialogue.

It leads him to important insights and unusual readings of the dialogues. In his discussion of the important notion of "The Good" in the *Philebus*, for example, Gadamer again and again emphasizes that the Good is not so much an abstract idea as a condition of a human life: "Thus the good is understood in advance as a condition of the human soul. So it is not something that man has (as *agathon* = "good" commonly means, to begin with) but a manner of his very being" (PDE, 105). What the question of the Good always addresses, then, as Gadamer understands it, is nothing abstract but "human Dasein as something that desires and chooses and reveals in its desires and its choices what is the good that it seeks" (PDE, 105). This leads him to the important conclusion that "Thus the good of human life does not confront us as a norm located in the beyond, but as the beauty, measuredness, and truth of human being and conduct" (PDE, 209). In his later (1978) work, *The Idea of the Good in Platonic-Aristotelian Philosophy*,[3] Gadamer will radicalize this insight into the claim that the famous "idea of the Good" cannot be, in any strict or technical sense, an idea at all: "The good is the being of the ideas generally and not an idea itself" (IG, 124). Whatever the specifics both of Gadamer's argument here and our evaluation of his claims, what I want to point to is the way in which he derives from the fact of the dialogue form a sustained existential reading of the dialogues, and so of "Plato's philosophy."

This existential element derives from what Gadamer takes to be an important, though always implicit, teaching of the dialogues, that philosophy as Socrates and Plato took it is always founded in conversation between humans, conversations that seek first and always *agreement*.[4] Again, the force of this recognition is to deny that Platonic philosophy is fundamentally about doctrines or abstract arguments. The dialogues teach us that philosophy is always concrete, always philosophic discussion, and so must be assessed in terms of a lived conversation, not the logic of an abstract argument. This leads Gadamer to a remarkable reading of the myriad "logical fallacies" that analytic philosophers regularly discover as flaws in this or that theory of Plato. For Gadamer, these logical flaws are to be understood not as unintentional lapses of logic on Plato's part, but as quite intentional, dramatic elements in the portrayal of concrete human conversations, which always proceed according to different measures of rigor and consistency.

> This is, incidentally, the way to assess Plato's logical errors in general: Socrates' logical traps are not meant to be the manipulations of a virtuoso technician which are simply applied where they promise success; instead, *they are living forms of a process of seeking shared understanding* which always has the facts of the matter themselves before it and which finds its criterion solely in its success in developing its capacity to see these facts. This has nothing to do, either positively or negatively, with the state of the science of logic. (PDE, 58; my italics)

As Gadamer later notes in his analysis of the development of the more rigorous notion of dialectic and diairesis in the *Philebus*, even after having developed this rather technical, quasi-scientific "method," Socrates does not adopt it in his own conversation but continues in the more loose dialogical procedure (complete with its occasional logical oddities), which is his wont.

> Socrates makes a new start, while seeming to forgo the rigorous path of dialectic. We find this kind of forgoing of the rigorous mode of presentation frequently elsewhere in Plato as well, and it is always motivated by a concern for the

partner in the conversation and for the concrete require-
ments of the situation. (PDE, 125)

So once again, the guiding interpretive principle for Gadamer is
to take seriously the dialogical character of Plato's dialogues and of
his conception of philosophy. The locus of philosophy is human conversation, and its efficacy must be measured by standards appropriate
to that situation.

We know from *Truth and Method* the fundamental importance
that Gadamer attributes to language, to the tradition which it at once
determines and by which it is determined. As is obvious from the
stress he places on dialogue and conversation in this Plato interpretation, Gadamer finds in Plato very much a kindred spirit in regard to
the decisive importance of language. What I think Gadamer finds so
compelling in Plato is that the latter's concern with language finds its
expression not in a "philosophy of language" that is developed in the
abstract, but in the human conversations that the dialogues imitate.
That is why Gadamer takes the drama of the dialogues with such
utmost seriousness. Even so, within those dialogues, there are more or
less explicit acknowledgments of the importance of language, logos,
and Gadamer regards them as seminal. Of particular importance to
him, in this regard, is the well-known passage in the *Phaedo* where
Socrates describes his "second sailing" (99d) after his disappointment
at the physicalist investigations of Anaxagoras and other presocratics.
That second sailing, as Socrates explicitly acknowledges, begins with a
"turn to the *logoi*" (99e). This turn for Gadamer is decisive, and is obviously inseparable from Plato's use of the dialogue form. For the turn
to logoi represents, in Gadamer's view, a return from the imagistic
character of the passing appearances that constitute our perceptual world
to the greater stability, even if not the complete stability, of language.

> What one is looking for is, after all, a reason or cause that
> *stays the same*: for each entity, that which it at bottom al-
> ways is. Now this claim is fulfilled, in a certain way, in
> *language*. Language already contains an understanding of
> the world in those respects in which it remains the same.
> (PDE, 70; Gadamer's italics)[5]

Thus for Gadamer, the dialogue form in which Plato writes, the
images of spoken conversations that they present, are the very embodiment of Plato's recognition of the decisiveness of language that

occasionally gets articulated within their pages. To ignore that form and the significance it embodies is therefore to ignore one of the fundamental elements in Plato's philosophic thinking.

Another crucial Gadamerian conviction that Gadamer finds exhibited so well in the Platonic dialogues concerns the important hermeneutical notion of a "pre-understanding," or what Heidegger had often called our "average everyday understanding" that we bring to every situation and to every question. In Gadamer's view, what Socrates raises questions about in the dialogues is nothing esoteric but precisely the instability of that pre-understanding, a version of the hermeneutic circle, which almost everyone has experienced. It is no abstract, esoteric set of philosophic doctrines but precisely that average everyday understanding that Socrates calls into question, and so, Gadamer clearly holds, that Plato recognizes to be the guiding philosophic issue. This is what separates the Socratic questioning, and so the dialogues, from both previous and subsequent more esoteric understandings of the philosophic enterprise.

> For the claim to knowledge which Socrates tests is a distinctive claim. What is in question is not a knowledge that one person has and another does not have, that one person claims and another does not claim; that is, it is not a knowledge by which only the "wise" are distinguished but a knowledge that everyone must claim to have and must therefore seek continually insofar as he does not have it. For the claim to this knowledge constitutes the manner of being of human existence itself. (PDE, 52–53)

It is the presumption of this pre-understanding, of always already comprehending the situation, that the Platonic Socrates both recognizes and calls into question in the dialogues.

> The Socratic discovery is that this claim, which seems to be such a matter of course, is not fulfilled as a matter of course: that Dasein's average self-understanding contents itself with the mere appearance of knowledge and cannot give an accounting of itself. So the Socratic question as to what arête is, is a demand that an accounting be given. (PDE, 54)

It is thus that Gadamer finds, not in any theoretical presentation of one of the characters but in the existential drama of the dialogue

itself, a profound recognition of and questioning of the very hermeneutical situation that he himself sets out in his own major work.

It is for this very reason that as soon as we translate the dramatic
action of the dialogues into a theoretical statement of Plato's view of
this or that, or in Gadamer's language, as soon as we express it in the
language of concepts, we risk seriously distorting it. This is why,
Gadamer argues, Aristotle's understanding of Plato and subsequent
critique of his master, while accurate enough as a translation into the
language of concepts, at the same time is a distortion of the richness
of Plato's presentation. At this point, Gadamer moves into delicate
territory, for as we have seen, his own teacher, Heidegger, has argued
at length that Plato can and must be understood through Aristotle,
who correctly understands, correctly criticizes, and is therefore superior to and clearer than Plato. While acknowledging in a qualified way
that Aristotle does understand Plato correctly insofar as the latter's
thinking can be translated into concepts, Gadamer sees that very translation as problematic.

> The conclusion that Aristotle misunderstood Plato is rightly
> felt to be impossible. But it is equally certain that in this
> critique what is truly Platonic does not make itself felt in
> the positive character that it still has even today, for us.
> Aristotle projected Plato onto the plane of conceptual expli-
> cation. The Plato who presents himself in this explication is
> the object of Aristotle's critique. What makes this critique
> problematic is that this projection cannot also capture the
> inner tension and energy of Plato's philosophizing as they
> speak to us, with such incomparable convincingness, in his
> dialogues. (PDE, 7)

Gadamer goes on to say that this translation into "conceptual
explication" of the thinking of the dialogues constitutes a "flattened
version" (7) of the richness of the dialogues.

Clearly, Gadamer is beginning here a cautious struggle with the
much more strongly pro-Aristotelian interpretation of Heidegger. He
acknowledges that if one embarks on the project of the "conceptual
explication" of Plato's thinking, Aristotle's is a correct understanding
and critique. So far forth, he seems to go along with Heidegger's
reading. But unlike Heidegger, Gadamer seems at least as troubled, if
not indeed more so, by what is lost in this conceptualization of the
thought of the dialogues. His own positive interpretation of the dialogues, even in this early work, thus pays much more attention to

those dimensions in the dialogues that are lost in the conceptualization of Plato that Aristotle initiates and that Heidegger endorses.

Still, it is clear that at this early stage of his own development, Gadamer is very much under the influence of Heidegger, and this influence, I want now to show, complicates and in certain ways undercuts his positive interpretation. We see that influence first and perhaps most obviously in the terminology and basic conceptual framework that Gadamer employs, which he clearly derives from Heidegger. More importantly, he largely accepts at this stage—in however qualified a way as we have seen—Heidegger's conviction that the appropriate way to understand Plato, at least at the level of concepts, is to read him "back" from Aristotle. Although he is already more uneasy with this procedure than is Heidegger, who employs it with an almost unqualified self-assurance, he nevertheless does follow his teacher in this conceptualization. Thus, "It might seem strange that the problem of Plato's dialectic is approached here from (of all things) the angle of the strict Aristotelian concept of *episteme* (knowledge), which is *apodeixis* (demonstration)" (PDE, 17). Nevertheless, he does so, and his long explication of Platonic dialectic (see especially pp. 17–29) is very much derived from Aristotle as seen through the eyes of Heidegger. Hence he emphasizes, I would say exaggerates, the sense in which Platonic dialectic is intended to be a "science of dialectic" in the Aristotelian sense of science. To arrive at this Aristotelian sense of science as applied to dialectic, Gadamer at times seems to forget his own best insights into the significance of the dialogue form. In such passages, he finds in them, bizarrely in terms of his deeper reading elsewhere, a "stylized uniformity" (PDE, 20) that paves the way for the transformation into science. In these contexts he ignores what he says elsewhere about the *importance* of the existential contingency of lived human conversation and says instead, "But this means—however paradoxical it may sound—that Platonic dialectic does not embody the contingently given dialectic of discussion, the questioning and answering *synousia* (being together, meeting) with its animation, which is specific to the situation" (PDE, 20). This tendency to go along with the Aristotelian/Heideggerian "conceptualization" of Plato, I suggest, is in manifest tension with the concrete richness of Gadamer's Plato interpretation in general.

Perhaps the most pervasive and troubling way that the influence of Heidegger shows itself in this early work is in the ease with which Gadamer, despite what the force of his dramatic interpretations should lead him to say, attributes this or that doctrine to Plato. In my chapter on Heidegger and throughout, I have tried to say why I find this

attribution so problematic. Gadamer's own hermeneutic of the Platonic dialogue, I here argue, should lead him to be no less troubled by
such attributions. Yet, apparently still deeply influenced by Heidegger's
reading, he still regularly finds various "Platonic doctrines" in the
dialogues. Thus, in addition to the Aristotelian scientific dialectic that
I addressed above, Gadamer finds in the *Philebus* a Platonic "theory of
dialectic" (52), or a "doctrine of science" (197).[6]

It is just this tension between his own hermeneutic insights and
his occasional conceding to Heidegger the latter's more Aristotelian
reading of Plato that I believe makes sense of what I hope now to
show is Gadamer's development as, in his later work, he follows out
with greater consistency his own hermeneutic of the dialogue form
and increasingly leaves behind the more doctrinal reading of his
teacher. To that end, let us turn to an examination of some of his later
work on Plato.

Gadamer's engagement with Plato is sustained throughout his
life. In addition to his major work of 1978, *The Idea of the Good in
Platonic-Aristotelian Philosophy,*[7] he wrote articles and essays on Plato
throughout his career.[8] One of the first things germane to our inquiry
that one notices in these later essays is that the very quiet criticisms of
Heidegger in the earlier work, in which Heidegger's name is not even
mentioned in the context of criticism, is now replaced by an explicit,
if always polite and respectful, confrontation with Heidegger's reading of Plato. We see this very clearly in the Preface to *The Idea of the
Good in Platonic-Aristotelian Philosophy,* where Gadamer characterizes
part of his enterprise in his then recently published *Truth and Method*
(1965) as an effort to "withstand the challenge" of Heidegger's "interpretation of Plato as the decisive step toward 'metaphysical thought's'
obliviousness to being" (*Sein*). (IG, 5). Moreover, in that work he explicitly counters Heidegger's acceptance, by and large, of Aristotle's
criticisms of Plato by again and again calling into question Aristotle's
way of reading Plato, his transformation of the drama of the dialogues
into the language of concepts. Such criticisms, he now says, are "one-
sided," (60), they derive from Aristotle's "always tak[ing] Plato word
for word," (95) and are based on his "literal reading of Plato's metaphorical statements within the framework of his own conceptual ap-
paratus. But for just that reason, they miss what Plato actually intended"
(145). Though these observations are directed to Aristotle's reading of
Plato, it is impossible not to notice that they are at least as true of
Heidegger. Again, in his 1968 *Amicus Plato Magis Amica Veritas,* reflect-
ing on his own development over the years and commenting on his
early work on Plato, Gadamer says,

> At that time I was strongly influenced by Heidegger's in-
> terpretation of Aristotle, the real intention of which was
> still not completely evident, namely, its critique of ontology,
> and which in essence repeated Aristotle's critique of Plato
> in the form of an existential situation-oriented critique of
> the idealist tradition. But does that suffice? (198)

To this one might add perhaps Gadamer's most poignant critique of his teacher on this matter, his reflection in *Heidegger's Ways*
that despite the richness of Heidegger's readings of thinkers in the
history of philosophy, "Only the thought-event of the Platonic dialogues—the first philosophical texts that we still have—remained in-
accessible to this impatient questioner in spite of all the momentum
behind his appropriations."[9] So by now, Gadamer has become more
explicitly critical of the inadequacy of Heidegger's Plato interpretation, and on many of the same grounds that I have been eliciting.

Still, notwithstanding Gadamer's regular acknowledgment of the
inadequacy of Aristotle's criticisms of Plato, one of the more striking
aspects of his later work is what he comes to call his "unitary effect"
thesis, his conviction that what Plato and Aristotle share is even more
fundamental than their differences, however important those differences
may be. For both Plato and Aristotle, he argues, the Good functions
both ontologically and practically (IG, 26). He astutely points out that
the Good functions both in Aristotle's physics, through the role played
by final cause, as well as in his ethics, just as it does for Plato (IG, 1128–
129). More generally, he regularly brings Plato and Aristotle together in
what he takes to be their common emphasis on praxis (IG 121–122).
Even when in a critical mode, Gadamer notes the irony that despite
Aristotle's criticism of what he takes (mistakenly in Gadamer's view) to
be Plato's separation of forms and things, his own separation of his god
from the rest of the cosmos constitutes a more radical "chorismos" than
anything in Plato (158). All this leads to a conclusion that, while sharing
to a certain extent Heidegger's view that Aristotle somehow completes
the Platonic project, is stated in a way that is altogether more sympathetic to Plato. Gadamer says, "But in the end, did not [Aristotle] carry
out what Plato intended to do—indeed even go beyond it in fulfilling
it." (177). But this is done, he adds, in the following way: "In Aristotle's
thought, what Plato intended is transferred to the cautious and tentative
language of philosophical concepts (178)." We can hear in the sentence
the loss in that transference as much as any "fulfilling."

Perhaps the most abiding theme of Gadamer's later work
on Plato, however, is that of the pervasive sense of finitude and

incompleteness that he finds in the thinking of the dialogues. This is more controversial than it may at first sound. Many of the orthodox interpretations of Platonism, even the Continental ones that we have considered, include the conviction that the theory of forms, coupled with the ideal state of the *Republic* taken as a serious blue-print for a real state, entail a systematic completeability, if not actual completeness, a "totalization" that is virtually definitive of what comes to be criticized by Heidegger and others as "metaphysics." Such a claim to totality or completeness Gadamer finds again and again undercut in the dialogues. Both the *Republic* and the *Philebus,* properly interpreted, suggest instead that "the ideal of dialectical derivation of all things from a single *arche* could never be carried out completely" (IG, 92). Perhaps his most sustained elucidation of this pervasive noncompleteability or finitude in the dialogues is his remarkable 1962 essay, "Dialectic and Sophism in Plato's *Seventh Letter.*" There, he shows in detail that the various modes of knowing that Plato sets out, ("name or word, explanation or conceptual determination (logos), appearance, illustrative image, example, figure (*eidolon*), and the knowledge or insight itself") (100), are each of them and together at once constitutive of the knowledge we have but at the same time always a limit on the completeness of any possible knowledge. "And now Plato begins to demonstrate the point toward which the whole exposition had been leading. These four are indeed indispensable for true knowledge. But they are of such a nature that if one avails oneself of them, *one can never grasp the thing itself with complete certainty"* (104; my italics). This is because of the very nature of *aletheia,* truth, the understanding of which Gadamer takes over from Heidegger. Every revelation of truth is always also a concealing. This is constitutive of the finitude of human knowing per se. "Plato's thesis is this: all these means assert themselves as whatever they are, and in pushing to the fore, as it were, they suppress that which is displayed in them" (105). This is true, he insists, even of the presumably highest mode of access to truth, full knowledge or insight. "And the state of the soul which we call knowledge or insight into the truth must also be of such a nature that it asserts itself and thereby conceals the thing itself" (112). So there can be no question in the dialogues, as the later Gadamer sees it, of the kind of complete, unqualified, "clear and distinct" knowledge that is so often attributed to Plato as a function of the "theory of forms" and the dream of an educational system so thorough as to lead humans to wisdom. This is so even if the four modes of knowing are taken together cumulatively as it were: "The entirety of the logoi is a true entirety but one which is given to finite human knowing only in its basic structure and only in concretizations of it in specific contexts" (120). Of decisive importance, given Gadamer's sustained interest in dialectic and his early claims in behalf of a "science of dialectic" in Plato, is that this necessary incompleteness of knowing is true even of dialectic.

> The labor of dialectic, in which the truth of what is finally flashes upon us, is by nature unending and infinite. And that infinitude is displayed in the impediment to understanding in the human realm, the impediment which corresponds to the function of the receptacle of all becoming in the *Timaeus*. Plato's Pythagorism is not a Pythagorism of the world but of human beings. The Many, the unlimited Two, sustains [*and restricts*] both the order of the world and, equally, the possibilities of human knowing. (121; my italics)

The upshot of all this, again in clear opposition to the assumptions of Platonism, is that in the most pervasive sense,

> What Plato describes here as the untiring movement back and forth through the four means of knowing is in fact the art of dialectic—a perpetual passing from one thing to another which nonetheless perseveres in the single direction of what is meant and which, for want of cogent deductive proofs, *remains in proximity to what is sought without ever being able to reach it.* (122; my italics)

There is, as Gadamer interprets Plato, a metaphysical, indeed a mathematical, basis for the necessary incompleteness of human knowing. In order to make his case, Gadamer turns astutely to the very theme which might seem to argue most strongly in favor of the totalizing metaphysical view ascribed to Platonism, Plato's sustained and clear interest in mathematics. It is precisely this mathematicizing Plato, this Plato who is presumably at heart a Pythagorean, who is usually taken to be the Plato of totalizing Platonism. Gadamer is deeply interested in and affirmative of Plato's engagement with mathematics and the mathematical understanding of the world, even to the point of acknowledging in a qualified way the notion present in Aristotle that the forms might be number ("Amicus Plato Magis Amica Veritas," 209). Gadamer takes Plato's thinking to be grounded fundamentally in the crucial mathematical notions of, on the one hand, the One, which is determinate, and the Two, or as he calls it, the indeterminate dyad.

The determinacy of the One, clearly, gives humans whatever definitiveness they can have, particularly in terms of their knowledge. But what especially interests Gadamer, and that on which he concentrates his attention, is the *indeterminacy* of the Two or the Many. That indeterminacy, inherent in the very notion of the many, is what makes any human knowledge always incomplete, always ongoing. For this reason, it is the crux of the mathematical issue for Gadamer's Plato: "*The thesis, then, which I would like to propose for discussion is that the problem of the Many is from the beginning the problem of the Two*" (*Plato's Unwritten Dialectic*, 133; Gadamer's italics). As long as the Two or the Many is indeterminate, and it is indeterminate in its very nature, then the very fact that the world *is* deeply mathematical guarantees not a completeable certainty but precisely the incompleteness , or we could now say, the indeterminacy, of human knowing. Shades of Godel! Gadamer can thus conclude as follows:

> Thus in teaching that dialectic could never be brought to a completion Plato seems to have drawn the appropriate conclusion from the fundamental experience of the early Greek thinkers. The doctrine of the indeterminate Two is a doctrine of the primordial discrepancy between essence and phenomenon, a discrepancy which is as inchoately expressed in the *Timaeus* as it is in Parmenides' doctrinal poem, a poem which appends a description of the dual world of oppositions to the Eleatic teaching of unity, without clarifying the connection between its first and second parts. (*Amicus Plato Magis Amica Veritas*, 205–206)[10]

So, strange as it may seem in the light of the usual understandings of Platonism, the mathematical doctrine of the One and the Two that Gadamer argues is the metaphysical foundation of Plato's thinking in the dialogue founds not Platonism but precisely the ongoing, dialogical, incompleteable understanding of philosophy that Gadamer espouses himself and in which he finds a kinsman in Plato.

It is in the light of this hermeneutic and the interpretation of the dialogue form that follows from it that we can understand the originality (and the controversial character) of many of the specific insights that Gadamer's reading elicits over the years. Let us consider a few of the most striking, as a way of testifying to their consistency with his hermeneutic and the richness that it allows.

Begin with his sustained engagement with the question of dialectic, recalling that in the early *Plato's Dialectical Ethics*, still under the explicit influence of Heidegger, he saw dialectic in the dialogues primarily in terms of its proximity to a "science" of dialectic. Soon, however, Gadamer distances himself from the notion of a science of dialectic, whether phenomenological science or not, in favor of what we may call a much more existential notion of dialectic, a notion that keeps dialectic related to what Gadamer had always insisted were its roots in dialogue. Those roots, he now affirms, are not to be left behind somehow in favor a move toward rigorous science, but preserved. In a striking statement of this movement, in *The Idea of the Good*, he speaks of dialectic now as "that Doric harmony of logos (word) and ergon (deed) that gives Socrates' refutational enterprise its particular *ethos* (character)" (IG, 44). Such a "harmony of word and deed" will of course be invisible if one reads a Platonic dialogue as a treatise, a compilation of philosophic arguments. To witness either the harmony or the lack thereof, one simply must pay attention to the drama of the dialogue in something like the way that Gadamer calls for. As he applies the question of this harmony concretely to the *Lysis* in his 1972 article, "*Logos* and *Ergon* in Plato's *Lysis*," he discovers that

> if one follows the evolution of the discussion in regard to the reciprocal relation between logos and ergon, things take on a meaningful, sequential order. One suddenly recognizes that any discussion which Socrates conducts about friendship with two young boys *must* end in *aporia*, for children do not yet know what friendship is and how complex a relationship an enduring friendship creates between the friends. The confusion in which these half-children are left is not to be viewed as negative per se; rather, it is an indication of their incipient maturation in their own existence as human beings. (6; Gadamer's italics)

Thus the reason that the various efforts of the boys fail is that "these logical disjunctions are not being tested against a *real* knowledge of friendship" (11; Gadamer's italics). As Gadamer sees it, then, Plato's dialectic can be seen only by noticing the connection, either of harmony or disharmony, between what the various characters say (which is what most philosophic readers pay exclusive attention to) and what they do, to the dramatic action of the dialogue. Thus in regard to the young Lysis, "Like Socrates' irony and like his complicity in aiding Hippothales woo his beloved, Lysis' shyness and his unwillingness to accept the result are intended by Plato to show indirectly how the discussion now touches upon its actual subject matter, the word, upon the deed" (19). We are here very far from the Heideggerian notion of a science of dialectic, and much closer to the origins of dialectic in dialogue, much closer, as well, to Gadamer's own emphasis on dialogue, on conversation, on the precariousness of logos.

This movement, from an abstract and abstracting, doctrinal version of Plato that he derives largely from Heidegger, to a more concrete, existential, dialogical, and aporetic Plato, is repeated in a number of ways. One of the most striking is in Gadamer's brilliant and unorthodox interpretation of the "idea of the Good" in Plato. Once again, Gadamer moves away from any abstract notion of the Good in favor of one that has to do, as we have already seen, with the *good of human life*. In *The Idea of the Good*, Gadamer connects the good at length with beauty, with its concrete appearing, its measuredness. "The dynamis of the good has taken refuge in the *physis* of the beautiful: measure and measuredness constitute what beauty and arête are everywhere" (IG, 115). Of this concretizing of the good, Gadamer comments immediately, "We are far removed here from some esoteric, abstract, dialectical doctrine" (IG, 115). Indeed, for what is of interest to Gadamer is the extent to which the good is visible as the *playing out of itself* in human lives. "Of itself and according to its own nature, the good is appearance (*erscheinen*), lighting up (*aufscheinen*), shining forth (*herausscheinen*), or in Greek, *ekphainesthai*" (IG, 116). The upshot of all this, in a striking passage that I have quoted earlier, is that "The good is the being of the ideas generally and not an idea itself" (IG, 124).

The crucial consequence of this existential concretizing of the good concerns our knowledge of it. For since it is not itself an abstract idea or even an object, knowledge of it cannot be a techne, cannot be any sort of technical or epistemic knowledge but somehow a *lived* knowledge. Gadamer makes this striking conclusion explicit:

> Plato himself saw that knowledge of the good cannot be understood using techne as a model, although—or better said, precisely because—Socrates continually uses the techne model in his critique and refutation of the views of his partners in the discussion. (IG, 33)[11]

Indeed, Gadamer generalizes this to the entire Socratic/Platonic project of the knowledge of virtue: "Knowledge in arête can have the character of neither knowledge in techne nor the knowledge of this new paideia (sophistry), which boasts of being techne" (IG, 50).

Together with this existential reading goes a sustained recognition, which we have already noted, of the pervasive incompleteness of the human project of knowledge. The concrete ways that Gadamer develops this point brings occasionally stunning results. He notes, for example, something that scholars who constantly refer to Plato's "theory of forms" regularly overlook, that the forms are never *proved*, but always assumed, hypothesized.

> Aristotle's syllogisms or a deductive system, Euclid's geometry, for instance, can construct proofs which by virtue of their logical cogency compel everyone to recognize the truth, but this, according to Plato, is not to be achieved in the realm of the philosophy of ideas. ("Dialectic and Sophism in Plato's *Seventh Letter*" 99. See also 100, 116, 190)

In a perhaps even more controversial observation, Gadamer argues that the so-called "proofs" of immortality in the *Phaedo* are not intended by Plato as proofs at all.

> Thus it seems appropriate to me to first examine Plato's mode of demonstration to see if it indicates whether Plato was fully aware of the insufficiency of these proofs and, if we find that he was, to ask then what the actual intent of his demonstration is. It seems clear that despite the inadequacy of all these proofs they have a sort of logical order to them and display increasing cogency, but it is just as clear that ultimately these arguments must be thought of only as expositions of an assumption and not as conclusive demonstrations. ("The Proofs of Immortality in Plato's *Phaedo*," 22. See also 25, 36)

Indeed, in a way they must be regarded as Plato's joke! (28).

Finally, a crucial consequence of Gadamer's hermeneutic is to recognize that certain fundamental tenets usually attributed to "Platonism," and used as a criticism by the very continental philosophers we have considered in this book, simply cannot be sustained in a reading sensitive to the drama of the dialogues. Two of these are worth noting in conclusion. First, Plato's supposed "dualism" simply cannot be sustained. Plato is not a dualist (see "Idea and Reality in Plato's *Timaeus*," 156ff). And finally, it is Aristotle, and not Plato, who is the true founder of western metaphysics (*Amicus Plato Magis Amica Veritas*, 200). With that recognition, Gadamer has fully "withstood the challenge" of Heidegger's interpretation of Plato which places the latter at the foundation of the "forgetting of Being" which is western metaphysics.

I have tried to show in this chapter that the kind of reading that I advocate, a reading sensitive to the dialogical, aporetic, existential character of Platonic thinking, is not only compatible with the guiding assumptions and commitments of Continental philosophy but has been exhibited by one of its leading representatives, Hans-Georg Gadamer. If I have succeeded, I hope that it makes still more persuasive the larger argument that I have tried to make in this book, that it is most of all imperative for continental philosophers, given their own commitments, to rethink the surprisingly orthodox readings they have tended to give of Plato, and to find in the dialogues not the beginning of the "forgetting of Being" or of "logocentricism" or of "phallocentricism," but a rich and in many ways compatible source of engagement in the never ending and uncompleteable task of philosophic thinking.

Notes

INTRODUCTION

1. Borrowing from the translation by Eva Brann, Peter Kalkavage, and Eric Salem, *"Plato's Sophist: The Professor of Wisdom,"* (Newburyport, MA: Focus Philosophical Library, 1996), 16.

2. See Mitchell Miller, "Platonic Provocations: Reflections on the Soul and the Good in the *Republic,"* in *Platonic Investigations,* edited by Dominic J. O'Meara (Washington, DC: Catholic University Press of America, 1985), 163–194.

3. Plato, *Phaedo,* 63b, 68a, 69e, 70b, 77a, 91a, 92a, 114d.

4. Ibid., 64a, 67c, 68a.

5. Ibid., 59b.

6. See my *Finitude and Transcendence in the Platonic Dialogues,* (Albany: State University of New York Press, 1995).

7. I owe the gist of this formulation to my friend and colleague, Richard Lee, whom I thank.

8. The decisive refutation is that of Jacob Howland, "Re-Reading Plato: The Problem of Platonic Chronology," *Phoenix,* 45, no. 3 (1991), 189–214.

9. As an especially pertinent example I cite an interesting book whose title might suggest that it is most germane to my project: Catherine Zuckert's *Postmodern Platos* (Chicago: University of Chicago Press, 1996). However, Zuckert's project, completely legitimate in its own right, is almost entirely different from mine. Her project is to find in a number of Continental philosophers "Platonic" elements of one sort or another, whereas my project is more addressed to calling into question the hermeneutical principles by which they read Plato.

CHAPTER ONE

1. Nietzsche, *The Birth of Tragedy,* translated by Walter Kaufmann (New York: Vintage Books, 1967), 86.

2. Ibid., 96.

3. Nietzsche, *Twilight of the Idols*, in *The Portable Nietzsche*, translated by Walter Kaufmann (New York: Penguin Books, 1976), 473–479.

4. Published in German as Martin Heidegger, *Gesamptausgabe*, Band 19 (Frankfurt: Vittorio Klostermann, 1992). Translated by Richard Rojcewicz and Andre Schuwer as *Plato's Sophist* (Bloomington: Indiana University Press, 1997). My translations will usually follow this text.

5. For an excellent example of such an interpretation, see Stanley Rosen, *Plato's Sophist: The Drama of Original and Image* (New Haven: Yale University Press, 1983).

6. Depending on one's interpretation, it is even possible that there are two other dialogues during this period. At the end of the *Statesman*, they agree to meet tomorrow to discuss "the philosopher," a dialogue that Plato never writes. In addition, there are hints within the *Cratylus* that it, too, may take place during this period. If we add these two dialogues, it serves to increase the intensity.

7. See, for example, *Apology*, 19b–20d.

8. See especially the formulation at 230–231 of the sophist as one who cross-examines others to reveal their sham wisdom, that is, as one who almost exactly resembles the activity of Socrates!

9. *Theaetetus*, 146b, 162a, 165a–b, 168e, 169b, 177c, 183c.

10. *Theaetetus*, 142a–c.

11. Present but silent in both the *Theaetetus* and *Sophist* is "the young Socrates," a friend and contemporary of Theaetetus who finally takes a more significant role later in the day, after the discussion in the *Sophist*, in the *Statesman*. That Plato makes a point of describing Theaetetus as looking like Socrates (both with bulging eyes and snub nose, hence ugly) and also invokes Socrates' younger namesake, raises implicitly the question of resemblance and the relation of resemblance and original, issues of importance in both dialogues but especially the *Sophist*.

12. Stanley Rosen has regularly addressed the way in which the dialogues as a whole suggest that an understanding of the human soul requires *both* "the mathematical," (broadly construed) *and* the poetic or mythic. Certain dialogues exaggerate the one or the other, or try to suppress the one or the other, and for this reason fail. For one early statement of this issue, see Rosen's *Plato's Symposium*, (New Haven: Yale University Press, 1968), xxi–xxii. "Since the psyche is both mathematician and poet, in the broadest sense of those terms, so too are the dialogues mathematical and poetic."

13. The judgment of the Stranger's methodological superiority is presumably the result of *modern* prejudices in favor of "methodological rigor," joined with speculations about the later date of authorship of the *Sophist*. It is important to emphasize that nothing in the dialogues themselves point to such superiority.

14. Heidegger, Martin, *Plato's Sophist*, translated by Richard Rojcewicz and Andre Schuwer (Bloomington: Indiana University Press, 1997), 8. Hereafter, PS.

15. For some other of the enormous number of instances where Heidegger speaks in these sorts of terms, see PS, 1140, 157, 158, 170, 172, 176, 177, 217, 223.

16. PS, 15. The German is *"Sich-Auskennen—im Besorgen, Hantieren, Herstellen -, Wissenschaft, Umsicht—Einsicht -, Verstehen, vernehmendes Vermeinen."* Martin Heidegger, *Gesamptaufgabe,* Band 19 (Frankfurt: Vittorio Klostermann, 1992) p. 21.

17. See for example Richard McKeon, editor, *Introduction to Aristotle,* (New York: Modern Library, 1947), 426.

18. I do not mean to imply that the metaphor of seeing for knowing is not profound and in some ways problematic. It surely is, and much could be said about it.

19. PS, 16. The German for "perception" here is again *"vernimmt."* (*Gesamptausgabe,* 19), 22.

20. See my *The Virtue of Philosophy: An Interpretation of Plato's Charmides* (Athens: Ohio University Press, 1981) especially chapters 3 and 5–7, and *Finitude and Transcendence in the Platonic Dialogues* (Albany: State University of New York Press, 1995), especially chapter 7.

21. See PS, 42ff. On the other hand, consider Aristotle's important reminder in *Ethics* I that we can only seek as much certainty in knowing as is appropriate to the subject matter, that "It is evidently equally foolish to accept probable reasoning from a mathematician and to demand from a rhetorician scientific proofs." (1094b25). This is a quite Platonic recognition.

22. Though Heidegger, strangely, does attribute an idea of eros to Plato. PS, 230.

23. See John Sallis's *Chorology: On Beginning in Plato's Timaeus* (Bloomington: Indiana University Press, 1999), for a profound discussion of the role of the *chora* in the *Timaeus*.

24. Vlastos, Gregory, *Socrates, Ironist and Moral Philosopher,* (Ithaca: Cornell University Press, 1991), 117. In a note (#50), Vlastos helpfully adds that this is "the grand methodological hypothesis on which my whole interpretation of Socrates in Plato is predicated." As we shall see, the same is true for Heidegger.

25. PS, 165, 224, 232, 235.

26. A partial list of the explicit identifications would include PS, pages 184, 188, 197, 199, 259, 260, 263, 279, 282, 283, 313, 331, 337, 357, 362, 364, 377.

27. The best critical evaluation of Heidegger's critique of Platonic dialectic is Francisco Gonzalez's "On the Way to *Sophia:* Heidegger on Plato's Dialectic, Ethics, and *Sophist"* in *Research in Phenomenology,* vol. XXVII, 1997, 16–60. I should say here that I have learned much from this rich and provocative criticism of Heidegger's reading of Plato.

28. This begs a very large question to which I shall turn subsequently: Heidegger simply *assumes* but never shows, that the Stranger's procedure is identical with *Platonic* dialectic (in its latest version).

29. Heidegger's account is complicated still further by his acknowledgment, in passing, that "The general opinion inclines today rather in the direction of placing the *Phaedrus* in the time of the *Theaetetus, the*

Sophist, and the Statesman, i.e., in the time of the properly scientific dialogues" (PS, 217).

30. Dialectic is not mentioned in this brief examination of the *Gorgias*, although Heidegger may be alluding to it when he concludes that "What is remarkable, however, is that already in this dialogue Plato holds in his hand positive possibilities for a real understanding, without letting them become effective" (PS, 215).

31. See especially pages 238–239 for the way in which Heidegger interpolates into the critique of writing a parallel critique of *logos* altogether.

32. Though at one point, and in passing, Heidegger does offer an intriguing, though abrupt, characterization of Eros as "the urge toward Being itself" (PS, 219).

33. It is especially instructive to note that in this passage at 266b, Socrates, with extreme tentativeness, associates these "divisions and collections" with dialectic: "Moreover, up to now, I've called those who are able to do this dialecticians, though whether I address them correctly or not only a god knows." Heidegger, not surprisingly, ignores the tentativeness.

34. Heidegger adds in a reference note that the "train of thought goes back to the Freiburg lecture course of winter semester 1930–31, "On the Essence of Truth." It later was published as part of the collection, *Wegmerken* (Frankfurt am Main: Vittorio Klostermann, 1967). Available in English as *Pathmarks,* edited by William McNeil (Cambridge: Cambridge University Press, 1998). The essay is pp. 155–182, the "reference" note on p. 380. The essay is translated by Thomas Sheehan, whose translation I shall usually follow.

35. Heidegger, *Vom Wesen der Wahrheit: zu Platons Hohlengleichnis und Theaetet,* first published as vol. 34 of Martin Heidegger's *Gesamtausgabe.* Translated as *The Essence of Truth* by Ted Stadler (New York: Continuum Books, 2002). Hereafter ET.

36. Published first as a contribution to the *Festschrift fur Hans Jantzen,* edited by Kurt Bauch (Berlin, 1951), pp. 7 ff., and later in Part III of *Vortrage Und Aufsatze* (Pfullingen: Gunther Neske, 1954). Translated by David Farrell Krell and Frank A. Capuzzi in *Early Greek Thinking* (New York: Harper & Row, 1975), p. 72.

37. David Lachterman, in "What is 'The Good' of Plato's *Republic?"* in *Four Essays on Plato's Republic* (Double issue of the *St. John's Review*) 39, nos. 1–2 (1989–90), shows that there has been an historical tendency to interpret the idea of the Good in one of two different ways: "ontological" interpretations focus on the epistemological function of the Good and tend to ignore its ethical or normative significance, whereas other interpreters concentrate their attention exclusively on the ethical significance; that it is the idea of the *Good,* after all, and ignore its epistemological function. Heidegger would clearly belong in the first category. Lachterman's altogether plausible point is that we must endeavor to think through *both* dimensions of this at once crucial and peculiar idea. For an extended critique of Heidegger's refusal to consider the Good as "the good," see Francisco Gonzalez's previously cited article, "On the

Way to Sophia: Heidegger on Plato's Dialectic, Ethics, and *Sophist*" (*Research in Phenomenology,* vol. XXVII, 1997), 16–60.

38. We see how little Heidegger has moved from the assumptions of the *Sophist* lecture course when we note that Heidegger cites as confirmation of this change in the essence of truth in Plato that *Aristotle* holds to a similar position when he says at *Metaphysics* 1027b25 that "In fact, the false and the true are not in things (themselves) . . . but in the intellect" (178). So Aristotle is still stating the same positions "more clearly" than Plato!

39. Translated in *Pathmarks* edited by William McNeil (Cambridge: Cambridge University Press, 1998), 323–336.

40. *Being and Time,* translated by Macquarrie and Robinson (New York: Harper & Row, 1962), 270, 272.

41. Translated in *On Time and Being,* edited by Joan Stambaugh (New York: Harper & Row, 1972), 70.

42. *Gesammtausgabe 54.* Translated as *Parmenides* by Andre Schuwer and Richard Rojcewicz (Bloomington: Indiana University Press, 1992). My translations will usually follow this text.

43. In addition, throughout the book, there is a continuation of the assumption that "Socrates=Plato." See for example 125, 126.

44. Nor is this the only place in this work where Heidegger attributes such a lack of self-awareness to Plato. In a striking passage discussing the question of writing at the end of the *Phaedrus,* Heidegger says, "In Plato's dialogue 'Phaedrus,' in the discussion of 'the beautiful' (concluding part), we see in addition that Plato recognized very clearly the priority of the immediately spoken word over the merely written one. But where would Plato's dialogues be if they never had been written down themselves" (89). Apparently, Plato did not appreciate the tension between the critique of writing and his own written dialogues, did not present that tension as a provocation to the reader.

45. Martin Heidegger, "*Aus einem Gesprach von der Sprache: zwischen einem Japaner und einem Fragenden,*" in *Unterwegs zur Sprache* (Verlag Gunther Neske Pfullingen, 1959: hereafter *US*), translated as "A Dialogue On Language" in *On The Way to Language* (trans. Peter Hertz, New York, Harper & Row, 1971: hereafter *OWL*), and "*Zur Erorterung der Gelassenheit,*" in *Gelassenheit* (Verlag Gunther Neske Pfullingen, 1959: hereafter *G*), translated as "Conversation on a Country Path About Thinking," in *Discourse On Thinking* (trans. John Anderson and Hans Freund, New York, Harper & Row, 1966: hereafter *R*). All page references will refer first to the German edition, then the English.

46. US, 269; OWL, 199.

47. If so, it is not. There are numerous occasions in the Platonic dialogues when speakers finish each other's sentences, some helpfully, some by way of interruption. Not to mention Socrates' regular insistence within dialogues that the *logos,* not individuals winning or losing, is what is at stake in genuine dialogue. This is precisely what distinguishes Socratic philosophy from sophistry.

48. For other passages where the scientist has the most difficulty of the three overcoming representative thinking, see G 41, 56, 62; R 67, 78, 83.

49. How can one avoid at this point thinking of the *Phaedrus*, which also occurs outside of the city, and where the erotic character of the human soul is addressed focally?

50. Heidegger, *Der Ursprung des Kunstwerkes* (1935–36) (Stuttgart: Reclam, 1960), translated as *The Origin of a Work of Art* by Albert Hofstadter in *Poetry, Language, Thought* (New York: Harper & Row, 1971), 33–34.

51. Heidegger, *"Bauen Wohnen Denken"* in *Vortrage und Aufsatze* (Pfullingen: Neske, 1954) translated as "Building Dwelling Thinking" by Albert Hofstadter, Ibid.

52. Compare, as one of many examples, *Symposium* 201c, where Agathon takes himself as "refuted" by Socrates and Socrates denies it: "I myself cannot refute you, Socrates, he replied, Let it be as you say." "No, Agathon, my friend, it's the truth you're unable to refute, since it's not difficult to refute Socrates."

53. One possible objection: at the closing reference to the night "nearing the distances" of the stars, the scientist responds, ". . . at least for the naïve observer, although not for the exact scientist" (G, 71; R, 89). This might be taken as a "return" on his part to his "subjective" status as a scientist. However, by this time in the dialogue, I take this remark of his as not serious but ironic, a reference to how he *might* have felt at one time. After all, the scientist immediately rejoins the mutual completing of each other's sentences with the imagistic "She neighbors; because she works only with nearness." (G, 71; R, 90).

CHAPTER TWO

1. For the development of a similar position, see Stanley Rosen, *Plato's Sophist: The Drama of Original and Image* (New Haven: Yale University Press, 1983), especially the section of the "Prologue" entitled "Dramatic Phenomenology," 12–16.

2. Speaking of those who have claimed to speak authoritatively about "Plato's philosophy," he says, "such writers can in my opinion have no real acquaintance with the subject. I certainly have composed no work in regard to it, nor shall I ever do so in the future, for there is no way of putting it in words like other studies. Acquaintance with it must come rather after a long period of attendance on instruction in the subject itself, and of close companionship, when, suddenly, like a blaze kindled by a leaping spark, it is generated in the soul and at once becomes self-sustaining. Besides, this at any rate I know, that if there were to be a treatise or a lecture on this subject, I could do it best. I am also sure for that matter that I should be very sorry to see such a treatise poorly written. If I thought it possible to deal adequately with the subject in a treatise or lecture for the general public, what finer achievement would there be in my life than to write a work of great benefit to mankind and to bring the nature of things to light for all men?" (Letter VII, 341c–e). Letter

II is even more blunt: "That is the reason why I have never written anything about these things, and why there is not and will not be any written work of Plato's own. What are now called his are the work of a Socrates grown young and beautiful" (Letter II, 314b–c). I submit that if these letters were not written by Plato himself, they were written by a writer who understood what is happening in the dialogues far better than we do.

3. See, among others, "Why Plato Wrote Dialogues," in *Philosophy and Rhetoric*, vol. 1, no. 1, 1968; *The Virtue of Philosophy: An Interpretation of Plato's Charmides*, (Athens, Ohio: Ohio University Press, 1981); *Finitude and Transcendence in the Platonic Dialogues*, (Albany: State University of New York Press, 1995).

4. An excellent work that addresses this precise point is Jill Gordon's *Turning Toward Philosophy: Literary Device and Dramatic Structure in Plato's Dialogues* (University Park: Pennsylvania State University Press, 1999). Gordon deploys aspects of "reader response theory" to argue persuasively that the give and take *within* the dialogues is an image of the sort of give and take that Plato hoped for with the reader.

5. The similarity to Heidegger's interpretive principle will be obvious.

6. Page 138. A footnote gives the entire sentence in Greek and locates it at *Lysis* 221e.

7. One might suggest that what Derrida is deconstructing is not the text of Plato but Platonism, (a project with which, as is obvious, I would be entirely sympathetic). But as this citation and others that I shall use make clear, Derrida does not sustain such a plausible distinction. He seems utterly comfortable in attributing this or that citation to Plato.

8. *Republic*, 592 a–b.

9. For some other instances, see 29, 30, 77, 78, 90, 91, 93, 94, 103, 114, 116, 138, 153, 154, 163.

10. Derrida, *The Post Card: From Socrates to Freud and Beyond*, translated by Alan Bass (Chicago: University of Chicago Press, 1987), 236.

11. That is, what if Plato's writing is much closer to the spirit of Derrida's own deconstructive strategies than Derrida is apparently able to recognize?

12. Derrida, *Specters of Marx*, translated by Peggy Kamuf (New York: Routledge, 1994), 59, 169.

13. For an elaboration of this general point, see chapter 3 of my *Finitude and Transcendence in the Platonic Dialogues*.

14. It also follows from those principles, as we have seen, that passages may be cited without context from any dialogue and attributed to Plato. "Plato's Pharmacy" is a veritable *tour de. force* of citation without context. Within its pages I find citations without context from the following dialogues: *Phaedrus, Symposium, Republic, Timaeus, Charmides, Phaedo, Theaetetus, Crito, Laws, Sophist, Philebus, Critias, Apology, Cratylus, Meno, Hippias Major, Hippias Minor*, and *Letters*. This constitutes almost half the entire Platonic corpus!

15. I first attempted to address this issue in "Why Plato Wrote Dialogues," in *Philosophy and Rhetoric*, vol. 1, no. 1, 1968. See also my *Finitude and Transcendence in the Platonic Dialogues*.

16. Derrida, *On The Name*, translated by David Wood, John P. Leavey, Jr., and Ian McCleod (Stanford: Stanford University Press, 1995). Originally published in French as three separate booklets in 1993: *Passions, Sauf le nom, and Khora* by Editions Galilee.

17. Fortunately, this sort of contextualized interpretation has recently been given in an excellent way. See John Sallis's fine book, *Chorology: On Beginning in Plato's Timaeus* (Bloomington: Indiana University Press, 1999). In this book, Sallis does what Derrida fails to do, places the discussion of the *khora* within a rich interpretation of the dialogue as a whole. The result, without being characterized as such by Sallis, constitutes a powerful critique of the deconstructionist disregard of context, and more positively, an illustration of the much greater richness of an interpretation that adequately places a given issue in its existential context.

18. As the subtitle of Sallis' book indicates, this is the way he begins his interpretation, and it is the way any adequate interpretation of the *Timaeus* must begin.

19. Interpreters who are inclined to take this last-mentioned account as a serious "Platonic" account will presumably also take the *next* point in the text as a serious teaching, that men who look at the stars too much and imagine that by looking they will understand, become birds in the next life (91d)!

20. *Timaeus*, 29d, 30b, 40e, 44d, 48d, 54d, 55c, 56a, 56b, 56c, 57d, 59c, 68d, 72d.

21. A further problem with identifying the Pythagoreanism of the dialogue as "Plato's view" comes to light when we note the previously mentioned presence in the dialogue of the notorious Pythagorean misogyny. "Today," Timaeus the Pythagorean affirms that misogyny as part of his view of the cosmos. "Yesterday," however, if the strange account at the beginning of the dialogue is to be taken as referring to the *Republic, Socrates* explicitly contested this misogyny.

22. Sallis, however, does, in an excellent way. *Chorology*, especially chapters 1 and 4.

23. I thus share with Derrida one crucial thesis: anything like Platonism is deeply and continually deconstructed in the Platonic dialogues. We disagree, however, in that I do not think that Platonism is asserted by Plato within the dialogues as his teaching.

24. These are my translations, which for our purposes here I make as literal as possible at the expense of smooth English.

25. N.B. Note the implication for "Plato's doctrine."

26. Derrida's passage includes the Greek of the passage from the *Timaeus* quoted.

27. Derrida here is obviously taking *logos* in a fairly narrow, technical sense, that Timaeus is claiming a rigorous account of the whole. If, however, we take Timaeus to be using *logos* here in the broader sense of simply "speech," (our speech has come to an end), it would avoid the problems Derrida is about to raise.

CHAPTER 3

1. Published in French as *Speculum de l'autre femme* (Paris: Les Editions de Minuit, 1974). Translated into English by Gillian C. Gill as *Speculum of the Other Woman* (Ithaca: Cornell University Press, 1985). Unless otherwise noted, I shall use this translation for texts cited.

2. Published in French as *Ethique de la différence sexuelle* (Paris: Les Editions de Minuit, 1984). Translated into English by Carolyn Burke and Gillian C. Gill as *An Ethics of Sexual Difference* (Ithaca: Cornell University Press, 1993). Unless otherwise noted, I shall use this translation for texts cited.

3. *Engaging With Irigaray: Feminist Philosophy and Modern European Thought*, eds. Carolyn Burke, Naomi Schor, Margaret Whitford (New York: Columbia University Press, 1994), 81.

4. An intriguing article in the *Engaging Irigaray* volume, Dianne Chisholm's "Irigaray's Hysteria," shows in remarkable detail another dimension of Irigaray's mimetic style: she mimes *hysteria*, traditionally understood, especially by Freudians, as a "woman's" disease.

5. In *Textures of Light: Vision and Touch in Irigaray, Levinas, and Merleau-Ponty* (New York: Routledge, 1998), 7.

6. Bloom, *The Republic of Plato* (New York: Basic Books, 1968), 384.

7. We leave aside what this would mean regarding the explicitly stated necessity for those liberated philosophers to *go back down* into the cave to share what they have learned.

8. Irigaray, Luce, *An Ethics of Sexual Difference* (translated by Carolyn Burke and Gillian C. Gill, Ithaca, NY: Cornell University Press, 1993), 134. *Ethique de la différence sexuelle* (Paris: Les Editions de Minuit, 1984), 128. The italics are in Irigaray's text. Hereafter, page numbers in this text will be referred to in parentheses, the English pagination followed by the French. Occasionally, I may alter the translation.

9. The most interesting post-Platonic exception to this tendency is probably Nietzsche, who writes in a rich variety of philosophic styles, the most provocative being his *Thus Spoke Zarathustra*.

10. One might add, as an additional woman teacher of Socrates, his mother, Phaenarete, a midwife who, as Socrates famously describes it at *Theaetetus 149ff.*, passed on to him his own philosophical form of midwiferery, his interrogative philosophical standpoint. Again, it is most instructive in this regard that he mentions his mother, but not his father.

11. There is a lively debate today among feminist interpreters of Plato as to whether Plato is some sort of proto-feminist. As I emphasize in my "The Difference the Difference Makes: The Question of Woman in Plato" (presented at the 1998 IAPL conference, University of California at Irvine, May 1998), Plato's feminism seems primarily directed toward the character of philosophy itself as requiring both the feminine and the masculine, and therefore both women and men as participants. The dialogues do not exhibit a great concern for social justice for women.

12. For the development of this same stance of responsive openness as the stance of *play*, see my *The Question of Play* (Lanham, MD: University Press of America, 1984), especially chapter 4, "The Stance of Play."

13. I again note that Plato has already problematized this association by attributing Poros's—and so the male's—characteristics to Poros's own mother, Metis.

14. An inspection of Diotima's responses to Socrates throughout her speech reveals a sustained, sardonic mocking of his innocence in erotic matters.

15. I owe a debt of thanks to Professor Diane Perpich, who has added a second invaluable point: Part of the reason for beginning with and preserving the bodily is that the body is the genuine other. The rest of the stages (beautiful speeches, laws and institutions, knowledge, philosophy) I can in principle generate within myself; but the beautiful body of another, and so the bodily altogether, is what puts me genuinely in touch with an other, and so makes possible genuine dialogue.

CHAPTER 4

1. 38. This is also a reiterated theme of the book. See 30, 46, 56, 58, 65, 68, 99, 100. The influence of Irigaray's reading of the cave analogy in *Speculum of the Other Woman* is clear here.

2. I again cite and commend Jill Gordon's *Turning Toward Philosophy: Literary Device and Dramatic Structure in Plato's Dialogues* (University Park: Pennsylvania State University Press, 1999) who draws out this dimension of the dialogue between Plato and the reader superbly.

3. "Shadow Writing," unpublished manuscript presented as a paper at a meeting of the IAPL, January 2000.

CHAPTER 5

1. Contemporary American "Continental philosophy" now has a number of representatives of this same sensitivity. Perhaps the most distinguished representative of this work is John Sallis.

2. Gadamer, Hans-Georg, *Platos dialektische Ethic*, 2nd edition (Hamburg: Felix Meiner Verlag, 1931). Translated as *Plato's Dialectical Ethics: Phenomenological Interpretations Relating to the Philebus* by Robert M. Wallace (New Haven: Yale University Press, 1991). Hereafter, PDE.

3. Gadamer, *Die Idee des Guten zwischen Plato und Aristoteles* (Heidelberg, 1978), translated by P. Christopher Smith as *The Idea of the Good in Platonic-Aristotelian Philosophy* (New Haven: Yale University Press, 1986). Hereafter, IG.

4. The importance of conversation and agreement has clear resonance with Gadamer's setting out of his own theory of hermeneutics in *Truth and Method*.

5. This claim by Gadamer that Plato seeks in the dialogues "the same" may seem problematic, in that it may seem to fall prey to Irigaray's dissatis-

faction with the supposedly Platonic obsession with "the same" and corresponding distaste for "difference." But Gadamer's own understanding of language as radically historical guarantees that in the literal sense "the same" will never be fully achieved, that its extent will always be highly qualified. Gadamer captures this qualification, however skeletally, with the phrase "in a certain way" above. Given the historical character of language, "difference" is always co-primordial with "the same." The dramatic variations in the dialogues surely attest that Plato and Gadamer are in accord on this.

6. More generally, when writing under the influence of Heidegger, Gadamer often forgets his own hermeneutic principles and easily attributes whatever is said by someone in this or that dialogue to Plato. See for example PDE, 91–94, 188, 191, 197, 202.

7. Gadamer, *Die Idee des Guten zwischen Plato und Aristoteles* (Heidelberg, 1978), translated by P. Christopher Smith as *The Idea of the Good in Platonic-Aristotelian Philosophy,* (New Haven: Yale University Press, 1986), hereafter IG.

8. A seminal collection of these essays is P. Christopher Smith's translation of the collection entitled *Dialogue and Dialectic: Eight Hermeneutical Studies on Plato* (New Haven: Yale University Press, 1980). This includes essays from throughout Gadamer's career, including two early essays, "Plato and the Poets," (1934) and "Plato's Educational State" (1942), and a number of the most important later essays, including the 1962 essay, "Dialectic and Sophism in Plato's *Seventh Letter,*" the 1968 essays, "Plato's Unwritten Dialectic" and "*Amicus Plato Magis Amica Veritas,*" as well as "*Logos and Ergon* in Plato's *Lysis,*" (1972), "The Proofs of Immortality in Plato's *Phaedo,*" (1973), and "Idea and Reality in Plato's *Timaeus,*" (1974). One must not forget also the discussions of Plato in *Truth and Method.* In the interests of showing Gadamer's development in his reading of Plato, I shall concentrate my attention on the later essays in this volume.

9. Gadamer, Hans-Georg, *Heidegger's Ways,* translated by John W. Stanley (Albany: State University New York Press, 1994), 144.

10. P. Christopher Smith, in his insightful introduction to the *Dialogue and Dialectic* volume, puts the point this way: "Gadamer deals specifically with the doctrine of ideal numbers, the One and the indeterminate Two. What he finds is not at all a pair of principles from which a *system* of eidetic relationships might be deduced but, on the contrary, a statement of the limits of human insight and, therefore, of precisely the impossibility of systematization." (xii: Smith's italics)

11. This interpretation, or one similar to it, namely, that the "techne analogy" is not, as most analytic commentators hold, a serious model for the knowledge of virtue in Plato, is worked out in persuasive detail by David Roochnik in his *Of Art and Wisdom: Plato's Understanding of Techne* (University Park: Pennsylvania State University Press, 1996).

Bibliography

Aristotle, *Ethica Nicomachea,* edited by I. Bywater (Oxford: Oxford University Press, 1962).

Aristotle, *Ethica Nicomachea,* translated by W.D. Ross. In Richard McKeon (editor) *Introduction to Aristotle* (New York: McGraw-Hill Inc., 1947).

Brann, Eva, Peter Kalkavage, and Eric Salem, *"Plato's Sophist: The Professor of Wisdom,"* (Newburyport, MA: Focus Philosophical Library, 1996).

Burke, Carolyn, Schor, Naomi, and Whitford, Margaret, (editors), *Engaging With Irigaray: Feminist Philosophy and Modern European Thought* (New York: Columbia University Press, 1994).

Cavarero, Adriana, *In Spite of Plato: A Feminist Rewriting of Ancient Philosophy,* translated by Serena Anderlini-D'Onofrio and Aine O'Healy (New York: Routledge, 1995).

Cavarero, Adriana, "Shadow Writing," unpublished manuscript presented as a paper at a meeting of the IAPL, January 2000.

Cheah, Pheng, and Grosz, Elizabeth, "The Future of Sexual Difference: An Interview with Judith Butler and Drucilla Cornell," in *Diacritics* vol. 28, no. 1, spring 1998, 19–42.

Chisholm, Dianne "Irigaray's Hysteria," in Burke, Carolyn, Schor, Naomi, and Whitford, Margaret, (editors), *Engaging With Irigaray: Feminist Philosophy and Modern European Thought* (New York: Columbia University Press, 1994).

Derrida, Jacques, *On The Name,* translated by David Wood, John P. Leavey, JR., and Ian McCleod (Stanford: Stanford University Press, 1995). Originally published in French as three separate booklets in 1993: *Passions, Sauf le nom, and Khora* by Editions Galilee.

Derrida, Jacques, "Plato's Pharmacy," in *Dissemination,* translated by Barbara Johnson (Chicago: University of Chicago Press, 1981).

Derrida, Jacques, *Specters of Marx,* translated by Peggy Kamuf (New York: Routledge, 1994).

Derrida, Jacques, *The Postcard: From Socrates to Freud and Beyond,* translated by Alan Bass (Chicago: University of Chicago Press, 1987).

Ferlinghetti, Lawrence, *How To Paint Sunlight* (New York: New Directions Book, 2001).

Gadamer, Hans-Georg, *Dialogue and Dialectic: Eight Hermeneutical Studies on Plato*, translated by P. Christopher Smith (New Haven: Yale University Press, 1980).

Gadamer, Hans-Georg, *Die Idee des Guten zwischen Plato und Aristoteles* (Heidelberg, 1978), translated by P. Christopher Smith as *The Idea of the Good in Platonic-Aristotelian Philosophy* (New Haven: Yale University Press, 1986).

Gadamer, Hans-Georg, *Heidegger's Ways*, translated by John W. Stanley (Albany: State University of New York Press, 1994).

Gadamer, Hans-Georg, *Platos dialektische Ethic*, 2nd edition (Hamburg: Felix Meiner Verlag, 1931). Translated as *Plato's Dialectical Ethics: Phenomenological Interpretations Relating to the Philebus* by Robert M. Wallace (New Haven: Yale University Press, 1991).

Gadamer, Hans-Georg, *Truth and Method* (New York: Continuum Books, 1975).

Gonzalez, Francisco, "On the Way to *Sophia:* Heidegger on Plato's Dialectic, Ethics, and *Sophist*" in *Research in Phenomenology*, vol. XXVII, 1997.

Gordon, Jill, *Turning Toward Philosophy: Literary Device and Dramatic Structure in Plato's Dialogues* (University Park: Pennsylvania State University Press, 1999).

Heidegger, Martin, "*Aus einem Gesprach von der Sprache: zwischen einem Japaner und einem Fragenden,*" in *Unterwegs zur Sprache* (Verlag Gunther Neske Pfullingen, 1959), translated as "A Dialogue On Language" in *On the Way to Language* (trans. Peter Hertz, New York: Harper & Row, 1971).

Heidegger, "*Bauen Wohnen Denken*" in *Vortrage und Aufsatze* (Pfullingen: Neske, 1954), translated as "Building Dwelling Thinking" by Albert Hofstadter in *Poetry, Language, Thought* (New York: Harper & Row, 1971).

Heidegger, Martin, *Being and Time,* translated by Macquarrie and Robinson (New York: Harper & Row, 1962).

Heidegger, Martin, *Der Ursprung des Kunstwerkes* (1935–36) (Stuttgart: Reclam, 1960), translated as *The Origin of a Work of Art* by Albert Hofstadter in *Poetry, Language, Thought* (New York: Harper & Row, 1971).

Heidegger, Martin, *Gesamtausgabe* (Frankfurt: Vittorio Klostermann, 1992).

Heidegger, Martin, *On Time and Being*, edited by Joan Stambaugh (New York: Harper & Row, 1972).

Heidegger, Martin, *Parmenides* (*Gesamtausgabe 54*), translated by Andre Schuwer and Richard Rojcewicz (Bloomington: Indiana University Press, 1992).

Heidegger, Martin, *Pathmarks*, edited by William McNeil (Cambridge: Cambridge University Press, 1998).

Heidegger, Martin, *Plato's Sophist*, translated by Richard Rojcewicz and Andre Schuwer (Bloomington: Indiana University Press, 1997).

Heidegger, Martin, *Vom Wesen der Wahrheit: zu Platons Hohlengleichnis und Theaetet*, first published as vol. 34 of Martin Heidegger's *Gesamtausgabe*. Translated as *The Essence of Truth* by Ted Stadler (New York: Continuum Books, 2002).

Heidegger, Martin, *Vortrage Und Aufsatze* (Pfullingen: Gunther Neske, 1954). Translated by David Farrell Krell and Frank A. Capuzzi in *Early Greek Thinking* (New York: Harper & Row, 1975).

Heidegger, Martin, *Wegmerken* (Frankfurt am Main: Vittorio Klostermann, 1967).

Heidegger, Martin, *Zur Erorterung der Gelassenheit,"* in Gelassenheit (Pfullingen: Verlag Gunther Neske, 1959), translated as "Conversation on a Country Path About Thinking," in *Discourse On Thinking* by John Anderson and Hans Freund (New York: Harper & Row, 1966).

Howland, Jacob, "Re-Reading Plato: The Problem of Platonic Chronology," *Phoenix*, 45, no. 3 (1991): 189–214.

Hyland, Drew, *Finitude and Transcendence in the Platonic Dialogues,* (Albany: State University of New York Press, 1995).

Hyland, Drew, "The Difference the Difference Makes: The Question of Woman in Plato," (presented at the 1998 IAPL conference, University of California at Irvine, May 1998).

Hyland, Drew, *The Question of Play* (Lanham, MD: University Press of America, 1984).

Hyland, Drew, *The Virtue of Philosophy: An Interpretation of Plato's Charmides* (Athens: Ohio University Press, 1981).

Hyland, Drew, "Why Plato Wrote Dialogues," in *Philosophy and Rhetoric,* vol. 1, no. 1, 1968.

Irigaray, Luce, *Ethique de la difference sexuelle* (Paris: Les Editions de Minuit, 1984). Translated into English by Carolyn Burke and Gillian C. Gill as *An Ethics of Sexual Difference* (Ithaca: Cornell University Press, 1993).

Irigaray, Luce, *Speculum de l'autre femme* (Paris: Les Editions de Minuit, 1974). Translated into English by Gillian C. Gill as *Speculum of the Other Woman* (Ithaca: Cornell University Press, 1985).

Lachterman, David, "What is 'The Good' of Plato's *Republic?"* in *Four Essays on Plato's Republic* (Double issue of the *St. John's Review*) 39, nos. 1–2 (1989–90).

Miller, Mitchell, "Platonic Provocations: Reflections on the Soul and the Good in the *Republic,"* in *Platonic Investigations,* edited by Dominic J. O'Meara (Washington, DC: Catholic University Press of America, 1985).

Nietzsche, Friedrich, *The Birth of Tragedy,* translated by Walter Kaufmann (New York: Vintage Books, 1967).

Nietzsche, *Twilight of the Idols,* in *The Portable Nietzsche,* translated by Walter Kaufmann (New York: Penguin Books, 1976).

Plato, *Plato: Complete Works,* edited by John Cooper (Indianapolis: Hackett Publishing Company, 1997).

Plato, *Platonis Opera,* edited by John Burnet (Oxford: Oxford University Press, 1958).

Plato, *The Republic of Plato,* translated by Alan Bloom (New York: Basic Books, 1968).

Plato, *The Symposium and Phaedrus: Plato's Erotic Dialogues,* translated by William S. Cobb (Albany: State University of New York Press, 1993).

Roochnik, David, *Of Art and Wisdom: Plato's Understanding of Techne* (University Park: Pennsylvania State University Press, 1996).

Rosen, Stanley, *Plato's Sophist: The Drama of Original and Image* (New Haven: Yale University Press, 1983).

Rosen, Stanely *Plato's Symposium* (New Haven: Yale University Press, 1968).

Sallis, John, *Chorology: On Beginning in Plato's Timaeus* (Bloomington: Indiana University Press, 1999).

Vasseleu, Cathryn, *Textures of Light: Vision and Touch in Irigaray, Levinas, and Merleau-Ponty* (New York: Routledge, 1998).

Vlastos, Gregory, *Socrates, Ironist and Moral Philosopher* (Ithaca: Cornell University Press, 1991).

Zuckert, Catherine, *Postmodern Platos* (Chicago: University of Chicago Press, 1996).

Index